PENGUIN CLASSICS

THE CYNIC PHILOSOPHERS

ROBERT DOBBIN was born in New York City in 1958. He received a PhD in Classics from the University of California at Berkeley in 1989, and taught history and classics at college level for years. He is the author of *Epictetus Discourses: Book One* (1998), as well as articles on Virgil, Plato and Pythagoras. He has also translated Epictetus's *Discourses and Selected Writings* (2008) for Penguin Classics. Currently he works as a book editor in northern California.

T0176336

The Cynic Philosophers

from Diogenes to Julian

Translated and edited by
ROBERT DOBBIN

PENGUIN BOOKS

PENGUIN CLASSICS

Published by the Penguin Group
Penguin Books Ltd, 80 Strand, London WC2R ORL, England
Penguin Group (USA) Inc., 375 Hudson Street, New York, New York 10014, USA
Penguin Group (Canada), 90 Eglinton Avenue East, Suite 700, Toronto, Ontario,
Canada M4P 2Y3 (a division of Pearson Penguin Canada Inc.)
Penguin Ireland, 25 St Stephen's Green, Dublin 2, Ireland (a division of Penguin Books Ltd)
Penguin Group (Australia), 707 Collins Street, Melbourne, Victoria 3008, Australia
(a division of Pearson Australia Group Pty Ltd)
Penguin Books India Pvt Ltd, 11 Community Centre, Panchsheel Park, New Delhi – 110 017, India
Penguin Group (NZ), 67 Apollo Drive, Rosedale, Auckland 0632, New Zealand
(a division of Pearson New Zealand Ltd)
Penguin Books (South Africa) (Pty) Ltd, Block D, Rosebank Office Park,
181 Jan Smuts Avenue, Parktown North, Gauteng 2193, South Africa

Penguin Books Ltd, Registered Offices: 80 Strand, London WC2R ORL, England

www.penguin.com

First published in Penguin Classics 2012

020

Translation and editorial material © Robert Dobbin, 2012
All rights reserved

The moral right of the author and translator has been asserted

Set in 10.25/12.25pt Postscript Adobe Sabon
Typeset by Jouve (UK), Milton Keynes
Printed in Great Britain by Clays Ltd, Elcograf S.p.A

ISBN: 978-0-141-19222-2

www.greenpenguin.co.uk

Penguin Books is committed to a sustainable
future for our business, our readers and our planet.
This book is made from Forest Stewardship
Council™ certified paper.

Contents

Abbreviations

Ad Lucil. epist.	*Ad Lucilium epistulae*
Anth. Pal.	*Anthologia Palatina* or *Palatine Anthology*
Arist. Rh.	Aristotle's *Rhetoric*
Benef.	*De beneficiis*
Cic.	Cicero
Codex florent. of *John Damasc.*	*Codex Florentinus of St John of Damascus*
col.	column
comm. in Epict. enchir.	*In Epicteti enchiridion commentarium*
DK	*Die Fragmente der Vorsakratiker*, eds H. Diels and W. Kranz (Berlin 1954), 3 volumes
DL	Diogenes Laertius, *Lives of the Ancient Philosophers*
De off.	*De officiis*
Gnom. Paris.	*Gnomologium Parisinum*
Gnomol. Vat.	*Gnomologium Vaticanum*
Hercher	R. Hercher, *Epistolographi Graeci* (Paris 1873).
Il.	*Iliad*
In Epist. I ad Corinth. homil.	*In Epistulam primam ad Corinthios homilia*
Inst. epit.	*Institutionum epitome*
Joann. Chrysost.	Joannes Chrysostomus
Mem.	*Memorabilia*
Od.	*Odyssey*

Orat. ad Graec.	*Oratio ad Graecos*
Or.	*Oration*
Pl.	Plato
Plut.	Plutarch
Prov.	*De Providentia*
Sen.	Seneca
Simplic.	Simplicius
Smp.	*Symposium*
SSR	G. Giannantoni, *Socratis et Socraticorum Reliquiae* (Naples 1990), 4 volumes
Stob.	Stobaeus
Suid.	Suidas or The Suda
TD	*The Tusculan Disputations*
Xen.	Xenophon

Square brackets [ ] around a name indicate that the associated work is spurious, that is, probably not written by the accredited author but by someone else whose identity is uncertain. Ellipses between square brackets indicate that the passage has been abridged in translation. Text between < > (less than and greater than symbols) indicates that a lacuna has been filled with a phrase or sentence supplied *exempli gratia*.

Chronology

emperors, beginning with Augustus himself.

AD

c. 4 BC–65	Seneca the Younger
37–71	fl. Demetrius, the first Cynic of note in the city of Rome
c. 1st century	The (pseudonymous) Cynic epistles are composed
1st–3rd centuries	Age of the Second Sophistic
c. 40–112	Dio Chrysostom, sophist and rhetorician
c. 55–135	Epictetus
c. 70–170	Demonax
c. 125–180	Lucian, sophist and satirist
c. 200	Diogenes Laertius, author of the *Lives of the Ancient Philosophers*, which includes a chapter (6) devoted to the Cynics
331–363	Roman emperor Julian the Apostate
c. 450–500	Sallustius of Emesa, last known Cynic philosopher

Introduction

In his *Rhetoric* Aristotle cites notable instances of metaphoric language among his contemporaries. 'The Dog,' he reports, 'used to say that taverns were the mess halls of the Athenians.'[1] With this oblique reference, the Dog (Greek *cyn*, related to English 'canine') and by extension Cynicism, the movement the Dog did most to inaugurate, make their first appearance in the written record. The Dog is Diogenes of Sinope. Like many of the aphorisms (*chreiai*) transmitted under his name and the names of other members of the dog pack, it is typically no more than a sardonic barb. But it is eloquent of the speaker's moral stance – its style invariably wry, even cynical (with a small 'c') in the contemporary sense of the word. With his analogy, the Dog intends a contrast between the Spartan regimen and the Athenians' more relaxed mores, which included meals taken not in military-style barracks, but either in private houses or, more often, in public inns. Now, an abundance of restaurants may recommend a city to tourists. But to the Dog it seemed symptomatic of Athens' increasingly lax habits – especially when Sparta and its stern culture is adduced as a foil.

That Aristotle could allude to him by his nickname, the Dog, without further elaboration, suggests that he was a well-known character in fourth-century Athens. Athens was Diogenes' home at a time when it was well known for its distinctive personalities. The label 'dog' cannot pass without comment, since it was no more a compliment in his own day than it is now. Nevertheless Diogenes embraced the epithet. Undoubtedly he earned it originally through his 'shameless' behaviour, which included neglecting personal hygiene, as well as masturbating and defecating in public, in defiance of the most entrenched social taboos. Perhaps his motive in accepting the insult was to neutralize it through a defiant act of appropriation (we may compare, in modern times, the adoption of originally disparaging terms like 'Lollards', 'Quakers', 'queers', by the group members themselves), but there were other reasons that, owing in part to his own complaisance, the label stuck. Diogenes admired the 'honesty' of dogs: they were 'shameless' in demonstrating their obvious fondness or antipathy towards certain people; they survived on very little – though in this they could hardly be less like Diogenes' fellow Athenians, most of whom, it seemed, could never get enough of anything. Most of all Diogenes professed to have, and be ready to share, the secret to that most elusive of blessings, simple contentment. Dogs with their buoyant spirits (in the company of their masters, taking part in the hunt, subsisting on only one meal a day with water alone to wash it down) were evidently happy creatures. Why are humans, with our far greater resources, so often not? The solution, in part, was obvious – take a lesson from dogs and other beasts and the simplicity of their existence, and rely on nature to provide a sufficiency of life's essentials. Not that this could be accomplished overnight; through training (*askêsis*) we first have to cure ourselves of our greedy, pampered habits.

Relying on nature, as the Cynics understood it, entailed living almost entirely out of doors (unless spending the night in a wine vat qualifies as an exception), travelling the country with little protection against the elements except a heavy cloak (no tunic or undergarment, no shoes), living off lupins, pulses and other wild cereals, picking mustard to give their plain food flavour, and depending on natural springs to slake their thirst. For rest and relaxation Diogenes enjoyed nothing more than basking in the sun. And the Cynics were great ones for hunting (cf. sections 25 and 124 §11), never forgetting to cite the importance of the dog (by which, by implication, they drew attention to themselves) when they tired of an exclusively vegetarian diet.

CYNIC ETHICS

All ancient ethical systems identified a *telos*, a practical goal. Cynics agreed with just about every rival philosophy in claiming that their ethics aimed at, indeed guaranteed, happiness (*eudaimonia*). As a corollary they held that moral virtue was sufficient for happiness. This was not an original view; Socrates had argued for it already. The Cynics, in turn, influenced the Stoics to adopt as the foundation of their own ethics some such correspondence between virtue and happiness. Traditionally, virtue for the Greeks comprised justice, self-control (*sôphrosunê*) and courage. Plato elevated wisdom to a position of equal, even paramount, importance.

However, this will not do as a description of Cynic ethics. They promoted ideals other than the traditional virtues, qualities that hardly qualify as virtues at all: self-sufficiency, freedom, detachment, training aimed at instilling physical and moral toughness or endurance (*karteria*). Since no ethical treatise by Diogenes or any of the other early Cynics survives (perhaps because they wrote so few of them), we must try to present a coherent account of their ethical system on our own. The question, then, is what relation obtains between their declared *telos*, happiness (*eudaimonia*), the means – virtue – leading to it, 'life in agreement with nature' as a moral principle, and the qualities they prized and promoted such as self-sufficiency (*autarkeia*), freedom of speech, poverty and the rest. In addition, an obscure incident early in the life of Diogenes of Sinope, its official founder, made 'deface the currency' Cynicism's motto and mission. As generally interpreted, that amounted to what Nietzsche (a professed admirer of the Cynics) would call – and in turn endorse – the 'inversion of all values'. Cynics proposed a new ethics based on reducing material needs in pursuit of self-sufficiency, abetted in part by mental and especially physical training (*askêsis*). They renounced the pursuit of possessions, fame and power as illusory goods that had no real value in nature.

Although they extolled virtue at every opportunity, the Cynics had little that was original to say about it. They did not analyse it into its components, or address such standard questions as whether the possession of courage, say, entailed possession of the other virtues; or whether wisdom played a sovereign role in their collective deployment. So they certainly stood by happiness as their professed *telos*. 'Life in agreement with nature', as they understood the phrase, conduced to freedom, self-sufficiency and the rest of the distinctive values that they saw as the constituents of happiness. As a formula to live by, it displaced virtue as the means to happiness. As for 'defacing the currency', trading in the traditional virtues for poverty and the like can be seen as an aspect of that project. They championed qualities that were either an affront to traditional Hellenic values (such as active involvement in governing one's native polis), in favour of 'world citizenship', which amounted to a declaration of independence from any particular city and a profession of allegiance to nature, insofar as nature and the world were one. Even more unconventionally, conditions such as poverty by their reckoning were not misfortunes but paradoxical avenues to peace and contentment – to happiness, in a word.

We can go further and say that the Cynic life was 'a shortcut to virtue' (as the Stoics later called it) inasmuch as it presupposed a measure of self-control, of justice (in the sense that one did not want too much for oneself), and of bravery in that they submitted to a preliminary course of training (*askêsis*) and developed exceptional endurance (*karteria*). Wisdom in the sense of erudition they dismissed as otiose, thus making their way of life that much more abbreviated a route to virtue. They were nevertheless respected as 'wise men' (*sophoi*) because they professed to have that most precious thing, the secret to a happy life.

Six centuries after Diogenes' death we find Cynicism defended by no less a personage than the Roman emperor Julian (reigned AD 355 to 363). It penetrated not only Greek but also Roman civilization after Rome assumed political control of Greece and the rest of Alexander the Great's empire. For centuries Cynics could be found on street corners berating passers-by on their false values. Even before they launched into their characteristic harangue, they could be recognized by their untrimmed beards, matted hair, rough cloak folded in two (the better to protect them against the cold and double as makeshift bedding), a knapsack that held their food and few belongings, and a walking stick adapted to their nomadic way of life.

Unlike other ancient philosophies they had no school in the strict sense. There was no acknowledged place where they met and discoursed comparable to Epicurus' Garden, Aristotle's Lyceum, or Plato's Academy. For Diogenes and his successors, the streets of Athens provide the setting for both their teaching and their training. Moreover, the Cynics neglect, and very often ridicule, speculative philosophy. They are especially harsh critics of dogmatic thought, anticipating thereby the rise of scepticism among philosophers (Academics, Pyrrhonians) of the Hellenistic age.[2] They also dismiss metaphysics in the sense of abstract or immaterial substances – an area where they saw fit to subject Plato and his 'forms' to especial ridicule.

SOURCES

Like the writings of the old Stoics, the writings of the founders of Cynicism – Antisthenes, Diogenes of Sinope, Crates, Hipparchia, et al. – have, almost without exception, disappeared. Summaries of their works survive, however, and we have ample testimony to Cynic thought from the Roman period. In sum, it is fair to say that we are well informed about the movement, both in its outlines and as regards the lives and views of individual Cynics. In dealing with biographical details, however, we would do well to apply a measure of scepticism. Our chief source for the latter is one Diogenes Laertius, who wrote his *Lives of the Ancient Philosophers* in ten books, covering most of the principal philosophers and their schools of antiquity. Given that it was composed in the early third century AD, this represents a gap of over five centuries between the first Cynics and the lives and works he describes. Given, further, that ancient historians were cavalier to the point of indifference concerning the accuracy of biographical details – one has only to compare the different accounts of Socrates' life in Plato and Xenophon – it becomes clear that the opportunity for factual distortion was there. Diogenes Laertius' report on his Cynic namesake consists largely of *chreiai* – anecdotes capped by a wry remark from the philosopher that serves to encapsulate his characteristically 'Cynic' attitude towards the incident and the values of the people involved. These stories accumulated over centuries and cannot all be regarded as genuine, particularly when we find near copies in the analogous section of other Cynic lives. Truth has been mixed with fiction, legend with historical fact.

The same applies to what purport to be some of the principal incidents in Diogenes' life: his meeting with Alexander the Great, for instance, as well as his service as a slave, which begins with his capture by pirates, followed by a lively account of how boldly he behaved when he was put on the auction block. Yet the accuracy of these anecdotes is not as important as evidence of the Cynics' attitude to life and its vicissitudes. *Chreiai* and biographical detail predominate in Laertius' chapter (6), on Cynicism, because the Cynics put a premium on the practice of philosophy as opposed to its abstract proof and exposition. The *chreia* also combines the elements of wit and serious moral message – the seriocomic register that Cynics favoured because it suited the dry and mordant personality of its leaders but also because the synthesis proved an effective educational tool.

KEY CYNIC THEMES

Freedom of speech (*parrhêsia*)

In the most celebrated Cynic legend, Alexander the Great was induced by Diogenes' reputation to call on him while he was sunning himself in his favourite outdoor spot, the Craneum near Corinth – the site of a gymnasium. Alexander stood over him and offered to oblige him with any favour within his power to confer. 'Get out of my light,' Diogenes promptly responded. The anecdote illustrates several Cynic traits. Foremost, perhaps, is the reputation for *parrhêsia*, or frankness of speech. Clearly not impressed by Alexander's fame, Diogenes repays the great man's condescension with a bluntness and nonchalance that border on insolence. Asked to name 'the most valuable thing in the world', Diogenes did not think twice before nominating *parrhêsia*.[3] As a rule, ancient thinkers cultivated the patronage of rulers, either as a means to get official support for their philosophy or simply to provide themselves with food and shelter, philosophy not being a particularly lucrative profession: Plato was intimate with the tyrant Dionysius of Syracuse and his son, Xenophon attached himself to Cyrus the Younger, Aristotle tutored Alexander the Great in his youth and remained a regular at the Macedonian court for the rest of his life. So far from seeking such alliances, the Cynics seem to have actively alienated the political powers that be. Their licence to speak frankly and brazenly derived from the licence of the outsider who, paradoxically, acted as society's conscience.

In the event, legend has it that their outspokenness and indifference to worldly authority succeeded, actually, in gaining the respect of those they defied. The story of his interview with Alexander concludes with a remark to his entourage that 'if he were not Alexander, he would like to be Diogenes'. The consensus is that the story is no more than *ben trovato*. It nevertheless serves to illustrate the Dog's candour and independence and the (sometimes grudging) respect it elicited.

Self-sufficiency (*autarkeia*)

Independence or self-sufficiency (*autarkeia*) was a code of behaviour the Cynics equally prized. In devoting whole days to the enjoyment of nature's gifts (in this case, the sun's comfortable rays), Diogenes showed that he was content with little, and that little for free. Dismissing Alexander and his offer of material wealth or power reinforces the impression. Sources are consistent in reporting that, so far as material goods were concerned, all he owned he carried on his person: a rough cloak which he folded double in winter against the cold, and bedded down on at night; a knapsack to carry lupins, lentils, vetches and other plants gleaned by the wayside in his wanderings; and a walking stick. For shelter he resorted to public buildings such as temples, and occasionally spent the night in a large ceramic barrel or 'tub' (*pithos*) in Athens' marketplace. He only drank water. According to more than one source, a bowl could be found in his knapsack until he caught sight of a child once managing with just his hands, or a mere piece of bread, to carry food and water to his mouth. From that moment onwards his knapsack was lighter by the weight of a single ceramic bowl.

Training (*askêsis*)

'Self-sufficient' certainly applies to an existence that today would be described as homeless as well as stateless. It involved subsisting on just one (vegetarian) meal a day. In Diogenes' case, at least, it also entailed walking great distances, between Athens and Corinth, and from one Panhellenic festival to another, not only to spread the Cynic word but because by his own admission he liked to watch – not only the athletes but the crowds. This routine demanded and promoted an exceptional degree of physical fitness. In addition to these physical trials, the Cynics practised austerities apparently of their own invention. Diogenes went barefoot all year round; he would embrace marble statues in winter to inure himself against cold; and in the summer months he rolled about in scalding sand. It was intended to serve a pedagogical purpose: '[Diogenes of Sinope] used to say that he followed the example of the trainers of choruses; for they too set the note a little high, to ensure that the rest should hit the right note'.[4] In other words, he did not expect all his disciples to follow him in the extremes to which he carried his austerities. As public displays they nevertheless served to show that even such hardships were within the capacity of human nature to endure. *A fortiori*, hardships involving the loss of familiar physical comforts, to which chance subjects the majority of men at one time or another, had to be tolerable and nothing to fear.

Endurance / self-control (*karteria*)

More than anything else Cynics extolled the virtue of endurance or perseverance – *karteria* in Greek. There was one Homeric hero, Odysseus, who embodied *karteria* and served the Cynics as a model for their own code of conduct. They liked to quote Odysseus' famous lines urging patience and self-mastery:

> *'Bear up, my heart.*
> *You went through things worse than this that day*
> *the Cyclops, in his frantic rage, devoured*
> *your strong companions. You held out then,*
> *until cunning led you from that cave,*
> *where you thought you were going to die.' He said these words,*
> *to hold down the heart within his chest, and his spirit*
> *submitted, enduring everything with resolution.*[5]

Hercules was also treated as an honourary Cynic for his twelve labours, some of which, like the cleaning of the Augean stables, required more forbearance than heroic strength or courage. Cynics preached *karteria* not only as a tonic for the soul, but on altruistic grounds. They were not monastics, ascetics, proto-holy men in the cloister or on top of a pillar. They were very public figures who endured life outdoors and a meagre diet, and no doubt a steady stream of heckling, especially from the gilded youth in the urban centres, while servicing society with their prose hymns to virtue delivered on street corners and in the public square. They invoked the historical Socrates in this connection as well. His capacity to endure extremes of hot and cold, his patient acceptance of the death sentence imposed on him, the self-control he displayed in his steadfastly chaste relations with the handsome Alcibiades – all this served to inspire in them a character trait that naysayers misconstrued as sign of meekness and lack of spirit.

Undoubtedly they were encouraged in part by Socrates to cultivate an attitude of patient forbearance (and, in their turn, influenced the early Church to make it a characteristically Christian virtue). But the degree to which they incorporated this habit of mind into their lifestyle was unprecedented and helped make of them a new kind of philosophical hero.

As we saw in the case of Diogenes and Alexander, Cynics scorned the blandishments of the great ones of the world. Philosophers who succumbed to that temptation were despised. According to Diogenes Laertius, 'Plato saw [Diogenes of Sinope] washing lettuces, came up to him and said to him under his breath, "Had you paid court to Dionysius, you wouldn't now be washing lettuces", and [Diogenes], answered, in a similarly confidential tone, "If you washed lettuces, you wouldn't have to flatter Dionysius" '.[6] The lesson of the *chreia* is clear: not only did they prize their independence but accepted poverty as a condition befitting a philosopher and his spiritual values. They were the first – virtually the only philosophers – to eulogize poverty as a blessing in disguise. Related to this is their indifference to conventional society's judgement on their poverty as well as their squalor, outspokenness and sporadic indulgence in openly outrageous behaviour , such as eating and even masturbating in public. 'Ignominy', Antisthenes said, 'should be endured and even welcomed as one more test of one's mettle';[7] and 'he urged people who were maligned to bear it better than being pelted with rocks'.[8]

Tuphos

Tuphos was a principal Cynic theme, but not a virtue, unlike the themes discussed above. It was, in fact, one of their main points of attack. Originally it had the meaning of 'smoke' or 'vapour'. In our texts it has the metaphorical meaning of 'pretence' or 'imposture'. The Cynics regarded their contemporaries as a sad race of moral degenerates who valued appearance, prestige and wealth above all else. *Tuphos* in Diogenes et al. represents preoccupation with luxury and social standing. In this respect, more than any other, they approach the modern connotation attached to the epithet 'cynical' – bitter, cutting, pessimistic – about a society that had gained the world but lost its soul.

And yet how pessimistic could the Cynics have been when they believed that they could recall men back to the 'primitive' qualities embodied in archaic heroes such as Hercules and Odysseus?

INDIVIDUAL CYNICS

Antisthenes

A question of paternity hangs over the movement's very conception. We have been treating Diogenes as its founder, but his older contemporary Antisthenes deserves a share of the credit. Today the consensus is that Diogenes was the first authentic Cynic, but that Antisthenes, although he did not adopt the Cynic lifestyle (this was Diogenes' invention), exercised a formative influence through his ethical teachings.

Now, most of the sources that you find in this book speak of Antisthenes as the original Cynic. This view shapes not only the life of Antisthenes in Diogenes Laertius, for example, it determines his whole presentation of Cynicism and Stoicism. He says the tag *Haplokuôn* ('downright dog') was attached to Antisthenes in his lifetime.[9] The same tradition is assumed in other writers of the imperial period like Epictetus and Dio Chrysostom. Tradition, in fact, makes him Diogenes' teacher, the man who personally initiated him into the Cynic way of life. These sources are late, however, and have in part been discredited by modern research. That Diogenes was Antisthenes' pupil was effectively challenged by Dudley in his groundbreaking *History of Cynicism*.[10] He identified it as a Stoic fabrication, an effort to establish a respectable Socratic pedigree for their movement by making Antisthenes, who was a known intimate of Socrates, the teacher of Diogenes, who taught Crates the Cynic, who we know on good authority taught Zeno – the founder of Stoicism.

Thus Stoics could claim inspiration, albeit at a few removes,

from Socrates – the figure every philosophical sect after him
wanted a piece of. Whether Antisthenes and Diogenes even met
is open to doubt. But the points of similarity in their ethics are
too many and distinct to be coincidental. As John Moles puts
it, 'Antisthenic influence upon Diogenes has been widely
accepted and is patent'[11] – even if that influence was transmitted indirectly. Consequently, no complete history of Cynicism,
or collection of Cynic sources, can be complete without
Antisthenes. With some degree of fairness he may be credited
with providing the theoretical underpinnings of the sect. Diogenes, to judge from our sources, put them into more consistent
practice (and perhaps took them to extremes that Antisthenes
himself would have recoiled from).

But if his association with Diogenes is unclear, there is no
doubt about his closeness to Socrates. In the first fifteen years
after Socrates' death (399 BC) he was regarded as the foremost
preserver of the master's moral legacy. The emphasis he placed
on moral and physical toughness (*karteria*), for instance, bears
witness to the influence not only of Socrates' teaching but also
the example of Socrates' life. And he certainly passed this value
on to the Cynics. He claimed, according to Diogenes Laertius,[12]
that virtue was sufficient for happiness, 'with the addition, perhaps, of Socratic strength'. He is mentioned by Plato as among
those present at Socrates' death,[13] and makes a frank profession of his allegiance to Socrates in Xenophon's *Symposium*.[14]

According to another ancient tradition, Antisthenes was a
student of Gorgias the sophist, and a teacher of rhetoric himself before he made Socrates' acquaintance. This background
helps explain the report that he intended to make speeches
both critical and complimentary of certain city-states at one of
the Panhellenic festivals:[15] capacity to argue opposed views
with equal facility was accounted a sign of rhetorical prowess.
The only works of his to survive, the display speeches *Ajax* and
Odysseus, are products of the same rhetorical training, arguing
in turn the claim of either man to Achilles' armour after Achilles' death. Giannantoni[16] rightly points out, in defence of the
speeches' authenticity, that several Cynic themes are touched
on in passing, which explains why we have included them here.

Little else in the way of biographical detail has come down to us regarding Antisthenes. His dates are reckoned to be *c.* 445–*c.* 365 BC. He lived most of his adult life in Athens, but was of non-Athenian (perhaps Thracian) origin on his mother's side. He fought with distinction at Tanagra in 424 BC and perhaps was rewarded with citizenship soon afterwards. He was a prolific author, and we have the names – but no more – of sixty additional works by him. Some of these were in dialogue form; the Socratic dialogue did not originate with Plato, it is merely the fact that they are the oldest to survive that accounts for this misconception. Works of logic and epistemology number among his productions as well. But the best surviving witnesses to the moral views that he espoused and taught are Diogenes Laertius 6. 1–19, and his contribution to Xenophon's *Symposium*. In the past, great ingenuity was exercised by scholars to supplement this rather meagre material by allegedly finding allusions to his doctrines in Plato, Aristotle and especially Xenophon. But this project has been largely abandoned as quixotic.

The value he placed on moral and physical toughness seems to have served an even higher principle, that is, *autarkeia* or self-sufficiency. He wrote works in praise of Heracles and Cyrus the Great, both of whom were presented as paradigms of autonomous virtue grounded in the capacity for endurance and sheer hard work. He claimed that virtue was teachable and sufficient for happiness but did not require a great deal of reasoning or erudition to gain. These ideas clearly bridge the characteristic views of Socrates and the Cynics. His militant anti-hedonism anticipates the Cynics also; he is famously quoted as saying that 'I'd sooner lose my mind than lose myself in pleasure'.[17] Much proto-Cynic thought is here, even if he did not become 'the Dog'; that distinction seems definitely to belong to Diogenes. But Diogenes' obvious borrowing of his beliefs is reason enough for having Antisthenes in our collection.

Diogenes of Sinope

Diogenes was born *c.* 410 BC in Sinope on the Black Sea. His father, Hicesias, managed the public bank. He became involved in a scheme to 'deface the currency', an incident that has been transmitted in various versions, particularly as regards the degree to which his son Diogenes was involved. In any case, as we have seen, he turned his reputation for 'defacing the currency' to account by explaining it as a metaphor for his life mission: he aimed to alter received values and replace them with ethical standards that were not just different but directly opposed.

If the details surrounding the scandal are obscure, sources at least agree that the result was Diogenes' exile from Sinope. Because an exile's life is difficult, particularly at first, it may have toughened him and taught him to be thrifty and abstemious by the time he settled in Athens. The status of outcast may also prefigure his renunciation of allegiance to any one city and his self-image as 'a citizen of the world' (*cosmopolitês*). Already we get a picture of someone who had a knack for making a virtue of necessity and turning misfortune to account. Such resilience and ingenuity developed into typical Cynic traits.

Athens was the nursery of philosophical schools and it was here that Diogenes, 'the Dog', made a name for himself by begetting one more. Making due allowance for the inspiration he undoubtedly received from Antisthenes, Diogenes is acknowledged as the founder of Cynicism because he made of Antisthenes' ethical principles the basis for a whole new way of life (and created the characteristic Cynic 'look'). From Socrates he adopted the habit of engaging in philosophical discussions *al fresco* with anyone he happened to run across. As we have seen, Diogenes travelled a fair bit but his home was in Athens; and the Athenians, despite his gruff demeanour, took him to their collective heart. He became one of the city's favourite 'characters', and when his 'tub' or *pithos* broke, the city voted to replace it at public expense.

Beyond this the biographical tradition presents us with a mass of anecdotes (*chreiai*) that are often very entertaining and attest to a consistent set of habits and beliefs that, taken as a whole, inspire confidence that they are at least true to the spirit of the man and his philosophy. But when we find practically the same story repeated in connection with other Cynics, we realize that some must be spurious; Diogenes was a character who attracted good stories to his name without regard to their original context.

Doubts apply not just to the minor incidents around which the *chreiai* are built but to major episodes in his biography – the meeting with Alexander, for instance – and again, differing versions of the event were in circulation that contain significant variations in detail.[18] Besides internal inconsistencies, there are external reasons for questioning the entire business. After sacking Thebes, Alexander remained in Greece only a short time; he hardly had the leisure (or inclination, considering the grand expedition preoccupying him) to go out of his way to meet with a (still obscure) philosopher. And he was relatively obscure himself. True, he had conquered Thebes, but he was not yet 'Alexander the Great', world conqueror, which detracts from the piquancy of this supposed encounter between archpotentate and arch-philosopher.

Historians find the tradition of his capture by pirates, sale and term of enslavement as dubious as that involving him and Alexander.[19] Once more we are faced with many different versions of the tale. This immediately raises questions. Then, too, such disagreements aside, they all are meant to show that happiness can survive circumstances as dire and degrading as enslavement; so Diogenes dared advertise himself when put up for sale as a born leader just made for someone who needed to be taken in hand and governed. Such freedom of speech (*parrhêsia*) in a slave would not have gone unpunished. But fortunately for Diogenes (and the story) he found a taker in one Xeniades of Corinth. Diogenes, of course, endured his condition manfully, raising Xeniades' boys (of course) as apprentice Cynics. Yet the boys came to love him despite (or because of) his strict management; and Xeniades, for his part, boasted that with the acquisition of Diogenes something like a spirit from heaven had been sent into his home.

This puerile romance apparently draws on an imaginary tale composed by the Cynic Menippus. Older literary treatments of the same or similar motif, including a lost play by Euripides in which Hercules is put up for sale, have been cited as influences on Menippus. Heracles was a Cynic icon; and it is not unlikely that in Euripides' drama he, like Diogenes, emerges from his ignoble ordeal with his dignity intact. Unfortunately Diogenes Laertius, never overly judicious in his use of sources, presents the edifying theme as straightforward history.

Predictably, accounts differ as to how Diogenes died. But there seems no reason to doubt Laertius' report that it was in the 113th Olympiad – that is, between 324 and 321 BC – when he must have been nearing ninety.

Laertius' chapter on the Dog is a hotchpotch of aphorisms and legends, along with a few credible facts. As a biographer he was as disorganized as he was gullible. To impose some order on the mass of material included in Book 6 of his *Lives of the Ancient Philosophers*, where Diogenes features, I have borrowed from Giannantoni's disposition of the material under various headings, some chronological, the rest thematic. For reasons of space I could not include all the testimony Giannantoni musters but have had to be selective. The same applies to most of the other Cynics represented in this collection (which comprises most of the principal figures, although minor or marginal ones have by necessity been left out). But the editing process was made easier by how repetitious the sources often are; and I have tried to include the most interesting and revealing variant of a thought or incident where there was a choice to be made. This is also the rationale for including such yarns as Diogenes' capture by pirates and the exemplary way he acquitted himself under these trying circumstances; because in the case of philosophers it is their ideas, or ideals, that count more than their biographies. The tales may be bogus but they are meant to dramatize the principles that, especially in the case of the Cynics, they both practised and preached.

Laertius[20] transmits two lists of Diogenes' writings. For our purposes the most significant item is the *Republic*, because we have some idea of its contents from papyrus rolls preserved by the volcanic eruption that buried Herculaneum in AD 79. Unfortunately, the treatise in question, entitled *On the Stoics*, was written by Philodemus, an Epicurean and not always a reliable source for the views of Stoics or Cynics, whose ideas he deliberately conflates to help discredit the former by associating them with the more controversial views of the latter.

The feasibility of organizing a community along such lines as the fragments of the work permit us to reconstruct will not stand up to scrutiny. True, Diogenes proselytized, on what evidence suggests was almost a daily basis – but to individuals or audiences of a modest size. He was hardly the man to undertake organization of a wholly new and radical society. With no allowance made for traditional social conventions – for marriage, family, politics, office, civic institutions, coinage or a standing army – his republic amounts to a state of libertarian anarchy; as a state or 'republic' it is not only improbable, it is practically a contradiction in terms. When to these negative features we add its endorsement of parricide, cannibalism and incest, we are led to conclude that, while the work was a statement of some serious Cynic positions, it also reflects their collective tendency to parody serious philosophical pretensions (most obviously, in this case, Plato's *Republic*), and their incorrigible urge *à épater le bourgeois*. Certainly we do not find any of the later Cynics invoking the work as a blueprint for a Cynic society, insofar as such a thing was ever mooted again.

The problem of exactly which of the remaining entries on Laertius' lists of Diogenes' writings are genuine is probably insoluble. Nor does it much matter, since the works in question are otherwise lost, and Diogenes in any case seems to have made more of an impression in person than in print.

Crates

Diogenes' most notable successor was Crates of Thebes (*c.* 368– *c.* 283 BC). He began life as a wealthy landowner; his conversion to Cynicism, with the repudiation of wealth this entailed, is that much more remarkable. He was a hunchback, which makes the most significant aspect of his life – his love match with the fair and well-born Hipparchia – compelling testimony to his moral influence. Her parents denied her insistent requests that she be allowed to marry him; in desperation, she threatened suicide if this happiness were denied her. Hipparchia's parents managed to enlist Crates to their side in the dispute. Like so many professed Cynics, he did his best to discourage followers or imitators. Hipparchia, however, would not be put off by his or her parents' refusals and so the pair contracted the first and (as far as we know) the only *kynogamia* (Cynic union). This distinctive form of marriage, as they came to define it, involved living and sleeping together in public places. In his *anaideia* (shamelessness), then, Crates consciously emulated Diogenes. But in important respects their styles diverged. He was less well known for his acerbic wit than for his benevolence: Laertius recounts how he reconciled friends or family members who were at odds for one reason or another. He also helped establish Cynic literature as a genre with distinctive formal elements, as well as what was to become its characteristically seriocomic tone. He composed parodies in hexameters, such as the 'Pêra', modelled on a passage in Homer, purporting to describe an island, but in reality using the description to delineate the conditions of the typical Cynic life. He also wrote a hymn to frugality, and a squib entitled 'An Encomium to the Lentil'.

Hipparchia

Hipparchia was probably fifteen to twenty years younger than Crates. As with other of the Cynics, it is not so much her ideas that interest us, in large part because they did not interest Diogenes Laertius – it is her life that is her legacy. There was no precedent for a woman's wholesale commitment to philosophy and no parallel for another six centuries at least, until we come across the female Neoplatonist philosopher Hypatia. That she chose Cynicism is especially surprising, considering that it took its inspiration from Hercules and seemed less congenial to females of the species than any other ethical regime. As we saw, Crates, for Hipparchia's own good, conspired with her parents to cure her of her ambition to turn Cynic by emphasizing the hardships and lack of creature comforts it entailed. He emphasized, too, that if they were to marry she must adapt to Cynicism and its precepts with the same degree of commitment, no allowances being made for her gender. According to legend, she did not hesitate for a moment. She adopted the Cynic dress as well as the provocative behaviour that the mantle, satchel and staff signalled to strangers even at a distance. Greek women were circumscribed by any number of social rules and restrictions: Hipparchia openly defied them. She excited protest of a kind Cynics generally provoked, but more in her case since she was a woman. The appearance of women in public, unattended by relatives or a husband, was frowned upon in classical Greece; but Hipparchia associated with her Cynic peers in doing it all the time. She accompanied her husband, Crates, to symposia and dinner parties, normally the preserve of men; and on such occasions she dared to challenge the male guests to contests of rational argument on equal terms.[21]

Onesicritus

Onesicritus was a native of the Greek island Astypalaia; his dates are reckoned to be *c*. 360–*c*. 290 BC. According to tradition, he associated with Diogenes himself; there is certainly no mistaking the impact Diogenes had on his writing. But rather than works of a traditionally philosophical character, he is best known for writing a history of Alexander, whom he personally accompanied on campaign. This work is lost, but was drawn on extensively by later geographers, historians and ethnographers. It was also harshly criticized, however, for distorting facts in the interest of presenting its subject in the best possible light and for including as much fable as fact. The distortions begin with his representing himself as the commander of Alexander's fleet, when it appears he was only a pilot. An account of a meeting between Alexander and the queen of the Amazons was also included. Such transparent fictions served to discredit Onesicritus as an historian, even among the first generation of his readers. It appears he was also the original source for the legendary meeting between Alexander and Diogenes – the two great heroes in his life between whom he tried to find a common moral ground.

He is less important, perhaps, for enhancing our knowledge of Cynicism than for reporting information about the faraway lands laid open to the West for the first time by Alexander's expedition. But his bias appears, for instance, in the way he represents the Indian holy men as, for all intents and purposes, Oriental Cynics, devoted to the same physical and moral training (*askêsis*). Anticipating Julian, he is concerned to present Cynicism as a universal philosophy, and the Cynic himself as a genuine citizen of the world (*cosmopolitês*), instead of the product of any parochial mindset.

Bion

Bion is thought to have lived *c.* 335 to *c.* 245 BC. He sampled practically all the styles of philosophy in vogue at Athens in his time before declaring himself for Cynicism. In the history of Cynicism he figures most prominently in the domain of literature.

He was born in the Black Sea town of Olbia by the mouth of the river Borysthenes (the modern-day Dnieper). He came from the lowest stratum of society (his father was a fishmonger, his mother a prostitute); and owing to some criminal activity on his father's part ended up being sold as a slave while still a boy to a rhetorician from whom he received rhetorical training.

Laertius' biography reflects an overtly hostile tradition vis-à-vis Bion. Cynic by profession, he nevertheless travelled the Greek world giving speeches in the manner of a rhetorician, and charged for his performances. He also gladly accepted the patronage of Antigonus II Gonatas at the Macedonian court. He subsequently taught philosophy at Rhodes and died at Chalcis in Euboea – further proof that his life conformed as much or more to the model of a well-travelled sophist or rhetorician than a bare-footed Cynic with his walking stick.

His works (none of which survive) reportedly drew on all the stylistic resources he had learned as a boy at his master's feet. For all these reasons he was an atypical Cynic and one who must have been regarded by his nominal peers with some suspicion and resentment. Ultimately this must also account for Laertius' unsympathetic portrait of the man. Laertius gives no formal list of his writings but says 'he left many memoirs and sayings of useful application'. Horace alludes to his satires and caustic wit,[22] but Teles is our best source for Bion's contribution to Cynicism; he frequently cites him by name and paraphrases his moral theses. From Teles we get a good idea, too, of Bion's talent for finding apt metaphors and clever turns of phrase for the presentation of his ideas. He may not, for instance, have invented the comparison of life to a drama in which we are to play whatever role fate assigns, be it humble or exalted, a leading or a supporting part; but he formulated it in such a way as to ensure that it had a long life in popular presentations of Cynic-Stoic thought. And, like several other Cynics, his personal experience of slavery must have helped to make his treatment of this common Cynic-Stoic theme more compelling.

Teles

Virtually nothing is known about Teles. From internal evidence it appears that he was a Megarian schoolmaster practising in the second half of the third century BC. Seven extracts of the lectures of Teles are preserved by Stobaeus, in an anthology of morally improving extracts from classical authors compiled in the early fifth century AD. But Stobaeus' own excerpts from Teles derive from an earlier epitome by an otherwise unknown Theodorus. Thus what we have is a collection of extracts from extracts, and it is possible that between Teles and Theodorus, or Theodorus and Stobaeus, the writings were subject to at least one other stage of redaction.

Teles has been faulted both on stylistic and logical grounds; but we cannot discount the possibility that his deficiencies as a writer reflect the tangled editing process his works underwent. If nothing else, they are valuable for preserving fragments from Crates, Metrocles and especially Bion.

Demetrius

Demetrius was a Cynic philosopher from Corinth who lived in Rome from AD 37 to 71 during the reigns of Caligula, Nero and Vespasian. The dates of his birth and death cannot be determined. He was the intimate friend of the writer and Stoic philosopher Seneca, who invokes his idol often in his letters and essays. Seneca does not aim to chronicle his life after the manner of Laertius in his *Lives of the Ancient Philosophers*. Nor does he purport to be objective in his estimate of the man, or be interested in what to him seem like biographical trivia. The praise he accords Demetrius has a frank, if indirect, purpose: it is meant to present a model to inspire others to make progress more in line with the same Cynic-Stoic principles, and to endure certain austerities as a short cut to virtue.

Like Dio, Demetrius became involved in the so-called Stoic-Cynic opposition led by certain senators with whom he associated. He was probably exiled to Greece under Nero (AD 66). He was allowed to return, but only for a brief time, because in 71 the emperor Vespasian banished all the philosophers from Rome. In its ruder aspects Cynicism faced a more hostile reception among the Romans with their comparatively conservative culture than other Greek schools of thought. In certain circles it met with outright condemnation. Cicero's round proscription of the Cynic regimen is often cited: 'The Cynic philosophy should be rejected outright; it is incompatible with our sense of decency or shame. And without that, there can be nothing moral, nothing right.'[23] Stoic ethics was heavily indebted to Cynicism, as we have seen. But the Greek philosophers Panaetius and Posidonius, who did most to introduce Stoicism to Rome, took care to purge it of the more offensive features that were part of its Cynic legacy. And Cynicism itself – insofar as it is reflected in Seneca's descriptions of Demetrius – more often evokes the *prisca virtus* (old-fashioned virtue) of Rome in its presumptive golden age than the outlandish and anti-social behaviour that Diogenes and his circle were notorious for.

Dio Chrysostom

Dio Chrysostom was born T. Flavius Cocceianus Dio in *c.* AD 40 and died *c.* 120; he was also known as Dio of Prusa after the name of his native city (now Bursa) in the province of

Bithynia (now part of north-western Turkey). The epithet Chrysostom ('golden-tongued') appears for the first time in a rhetorical treatise of the third century AD.

Dio received a thorough training in rhetoric that prepared him to seek his fortune in Rome, probably soon after the death of Nero in 68. He made powerful connections among the political and intellectual elite of the capital and complemented his rhetorical training by studying philosophy with Musonius Rufus (who also taught Epictetus). Musonius is usually classified as a Stoic but the extracts of his surviving lectures show a strong Cynicizing bias. That Dio in his speeches evinces most sympathy for Cynicism from among the foremost doctrines of his day is easily explained as an effect of his introduction to philosophy by Musonius. It is no coincidence that Epictetus was also his disciple and looks favourably on Cynicism (as we will see) as well, besides making frequent flattering references to Diogenes en passant.

In Rome Dio got caught up in a struggle between Nero's successor, Vespasian (who ruled AD 69–79) and a group of senatorial aristocrats who found in philosophy, especially Stoic and Cynic philosophy, a sort of ideological basis for their resistance to the emperor's oppressive rule. Since Dio wrote works delineating the role of the ideal king, it was evidently not monarchy (or the principate) as such that he objected to, but tyranny – typified, for instance, by confiscation of the property of the rich to fill the royal coffers, arbitrary executions, and – most galling of all to Dio and his Cynic cohorts – ruthless suppression of free speech, especially speech critical of the emperor.

As a result of his association with the resistance Dio was sentenced to exile in 82 by Domitian, not to return to Rome until 96. During this decade and a half of wandering he took his commitment to Cynicism to the next level and put on the Dog's cloak and satchel.[24] As he writes of himself, 'People who met me judged from my appearance that I was either a vagrant, a beggar – or a philosopher. In time, without any conscious effort on my part, I became known as a philosopher ... And indeed, I profited from this designation, because many people consulted me on questions of good and bad; so that I was forced to reflect on those topics ... My reflections led me to conclude that practically everyone was devoid of sense ... that all were subject to the same distractions – money, reputation, physical pleasure – and that none knew how to escape them and free his soul ... So I blamed them all, and especially myself.'

Under Nerva, Dio's banishment was lifted and he was again permitted access to Rome. He retired his Cynic costume and turned to writing and delivering speeches. The following years were very productive and he composed eighty orations, all of which survive. We have included three in which Cynicism in general, and Diogenes in particular, make up the dominant subject matter.

Dio belonged to a social and literary phenomenon known as the Second Sophistic, which flourished in the context of the *pax Romana* from the early first century AD until the early part of the third. 'Sophistic' means it was a movement of sophists, that is, orators who declaimed in public and often taught rhetoric. As Dio saw it (in contrast, say, to Plato), there was no inherent conflict between rhetoric and philosophy. In fact, a good grounding in rhetoric was essential to philosophy practised on Dio's terms. He makes no pretence to originality or profundity as a philosopher; he only aims to promote it most effectively to the broadest possible audience. Dio uses the authority of Diogenes' persona in an important series of speeches to spread and support Cynic values such as autonomy and freedom of speech. In his presentation of Diogenes in Orations 6 and 8 we miss the humour that Diogenes displays in Lucian and Laertius; his Diogenes is a bit bland by comparison. But in the main, the impression he leaves is remarkably similar to Diogenes' image in the *chreiai* tradition.

Lucian

We have few details concerning Lucian's life. He was born in the eastern half of the empire, in a town called Samasota, part of present-day Turkey. He lived *c.* AD 125–*c.* 180. He was not a Cynic. In fact, he was not a philosopher. In his *Apology*, he disowns the title of *sophos*, and describes himself as 'a member of the common mob, who has devoted himself to literature'. Philosophy, nevertheless, features prominently in his *oeuvre*. Among comic writers of antiquity whose works we can read at first hand because by good luck they have survived, only Aristophanes perhaps surpasses him. Aristophanes' *Clouds* shows that in the classical age philosophers had already become sporadic figures of fun. Their eccentricity, both in their doctrines and their personal habits, provided material enough for sport; the fact that the various sects seemed unable to agree on anything made their abstruse views seem even less deserving of serious attention. Lucian exploited philosophy to similarly sarcastic effect while also adding original comic touches of his own. Yet his attitude was not wholly dismissive. His view of the *sophoi* was ambivalent. His piece on Peregrinus transcends satire, its harshness qualifies it as personal invective. But his *Demonax* is as reverent (and probably just as one-sided) as his *Death of Peregrinus* is reproachful.

In Lucian, contemporary Cynics function in a dual capacity, as both satirist and satirized. In his work on Demonax, the main character is represented as maintaining the honourable Cynic tradition of wry humour. When he prepared for a winter voyage, a friend asked how he relished the prospect of capsizing and becoming food for fish. 'It would be unreasonable of me to begrudge them a meal,' he said, 'considering how many they have provided me.'[25] But in Lucian the habit of lampooning false philosophers, such as Peregrinus, is well established; it only becomes more prominent during the Roman period. Cynicism certainly furnished the right set of circumstances for impostors to exploit: they had no credentials apart from their (very cheap) get-up, they depended on handouts for sustenance; by Lucian's time the content of their street-corner tirades had grown very long in the tooth; no diploma or certification process existed to prove that a declared Cynic had endured the requisite *askêsis* to qualify him for the *tribôn*. The early Cynics had criticized the morals of their degenerate generation. Epictetus and Julian are equally exercised by how Cynics of their day have declined from the high standard set by Diogenes and his immediate successors. Their works devoted to the theme of Cynicism are written above all in a spirit of revival. It is doubtful, however, if there is any such reforming agenda behind Lucian's *Death of Peregrinus*; nor should the *Demonax* be regarded as anything more than an uncritical eulogy. The value of his 'Cynic' works lies in the picture they provide of the movement in his time, besides the information they furnish about the Dogs Demonax and Peregrinus.

Epictetus

Epictetus' dates are reckoned to be *c.* AD 55–*c.* 135. Epictetus was not a Cynic but a Stoic. But we have seen that Cynicism and Stoicism were close from the beginning. His discourse 'On Cynicism' presents an idealized picture of Cynicism. He replaces the 'shamelessness' (*anaideia*) of the old Cynics with an ideal of honour (*aidôs*). This and other changes reflect the good scrubbing the old Cynic was subjected to at the hands of the Romans. Diogenes emerges gleaming, eloquent, dignified. Cynicism persists as an ideal even for Epictetus, who usually flies the Stoic flag.

Julian

Much the same applies to Julian, who reigned as emperor of Rome from AD 355 to 363. He is also known as Julian the Apostate because he was raised a Christian but reverted to paganism. Like Epictetus, Julian disapproves of his contemporaries in the Cynic fold, although he approves of an ideal Cynicism that he associates with Diogenes, the prototypical Dog. Like Epictetus, too, he was not a professed Cynic himself. He identified most with Neoplatonism, whose doctrines supply much of the substance of the first oration we have translated, usually in digressions when the focus on Cynicism is temporarily lost sight of. But in the process he followed Epictetus' lead in presenting an idealized Cynicism as a timeless moral paradigm. In the first extract, he is seen defending the rigours of Diogenes' regime against a contemporary critic. In the second he reflects on what place, if any, myth has a right to in philosophical discourse. In their shared Cynic sympathies, Julian, the Neoplatonic philosopher-king, as well as Epictetus, the professed Stoic, find the figures of Diogenes and Crates still helpful supports for their customary philosophical positions.

THE LEGACY OF CYNICISM

If imitation is the sincerest form of flattery, Stoic ethics, which is a development of Cynic ethics, suffices to establish the movement's importance. Diogenes Laertius[26] gets at the connection neatly, writing, '[Cynics] hold that life in agreement with virtue is man's goal (*telos*), as Antisthenes says in his *Heracles*: exactly like the Stoics. For indeed there is a close relationship between the two schools. Hence it has been said that Cynicism is a short cut to virtue; and after the same pattern did Zeno of Citium[27] live his life.' Zeno composed his own *Republic* in the tradition of utopian theorizing popularized by Plato. Contemporaries joked that it was 'written on the tail of the dog'[28] so much did it share with (or borrow from) Diogenes' treatise – in doing away with money, recommending that men and women wear the same clothes, and promoting the community of wives.[29] Chrysippus, Stoicism's leading theorist, approved of Cynicism for the prospective philosopher, calling it (again) 'a short cut to virtue'.[30] He also wrote a *Republic*. Citation of a single sentence should be enough to locate it squarely in the tradition of Diogenes' radical political tract: 'We should look to the beasts and infer from their behaviour that [incest and cannibalism] are not out of place or unnatural.'[31]

Identifying the *telos* as 'life in agreement with nature' is tantamount to saying that it is the key to happiness (*eudaimonia*). But attaining lasting happiness requires mental and physical training that enable a person – happily – to endure life's adverse circumstances. This training (*askêsis*) conduces to bravery, self-control and justice. Happiness entails possession of these virtues, and renders a person wise and free. External goods commonly considered necessary for happiness, such as wealth, fame and political power, have no natural value.

Cynics and Stoics held these moral propositions in common, and not by accident. By calling Cynicism 'a short cut to virtue', Stoics even allowed that it got them to their shared goal quicker. It was a short cut because it entailed a radical break with family, property, social comforts and social conventions – obviously not a project most people would contemplate, much less complete. Add to which, it disparaged as idle the study of physics and logic. In the Roman period we find the affinity between the two schools reaffirmed. Demetrius the Cynic is praised by Seneca *in extenso*, for values and character traits entirely consistent with the Stoic principles he normally upholds. Diogenes occupies a similarly exalted place in Epictetus' *Discourses*, and his favourable presentation of Cynicism in Discourse 3. 22 is one of the fullest and most important descriptions of the Cynic movement to survive from antiquity.

Similar approval, even if expressed in his less effusive style, is evinced in the *Meditations* of the Stoic Marcus Aurelius: 'Alexander, Caesar, Pompey; what are these to Diogenes, Heraclitus and Socrates? These penetrated into the true nature of things; into all causes, and all subjects: and upon these did they exercise their power and authority. But as for those, as the extent of their error was, so far did their slavery extend.'[32]

The historical Jesus as a Jewish Cynic

Some historians have noted the similarities between the life and teachings of Jesus and those of the Cynics. Certain scholars have argued that the Q document, the hypothetical common source for Jesus' sayings in the gospels of Matthew and Luke, has strong similarities with the teachings of the Cynics. The renewed quest for the historical Jesus has led others to point out that first-century Galilee was a world in which Hellenistic ideas collided with Jewish thought and traditions. The city of Gadara, only a day's walk from Nazareth, was a noted centre of Cynic activity. The verses in the Sermon on the Mount advocating poverty, and assuring Jesus' followers that nature will

provide, certainly evoke Cynic principles, albeit with a pro-
nounced religious colouring absent from most Cynic sources
owing to Jesus' virtual identification of nature with God:
'Therefore I say unto you, Take no thought for your life, what
you shall eat, or what you shall drink; nor yet for your body,
what you shall put on. Is not the life more than food, and the
body than clothing?'[33]

Cynics of course appealed to the example of animals as a
model of the carefree life: 'Consider the beasts yonder and the
birds, how much freer from trouble they live than men, and
how much more happily also, how much healthier and stronger
they are, and how each of them lives the longest life possible,
although they have neither hands nor human intelligence. And
yet, to counter-balance these and their other limitations, they
have one very great blessing – they own no property.'[34] The
passage inevitably evokes the verses immediately following the
passage from the Sermon on the Mount quoted above: 'Look at
the crows: they don't sow seeds, gather a harvest or put them
in barns or storerooms. Yet your father in heaven looks after
them . . . Can any of you live even a moment longer by worrying about it?'[35]

Other scholars, however, doubt that Jesus was much influenced by the Cynics. In their view, the Jewish apocalyptic
tradition is of much greater importance to the understanding of
Jesus' mission. They point to his baptism by John the Baptist,
who was certainly part of the apocalyptic strain in Palestine at
the time, and to the hope on the part of his disciples that Jesus
was the Messiah who would free Israel from Roman rule and
restore its independence.[36]

If scholars differ over the degree to which Cynicism influenced Jesus, there is general agreement that it helped shape the
direction of Christian asceticism from its origins in the figure of
the Holy Man of Roman Egypt and Syria, right through the
Middle Ages with its various orders of mendicant friars. Jesus'
charge to his disciples to adopt a nomadic lifestyle, relying on
the charity of whomever they chanced to meet and attempted
to convert ('Don't take anything with you on your journey
except a stick': Mark 6:8), already has obvious parallels with

the Cynic's voluntary indigence and vagrant habits. The Dominicans punned on their name and called themselves 'Domini canes' – the Lord's (faithful) dogs. The Franciscans – wandering the world, voluntarily living at subsistence level, accepting whatever menial work sufficed to survive, or more often begging for their bread – invite obvious comparison with Epictetus' idealized picture of the Cynics as god's elect.

NOTES

1. Arist. *Rh.* 1411a24.
2. Cf. A. A. Long, 'Timon of Phlius: Pyrrhonist and Satirist', *Proceedings of the Cambridge Philological Society* 204 (1978), pp. 68–90.
3. DL 6. 69.
4. DL 6. 35.
5. Homer, *Od.* 20. 18–21; cf. section 137 §204.
6. DL 6. 58.
7. DL 6. 11.
8. DL 6. 7.
9. DL 6. 13.
10. D. R. Dudley, *A History of Cynicism* (London, 1937), pp. 1–16.
11. J. Moles, 'Honestius quam ambitiosus: An exploration of the Cynic's attitude to moral corruption in his fellow man', *JHS* 103 (1983), pp. 103–23, at 104, n8.
12. DL 6. 11.
13. *Phaedo* 59b.
14. Xenophon, *Symposium* 8. 4.
15. DL 6. 2.
16. *SSR* note 26, IV. 257–64.
17. DL 6. 3.
18. *SSR*, note 43, IV. 443–51.
19. *SSR*, note 44, IV. 453–6.
20. DL 6. 80.
21. Compare section 89 § 97.
22. Horace, *Epistles* 2. 2. 60.
23. *De off.* 1. 148.
24. *Or.* 32. 22.
25. *Demonax* § 13.
26. DL 6. 105.

27. *Zeno of Citium*: A disciple of Crates and the founder of Sto-
    icism.
28. DL 7. 4.
29. DL 7. 33.
30. DL 7. 121.
31. Plut. *On Stoic Self-Contradictions* 1045A.
32. *Meditations* 8. 3.
33. Matthew 6:25.
34. Dio Chrysostom, *Or.* 10. 16.
35. Matthew 6:26.
36. Acts 1:6.

Further Reading

The basic sourcebook for the early Cynics is G. Giannantoni, *Socratis et Socraticorum Reliquiae* (Naples, 1990), 4 vols. The groundbreaking work of D. R. Dudley, *A History of Cynicism* (London, 1937), is dated in details but holds up well overall and remains, in my view, the best introduction to the subject. A valuable study that takes Cynicism into its purview is A. O. Lovejoy and G. Boas, *Primitivism and Related Ideas in Antiquity* (Baltimore, 1935).

Of more recent treatments, the best known to me is *Cynics (Ancient Philosophies)* by William Desmond (Berkeley, 2008); see also his companion volume, *The Greek Praise of Poverty: Origins of Ancient Cynicism* (Notre Dame, 2006).

There is a miscellany edited by B. Branham and M. Goulet-Cazé, *The Cynics: The Cynic Movement in Antiquity and Its Legacy* (Berkeley, 1996), which not only includes many useful articles but is enhanced by the inclusion of ancillary material such as a list of each known Cynic with a thumbnail biography, making of the collection an essential resource. *Le Cynisme ancien et ses prolongements*, edited by Marie-Odile Goulet-Cazé and Richard Goulet (Paris, 1993), is another collection of articles worth consulting.

More specialized monographs tend to focus on aspects of Cynicism's influence. A case for its influence on Jesus, arguing that in his social milieu he would have been immediately identified as an itinerant preacher in the Cynic mould, is argued in two books by F. G. Downing, *Christ and the Cynics: Jesus and Other Radical Preachers in the First Century Tradition* (Sheffield, 1988) and *Cynics and Christian Origins* (Edinburgh,

1992); see also J. D. Crossan, *The Historical Jesus: The Life of a Mediterranean Jewish Peasant* (New York, 1992). *The Cynic Enlightenment: Diogenes in the Salon* by Louise Shea (Baltimore, 2010) treats of Cynicism's revival in the eighteenth century, with special attention to Diogenes' influence on Rousseau and his radical politics.

A Note on the Translation

Wherever possible, I have translated from the Greek text edited by G. Giannantoni in his four-volume *Socratis et Socraticorum Reliquiae*. Volume II is devoted to the early Cynics, from Antisthenes through Crates and Hipparchia. For later authors I have used the texts available at the Thesaurus Linguae Graecae online project; my thanks to Prof. James Porter and the UC Irvine Classics Dept. for gracious permission to access this resource *gratis* for a year. Otherwise, I resorted to the texts available online as part of the Perseus Project. The translation of Epictetus' *On Cynicism* is reproduced with only minor changes from my edition of Epictetus' *Discourses*, also in the Penguin Classics series; permission to reuse it is gratefully acknowledged. All the translations, including the Homeric and other poetic passages, are my own.

THE CYNIC PHILOSOPHERS

[LUCIAN], THE CYNIC

This dialogue was probably not composed by Lucian, but is written in imitation of his style, and is included here because it serves as a useful introduction to our subject. The main speaker is supposed to be a typical Cynic; he is identified simply as 'the Cynic', in fact. Lycinus, the interlocutor, is not otherwise known and is probably made up – a mere device to challenge 'the Cynic' to prove the value of his vocation.

1 *KYNIKOS* – 'The Cynic' by [Lucian]

LYCINUS: [1] Hey you! Who are you with the beard and long hair, but no shirt, no shoes, and practically naked? who prefers a life of wandering more suited to a beast than a human being? who subjects their flesh to pain and hardship, unlike normal people, and who roams from place to place, prepared to sleep on the ground, so that your cloak is covered in filth – not that it was ever soft, fine, or pretty to begin with?

KYNIKOS: Yes, and I don't even need the cloak. But it's the kind that is easiest to get and gives its owner the least trouble to maintain, which is enough for me. [2] I'd like to ask *you* something, though: Don't you think there's something wrong about excessive luxury, and something right about thrift and economy?

L: Of course.

K: Then why, when you see me living more economically than most, do you criticize me instead of other people?

L: Because your life does not impress me as more economical than others', simply as more deficient – as quite empty, in fact, and impoverished. You're no better off than panhandlers who have to beg for their daily bread.

K: [3] The question, then, comes to this: what does it mean to have enough or too little? Shall we discuss it?

L: If you like.

K: The man whose needs are met can be said to have enough, don't you think?

L: I suppose.

K: And the man who has too little is described that way when his means fall short of his needs and don't match his requirements?

L: Yes.

K: Then nothing is missing from my life, because nothing in it fails to satisfy my needs.

L: [4] Explain.

K: Consider any of the things that we've come to depend on, such as shelter. We need it for protection, right?

L: Yes.

K: All right. And clothes, what are they for? Protection too, I suppose?

L: Yes.

K: But what in the world is 'protection' for? Presumably this 'protection' is meant to improve the quality of life?

L: I guess so.

K: Now do my feet look to be in any worse shape than other people's?

L: I can't tell.

K: Maybe this will help you. What are feet for?

L: Walking.

K: And do you think my feet do any worse a job of walking than most people's?

L: Well, probably not.

K: Then if they fill their function as well, it follows that their condition is in no way inferior.

L: I concede it.

K: Then as far as feet go, it seems I am no worse off than your average person.

L: Apparently not.

K: What about the rest of my body? Is it worse than others'? Because if it's worse, that means it's weaker, strength being the measure of a body's fitness. So is it weaker?

L: It doesn't seem to be.

K: Then I don't believe my body in general, or my feet in particular, come up short in the 'protection' department. They would be in poor condition if they were, since deficiency of any kind has a bad effect in any circumstance. Again, my body doesn't seem to be any less well nourished for depending on whatever fortune provides.

L: I would agree.

K: And my body is strong, which proves that the food I'm given is healthy; if the food were unhealthy, my body would be in poor health too.

L: True enough.

[5] K: Well, if that's true, then why fault my lifestyle and call it disgusting?

L: For heaven's sake, because nature – which you are always acclaiming – and the gods have given us the earth and its blessings for everyone to use, and not just use but enjoy. Yet you ignore these advantages – or most of them – and take no more account of them than do beasts. You drink water like beasts, you eat whatever you happen to find, like dogs, and like dogs you sleep just anywhere, as much satisfied with straw for a bed as they are. Add to which your coat is no better than a bum's. But if it turns out that you are the one justified in needing no more, then God was mistaken to supply sheep with wool, make vines capable of producing sweet wine, and create nature in all its wonderful variety, including different kinds of olive oil, honey and the rest, so that we have a choice of food, of drink that is pleasant, soft beds and other furnishings, fine houses and other cunning inventions. For the products of the arts are gifts of the gods too, which it is a pity to renounce as if we were men condemned to prison and dispossessed. It's even more deplorable when someone denies himself these benefits willingly; that is sheer madness.

[6] K: Well, there may be something in what you say. But consider: suppose a rich man in a spirit of warmth and generosity
   gave a feast and invited many people of different sorts, some
   healthy, others sick, and put out a large and varied spread.
   And let's suppose one of the company grabbed and ate all of
   it, not just the food put before him, but what was at a distance from him and intended for the less fortunate guests – and
   this though he was in perfectly good health, and having but
   the one stomach needed little enough to be satisfied but was
   apt to burst by devouring so much. What would you think of
   such a person? Would you consider him reasonable?

L: No.

K: Well mannered?

L: No.

[7] K: Now imagine that someone at the same table, ignoring
   the range of dishes, settled instead on the one closest to him
   which is sufficient for his needs, and ate it politely without
   even a glance at the other provisions. Wouldn't you think
   him better bred and better mannered than the other person?

L: Of course.

K: Well, do you get my point or must I spell it out?

L: Tell me.

K: God is that gracious host who provides many dishes of various kinds, so that his guests can have whatever suits
   them – the healthy, the sick, the strong, and the infirm. We
   are not supposed to eat all of them indiscriminately; each
   should take what is set in front of him and of that only as
   much as he really needs. [8] You resemble the guest who, in
   his greed and gluttony, helps himself to everything – and not
   just what's easy of access from local land and water. You
   import your pleasures from the ends of the earth, always
   prizing what's exotic over what's regional, what's expensive
   over what's cheap, what's hard to get over what's near to
   hand. In short, instead of a simple life you choose to fill it
   with unnecessary complication. Because all this expensive
   stuff which is supposedly so conducive to happiness and
   which you hold so dear costs a lot in terms of pain and aggra-
   vation. Just look at gold, which is so sought after, or silver, or

expensive houses, fancy clothes, and all that goes with them. Then consider at what price they're acquired in terms of trouble, pain and danger – or rather in terms of blood, death and shattered lives, not just because many people die at sea searching for these luxury goods or ruin their health manufacturing them, but because they are the source of so much intrigue and conflict among you, setting friend against friend, child against parent, even wife against husband.

[9] And these calamities all occur despite the fact that bright colours do nothing to make clothes warmer, gilded roofs afford no better shelter, drink tastes no more appetizing for being served in gold or silver cups, nor is sleep sweeter when taken in ivory beds. In fact, you will often find that people of status cannot get any rest in their ivory beds, wrapped in their expensive blankets. I need hardly tell you that rich and spicy foods are no more nourishing but can actually harm our bodies and induce disease. [10] Why add the things we do and suffer for the sake of sex? Yet how easy it is to allay this passion, unless we are addicted to perversions. Nor is it enough for us to show ourselves mad and dissolute in the pursuit of sex, nowadays we twist everything from its natural use – like people who would treat a coach not as a coach but a carriage.

L: And who does that?

K: Well, you do – when you order men about like beasts of burden, making them carry you on their shoulders in sedan chairs as if you were travelling by carriage, while you recline in state above, yelling directions down at them as though they were donkeys, 'Not this way, fool, that!' And the more often you indulge in such behaviour the higher the world regards you. [11] What about those who use edible things not just for food but for dyes, like the manufacturers of purple dye – aren't they also making an unnatural use of God's creatures?

L: I cannot agree with you there, the cuttlefish is just as suited to provide dye as food.

K: But that's not what it's for. In the same way you could make a punch bowl serve as a teacup if you had to; but that is not its purpose. In the end, though, no one can give a complete account of the misery such people create for themselves, it's too much. Yet you blame me for wanting no part of it when I live like that well-bred guest whom I described. I enjoy what's easily available, preferring what costs least to get, and don't hanker after delicacies imported from the ends of the earth.

[12] And there's this to consider: if my life reminds you of a beast's because my needs are few and meagre, then by the same argument the gods would be even worse off than animals since they have no needs at all. But to really appreciate what it means to have few wants as opposed to many, consider that children require more than adults, women more than men, the sick more than the healthy – wherever you look, in fact, you'll find that the needs of the inferior amount to more. It follows that the gods stand in need of nothing; and those who most resemble the gods need hardly anything at all.[1]

[13] Take Heracles, the best man that ever lived, practically a god and rightly honoured as one. Do you imagine that it was ill fortune that made him go about dressed in a lionskin, forgoing the things that you consider essential? No, Heracles could hardly be called unfortunate, he saved *others* from bad fortune, nor could poverty be the cause of his austere habits when he could go anywhere he wanted on land or sea. In all his labours he got the better of everyone, everywhere, and in his time among men he never met his match. Or is it your view that he could not afford shoes or a bed, which is why he travelled so light? No, the idea is absurd; the fact is he had strength and willpower, he chose to control, not indulge, his desires.

Theseus, too, the son of Poseidon, according to legend, the king of Athens, and the best man of his day – didn't he take after Hercules? [14] He chose to go about shoeless and barely clothed too, and let his hair and beard grow out. In this he was like all the men of ancient times. They were better men than you, and not one of them would have shaved any more than a lion would submit to having its mane cut off. Smooth,

soft flesh becomes a woman; but as they were men, they
chose to look like men. They believed that a beard enhanced
a man's appearance like a horse's or a lion's mane, which
God gave these animals for no other reason than to enhance
their majesty. In the same way God has given men the complement of a beard; and so it's the men of old that I admire
and choose to imitate. I disdain the rich food and fancy
clothes of the man of today, not to mention the unnatural
fashion for smoothing and shaving every part of the body,
the private parts not excepted.

[15] My prayer is that my feet be just like hooves, as Chiron's
were said to be; that I need bedclothes no more than do lions,
expensive food no more than dogs. Let the whole world be
bed large enough for me, let me call the universe my home;
and may I always prefer the food that's easiest to acquire.
May I never need gold or silver; and I wish the same for my
friends, since greed for money is the source of society's wars,
plots, murders and divisions. And behind it is the unceasing
lust for more. So let such desires keep their distance. I hope
never to hanker after more than others, but instead be
granted the capacity to do with less.

[16] There you have an outline of our ambitions – ambitions,
to be sure, different from those of the masses. And since we
differ from them so much in character it isn't surprising that
we should differ in appearance. What is surprising, rather, is
how you appreciate that actors and musicians should have a
characteristic dress and uniform, but don't afford philosophers the same privilege, believing instead they should look
the way most people do – though most people are hardly
worth emulating. But if a philosopher be allowed his own
uniform, what better one to have than one that shocks people
who have no principles – a uniform that is about the last
style of dress they would choose for themselves?

[17] So naturally my appearance tends towards the rough and
shaggy – with a worn cloak, long hair, and bare feet. Yours,
on the other hand, is indistinguishable from that of cat-
amites, with the same colour and softness of coat, having the
same large wardrobe, same hair, same shoes, same perfume.

Yes, you even smell like them now, the richest among you the most – and yet, what, in that case, can people like you really be worth? You are no more capable of work than they are, no less addicted to pleasure. You eat like them, you sleep like them, you walk like them – or, rather *don't* walk like them, but prefer to be carried around like baggage on litters or in coaches. *My* feet take me wherever I have to go. And I can put up with any amount of cold or heat and not complain about the gods and their works because I am poor, whereas you, because of your wealth, are never happy about anything but are always dissatisfied. You cannot put up with what you have, but must have whatever is lacking. In winter you want summer, in summer, winter, when it's hot you want cold, when it's cold you want hot – like people who are sick and never content but always complaining. But if in their case their sickness is to blame in yours it is *you* who are to blame.

[18] Next, you try to reform us and get us to change because we often are ill-advised in what we do. But you give no thought to your own actions, basing none of them on rational judgement, only on impulse and habit. You are just like people caught in a flood, carried along wherever the current takes them. You go wherever your desires lead. Your situation is like that of the man, they say, who mounted a wild horse. It dashed off with him, and with the horse in full flight he couldn't dismount. Then they passed someone who asked where they were headed. 'That's up to the horse,' the man managed to respond. Now if someone asks you where you're off to, if you're honest you will simply say that your desires will decide – the desires of pleasure, greed, and ambition, to be precise. Then anger, or some other emotion like fear, seems to direct you. For you are on the back of not one but many horses, and different ones at different times – but all of them out of control, which is why you end up in ditches or falling off cliffs. And you have no presentiment that any such calamity awaits you.

[19] This worn cloak, however, which you make fun of, my long hair, and this style of dress, are so effective that they afford me a life of quiet, doing whatever I like, with whomever I like.

No ignorant or uneducated person will come near me because of how I dress, and the fops turn around after spying me a long way off. Men of real refinement and intelligence seek me out, and those who aspire to virtue – the latter especially, since their company affords me the greatest pleasure. I don't hang about the doors of men that society considers happy. Their gold crowns and purple robes are absurdities to me, which I can only laugh at in derision.

[20] I would have you know that my appearance is suited, not just to men of virtue but to the gods, for all the fun you make of it. Examine the statues of the gods and see whether they resemble more you or me. And not just the Greeks', go and inspect images of foreign gods as well and see whether they are depicted in paint or marble with long hair and a beard like me, or close-shaven like you. Most of them, too, you will find are shirtless. So how dare you describe my appearance as scruffy when it even suits the gods?

SUMMARY OF CYNIC
DOCTRINES

At the end of his chapter on Diogenes the Dog, Laertius appends a summary of Cynic doctrines. We reproduce it here, to orient the reader to the basics of Cynic philosophy.

2 (DL 6. 103–5)

[103] Here now are doctrines found among Cynics in general, working on the presumption that Cynicism really is a distinctive school of philosophy and not – as some maintain – just a way of life.

Like Ariston of Chios they were content to focus on matters of ethics to the exclusion of physics and logic. What some assert of Socrates, Diocles reports of Diogenes when he quotes him as saying: 'Our business is to find out "What there is of good and evil within our home" (Homer. *Od.* 4. 392)'. Nor do they have time for the traditional Greek curriculum. [104] They dispense with geometry, music and the rest. And so, when someone showed Diogenes a clock, 'a useful thing', he said, 'to keep you from being late for dinner'.

They define the goal of man as life in accordance with virtue, a position the Stoics also endorsed. Certainly there is an affinity between the schools; the Stoics actually described Cynicism as a shorter route to virtue.

They believed in a simple life, eating just as much as we need to survive and wearing a single, shabby cloak. For wealth, prestige and aristocratic lineage they had nothing but contempt. Some were vegetarians and water drinkers and were satisfied with any kind of shelter or tub, like Diogenes. He used to say that it was characteristic of the gods to want nothing and of people most like the gods to want next to nothing. [105] They believed that virtue could be taught . . . and once acquired was ours for life; that philosophers were deserving of romantic relationships, were immune to error, and on naturally friendly terms with their peers. Nothing, they said, should be entrusted to luck. Like Ariston of Chios, they thought that virtue was the only good thing and vice the only bad thing. Nothing else had value either way.

ANTISTHENES

As someone who can be described as a proto-Cynic, Antisthenes occupies a transitional role in our story; he served to link Socrates through a putative chain of association with Diogenes, the Dog in full. However controversial this diadoche *(succession) may be, the consensus is that he planted the conceptual seeds of Cynic thought that in Diogenes advanced from theory to practice: thus the justification for his inclusion here. He is represented first by the testimony of Diogenes Laertius, then by an extract from a Socratic dialogue by Xenophon, another member of the Socratic circle, purporting to express his paradoxical values and singular habits that prefigure Cynicism in its mature form, followed by a pair of epideictic speeches from his own hand.*

3 (DL 6. 1–19)

[1] Antisthenes, son of Antisthenes, Athenian

He was said not to be of authentic Athenian birth. When reproached on this account he said, 'The very mother of the gods is Phrygian';[1] his own mother was supposedly from Thrace. When he distinguished himself at the battle of Tanagra, Socrates was moved to say that no child of two Athenian parents could have turned out braver. He himself would poke fun at the Athenians' claim to be born of the earth by pointing out that this made them no better than locusts or snails.

Antisthenes originally studied rhetoric under Gorgias. This

accounts for the rhetorical style found especially in his dialogues *Truth* and *Exhortations*. [2] According to Hermippus, he originally planned to attack and also to praise the Athenians, Thebans and Spartans at the Isthmian games, but dropped the idea when he saw many from those cities present.

Later he came to know Socrates, and gained so much from the association that he recommended to his own students that they become Socrates' students along with him. Every day he hiked the five miles from Peiraeus where he lived to Athens to hear Socrates speak. From Socrates he learned what it meant to be strong and resilient; and so he became the first Cynic philosopher. He proved that hardship can be a good thing by invoking the examples of the great Heracles and of Cyrus – one illustrious example each from Greek and foreign culture.

[3] He was the first to define reason, as 'the faculty that discloses the truth of a thing past or present'. He would always say, 'I'd sooner lose my mind than lose myself in pleasure.' And, 'Only have sex with women who will thank you for it.' A young man from the Black Sea area asked him what supplies he should bring to enrol in his school. 'Three things,' he replied. 'A brain, a brain and a brain.'[4] Asked what kind of wife to marry he said, 'If she's ugly you'll be swearing, if she's pretty you'll be sharing.' Told that Plato maligned him he said, 'It is the fate of great men to do good works and have bad things said about them.' . . .

[5] To the question, what was the most a man could hope for, he answered, 'To die happy.' A friend came crying to him because he had lost his notes. 'Well,' he replied, 'you should have inscribed them on your brain instead of on scraps of paper.' People are consumed by their own jealousy, he believed, the way iron is eroded by rust. He said that whoever would be immortal should live purely and honestly. He maintained that states begin to fail when they cannot tell the bad citizens from the good. Hearing that some worthless men had complimented him, he responded, 'Dear me, what offence could I have committed to deserve such praise?'

[6] The mutual support of a like-minded family was stronger than any fortified city, he said. And, the only things to bring on

a sea voyage are what will float with you if the ship wrecks. Criticized once for keeping bad company, he responded, 'Well, doctors keep company with the infirm without themselves getting sick.' It made no sense to him that we remove weeds from grain, and keep men unfit for service out of the army, yet when it comes to the state we don't bar bad men from participation.[2] Asked what he gained from philosophy, he answered, 'The habit of engaging myself in dialogue.'

When Diogenes asked him for a coat, he suggested folding his tunic in half instead. [7] Asked what was the most important thing to learn, he said, 'How not to forget what you have learned.' He used to urge people who were maligned to bear with it more than somebody pelted with rocks. Antisthenes had a cheap coat which he wore with the worn areas on the outside, where no one could miss them. 'I can see your vanity through the holes in your coat,' Socrates said to him.

[8] Someone wanted to know what he should do to become a better man. 'You must be ready to learn from those who know better what faults you have and how to rid yourself of them.' Someone once spoke in praise of the affluent life. 'Why, I wish for nothing else than affluence,' he said in answer – 'on my enemies and their families.'

[10] Here are his doctrines. He argued that virtue was a thing that could be taught. Virtuous people were the true aristocrats. [11] To be happy it was enough to be virtuous, with the assistance, perhaps, of Socratic fortitude. Virtue was a matter of deeds, not words or erudition. The wise man was self-sufficient, because what belonged to others also belonged to him. Ignominy should be welcomed as a form of hardship. The wise man would regulate his conduct as a citizen not by conventional laws but by the principles of virtue. He would marry to raise a family, selecting the most beautiful woman for his wife. And he would love her, because only wise men knew what was deserving of love.

[12] Diocles credits him further with the following views. To the wise man nothing is strange and nothing impossible. The moral man deserves love. Good men are friends. It is right to make the brave and just one's allies. Virtue is unremovable

armour. It is better to fight with a few good men against all the
bad ones than with many bad men against a few good ones.
Listen to your enemies, they are the first to point out your
faults. Value a just man more than a relation. A woman's virtue
is the same as a man's. What is good is beautiful, what is
wicked, ugly. Consider alien everything that is morally wrong.
[13] Good judgment is the most secure defence, since it can
never fall or be betrayed. We should make for ourselves a sure
defence of our impregnable powers of reason.

He used to lecture in the Cynosarges[3] gymnasium, just outside Athens' walls. Some people say that this is where Cynicism
derives its name. He himself was entitled 'Downright Dog'.
According to Diocles, he was the first person to fold his cloak in
two and wear nothing else; and was then the first to take up the
Cynic staff and shoulder pack. Neanthes also credits him with
first doubling the cloak. But Sosicrates says in the third book of
his *Teachers and Their Pupils* that Diodorus of Aspendos
already grew his beard long and carried a stick and knapsack.

[14] Theopompus singles him out from among all Socrates'
pupils for his cleverness and the charm of his conversation that
no one could resist. This verdict receives support from his own
writings and from Xenophon's *Symposium*. He is thought to
have inspired the virile Stoic school of philosophy. So Athenaeus the epigrammatist composed these lines on the Stoics:

> Stoic adepts, you entrust to sacred pages the noblest doctrines,
> that only virtue does our souls good, and that virtue alone is the
> salvation of men's lives and cities. If the pleasures of the flesh are
> preferred by other men, one of the Muses, daughters of Memory,
> is responsible.

[15] Antisthenes anticipated Diogenes in his composure,
Crates in his sobriety, and Zeno in his self-possession; he laid
the foundation for the city they afterwards built.[4] Xenophon
calls him the most charming man for conversation and the
most refined in other respects.

His writings survive in ten volumes. The first includes the
thesis *Diction*, or *Style*; *The Ajax*, or *Speech of Ajax*; *The*

Defence of Orestes, or *On Composers of Forensic Speeches*; *Similar Writing*, or *Lysias and Isocrates*; a reply to Isocrates' speech *No Witnesses*. The second volume includes *The Nature of Animals*; *On Procreation*, or *An Amatory Essay on Marriage*; *Experts in Anatomy*; [16] *On Justice and Courage*, a work of advice in three books; Books 4 and 5 are together called *Theognis*.

The third volume includes *On the Good*; *On Courage*; *On Law* or *The Republic*; *On Law*, or *On Justice and Morality*; *On Freedom and Slavery*; *On Belief*; *The Governor*, or *On Obedience*; *On Victory*, a treatise on household maintenance.

The fourth volume includes *Cyrus*; and *Heracles the Greater*, or *On Strength*. The fifth includes *Cyrus*, or *On Kingship*; and *Aspasia*. The sixth includes *Truth*; *On Dialogue*, a handbook of debate; *Satho*, or *On Debate* (three books); *On Language*.

[17] The seventh volume includes *On Education*, or *On Names* (five books); *On the Use of Names*, a handbook of argument; *On Question and Answer*; *On Opinion and Knowledge* (three books); *On Death*; *On Life and Death*; *On the Underworld*; *On Nature* (two books); *Natural Investigations* (two books); *Opinions*, or *The Debater*; *Problems of Epistemology*.

The eighth volume includes the treatise *On Music*; *On Interpreters of Prophecy*; *On Homer*; *On Crime and Impiety*; *Calchas*; *The Spy*; *On Pleasure*. The ninth volume includes a treatise on the *Odyssey*; *On Circe's Wand*; *Athena*, or *Telemachus*; *Proteus*; *Cyclops*, or *Odysseus*; [18] *On the Consumption of Wine*, or *On Drunkenness*, or *The Cyclops*; *Circe*; *Amphiaraus*; *Odysseus, Penelope*, and *Odysseus' Dog*.

The tenth volume includes *Heracles*, or *Midas*; *Heracles*, or *On Intelligence*, or *On Strength*; *Cyrus*, or *The Lover*; *Cyrus*, or *Spies*; *Menexenus*, or *On Government*; *Alcibiades*; *Archelaus*, or *On Kingship*.

These then are the titles of his works. Because of their great number, Timon criticized him as 'a prolific prattler'. He died of natural causes. While he lay sick Diogenes visited him with a dagger on his person. 'Could you use a friend?' he said. 'Won't someone release me from my agony?' Antisthenes asked. 'This will,' the other replied. 'From my agony, I said,' Antisthenes responded, 'not from my life.' [19] He seemed to betray some weakness in thus holding out against death.

Here are some lines I composed on him myself:

In life you were a dog, Antisthenes, though one born to bite the hearts of men with words instead of teeth. But you died by wasting away. Well, someone still could say, 'what's the difference? we all have to die of something.'

The following is an excerpt from the Symposium *of Xenophon. It is modelled on Plato's dialogue of the same name. Socrates and his friends each take a turn over their wine to give a discourse on a commonly agreed theme – in this case, what is each participant's greatest source of pride. Antisthenes in his speech nominates wealth – but his speech turns out to be a panegyric to poverty. It is a good example of how Cynics 'defaced the currency', that is, turned traditional values on their head.*

4

[33] 'What about you, Antisthenes, what are you most proud of?' Socrates asked him. 'My wealth,' he answered. Hermogenes asked if he had much money. 'I don't have a penny,' he said. 'A lot of land, then, I presume?' 'Enough dirt, perhaps, for Autolycus here to rub himself down with.'

[34] 'So explain how, with means so slight, you pride yourself on wealth,' Socrates asked. 'Because (he answered) in my view wealth and poverty relate not so much to a man's possessions as to his soul. [35] For instance, I see many affluent people who consider themselves so much in need that they will take any risk and suffer any hardship for gain. I know brothers with equal shares in their inheritance where one of them has more than enough to meet his needs while the other is impoverished.

[36] I see rulers who commit far worse crimes for money than the poorest of the poor. Of course poverty makes people steal, burgle and enslave. But there are rulers who will wipe out entire families, kill people in the thousands, even reduce whole cities to slavery, all for money.

[37] I pity their condition. They remind me of people of means who can never get enough to eat. As for me, my resources are so plentiful that I hardly know where they all are. Nevertheless, I have enough to eat to keep hunger at bay, enough to drink to slake my thirst, and enough to wear that I am no colder when I venture out of doors than Callias here, with all his millions.

[38] And when I am indoors, what shirts could be warmer than my walls, what coats thicker than my ceiling? My bedding is so adequate that it is actually hard to rouse me in the morning. If my body gets the itch for sex I scratch it with the first thing handy, and my partners are all the more enthusiastic for not being much sought after themselves.

[39] And I find all these things so pleasant that I am more apt to wish they were less so, since some of them seem distinctly more pleasurable than can be good for me.

[40] But this I reckon to be my most precious possession: if someone were to rob me of all of my wealth there is no work I know of so mean that it would not do to support me.

[41] For entertainment I do not go to the shop and buy something (that can get expensive). Instead I draw on my soul's own resources. And my pleasure is greater when I wait until the craving comes on me than when I partake of some luxury item – this Thasian wine, for instance, which I drink since it's here and not because I'm thirsty.

[42] And of course men of simple tastes are more ethical than men bent on amassing wealth since we are less likely to want what belongs to others when we are happy with what we have.

[43] It is worth noting, too, that my sort of wealth renders its owner generous. I got it from Socrates here, who took no notice of exactly how much he gave, but loaded me down with all I could carry. I in turn begrudge it to nobody. I make no

effort to hide my magnificence before my friends, and am ready to share my soul's riches with everyone.

[44] And, as you can see, leisure, the most enviable thing of all, is always mine to enjoy. It allows me to delight in those sights and sounds that I most prize and that merit my attention. But most of all it gives me whole days free to spend with Socrates. And he is not one to admire the person with the largest bank account. He associates with whomever he finds the most congenial company.'

[45] That was Antisthenes' speech.

These next two pieces purport to be speeches delivered by two heroes of Greek legend Ajax and Odysseus, both prominent Greek warriors in Homer's Iliad. *Odysseus, of course, is also the main character in Homer's* Odyssey. *Ajax is Telamonian Ajax, otherwise known as the greater Ajax (to distinguish him from a lesser Ajax of Greek epic.)*

After Achilles was killed in the Trojan War, the surviving Greek captains debated as to who should be awarded Achilles' armour, which amounted to acknowledging the most valuable warrior among them with Achilles gone. Ajax and Odysseus each set forth their claim to the armour of Achilles in the speeches Antisthenes puts in their mouths. The authenticity of the works – that is, whether they were actually written by Antisthenes or by someone else and only later ascribed to him – has come into question, but most now believe that they are genuine. As complementary rhetorical exercises, they are interesting in representing two very different, even antithetical, heroic ideals. Ajax was traditionally more remarkable for brute strength than brains, Odysseus contributed most to the Greek cause by virtue of his intelligence and talent for subterfuge and deceit. The tone of the speeches also serves to define their opposed characters: Ajax is blunt to the point of insolence; Odysseus is more tactful but also sometimes too subtle by half in deploying his arguments. Maybe in part because Ajax alienated the jury with his veiled threats and truculence, the surviving

Greek captains who judged the contest awarded Odysseus the
honour. This so enraged Ajax that he went mad and slaugh-
tered a great many livestock, under the delusion that he was
killing the same Greek leaders who had insulted him by deny-
ing him the prize. When Ajax recovered and realized what he
had done, he committed suicide – a fate Odysseus anticipates
when he says that his rival's emotional nature will some day
prove his undoing. (Note one relevant detail: after Achilles was
slain, it was Odysseus who retrieved his armour and Ajax who
brought back the body in the midst of heavy fighting.)

We have included the speeches here because they are among
the few original compositions by a Cynic to survive. They also
feature certain distinctively Cynic themes: Ajax is notable for
his frankness of speech (parrhêsia) *– a notable Cynic virtue,*
although one certainly made problematic by the context. Odys-
seus, for his part, emphasizes that he works alone, is self-sufficient,
cares nothing for what others think of him when he dresses in
rags and assumes the part of a slave or ruffian; has great powers
of endurance and tenacity; and, like a dog, is committed to the
role of guardian and protector at all hours of the day and night.
All these qualities served the Cynics as virtues, which accounts
for Odysseus' being made an honourable (founding) member of
the Cynic fraternity (see further sections 95 and 137).

5 The Speech of Ajax

[1] I would have preferred this dispute between us to be settled by
the same people who were witnesses to the action. Then I could
simply await your verdict in silence, while this man, Odysseus,
would for once have to keep quiet also while you deliberated.

Unfortunately, witnesses to the actual events are unavail-
able. So it is up to you, who know nothing of what happened,
to judge between us. And what kind of verdict are judges in a
state of ignorance likely to make – a verdict, too, based on
words – when action, not words, are what matter?

[2] Very well, I will give you my version of the story. It was

I who entered the fray to retrieve Achilles' body and bring it safely back to camp. Odysseus, in the meanwhile, was intent only on recovering Achilles' armour, despite knowing that the armour meant less to the Trojans than getting to Achilles' body before the Greeks did. They meant to abuse it, then use it to ransom Hector's corpse. The Trojans had no intention of making a votive offering of Achilles' armour to the gods. No, they would have hidden it somewhere – out of mistrust of Odysseus, this honourable man.

[3] After all, Odysseus had already profaned the sanctity of their temple by stealing the statue of Athena under cover of darkness. And since then he has been showing it off to the Greeks as if he had brought off an act of bravery.

Gentlemen, I ask for Achilles' armour with the intent of turning it over to his family. Odysseus, on the other hand, asserts his right to it solely in order to sell it. He would never dare wear it himself. A coward never wears recognizable armour, knowing it would only throw his comparative cowardice into sharp and awkward relief.

[4] But it's nearly always the same thing.[5] The so-called leaders who arranged this contest to determine who is the better man have handed the job over to others. And you are now charged with the duty of deciding matters you know nothing about. I can say this with certainty: no captain who is competent to judge a soldier's worth would delegate that duty to others, any more than a capable doctor would trust a layman to diagnose a patient's disease.

[5] Now, if I were matched against a man my equal in character, I would be ready to accept defeat with good grace. But the fact is that the two of us could hardly be less alike. This man does nothing openly and honestly. I, on the other hand, never presume to act on the sly. And while I will not stand to be ill spoken of any more than I would put up with ill treatment, Odysseus would submit to any form of abuse if there were something material to be gained by it.

[6] Just consider: he allowed his slaves to whip him, flog him on the back with sticks and pummel him in the face with their fists. Then, wrapping himself in rags, he gained access at night

behind the enemy's walls, posing as a common beggar in search of shelter. He then plundered their temple and escaped. And he readily admits to the whole thing, he may even convince some of you that it was all well done. But is a temple robber and a man without shame really deserving of Achilles' armour?

[7] You *soi-disant* judges and jurors, who know nothing – I urge you, don't take eloquence into account in deciding who the better man is. Only give actions consideration. After all, in war it is actions not words that matter. Debating the enemy is never an option. In the heat of battle you either kill your opponent or take him captive. And look to this too: if you err in your verdict, you will find that words are powerless against brute force.

[8] And no man, whatever he may say, will be able to help you. You will know with certainty that only because the means for action are lacking is many a long speech delivered in its place.

So either admit that you don't understand the issue, and recuse yourselves; or render the only verdict that is fair. And don't decide in secret, do it openly. That way you will learn that jurors, when their verdicts are wrong, are as liable to judgment as the accused. You should also realize sitting here and listening to speeches that your ruling amounts to no more than opinion and conjecture.

[9] I entrust you then to come to a determination about me and my actions; but I warn you all not to judge too hastily, especially in this case, involving, on the one hand, a man who was forced to come to Troy against his will,[6] and me on the other hand, always the first in line for battle, unattended, and outside the protection of the fortress walls.

6 The Speech of Odysseus

[1] I now take to my feet to deliver a speech directed not just at you, Ajax, but at the rest of you gentlemen. For I have accomplished more as a soldier than you all. I would have made the same claim even when Achilles was alive. Now that he is dead I dare to say it to you.

There was no battle that you fought where I was not there beside you. But none of you is aware of the dangers I undertook alone. [2] It must be said that in the collective battles, however well you fought, nothing much was accomplished. Whereas in my private exploits, success meant the realization of everything we came here to do. And even if I had failed, it would have only meant the loss to you of a single man – myself. Because, remember, we did not come here to fight the Trojans, but to recover Helen and capture Troy.

[3] Both goals relate to my exploits. Because whenever an oracle was consulted we learned that Troy could not be taken unless we first got possession of the statue of Athena – the one I personally stole. And who but I brought it back safely – I, whom you are pleased to call a temple thief? It's because you know nothing that you insult me and call me sacrilegious. What about Paris, who robbed the Greeks of Helen?

[4] You all pray to capture Troy, but condemn me as a temple robber when it was I who contrived a plan to do it. Look, if it was right to take Troy, then the means to achieve it were right as well. And while everyone else repays me with thanks, you repay me with insults. Only stupidity prevents you from realizing how much good has been done you. [5] But it's not your stupidity I find fault with – like everyone so afflicted, your fault cannot be helped – but that, besides being unable to see that you have been saved by my 'crimes', you even threaten to do the jurors injury if they elect to award me the armour. You may give them any number of threats, as many as you like, before you carry out the least of them. In all likelihood I think your insolence will only cause problems for yourself in the end.

[6] Now, because I did real harm to the enemy, you charge me with cowardice. You, on the other hand, exerted yourself in plain view and to little effect – and for this I call you a fool. Just because you fought beside the other troops, do you think this proves you my superior? Do you presume to teach me about honour? You don't know the first thing about how best to fight. You act like a wild boar on a rampage, liable to kill yourself some day by running straight onto an enemy sword. Don't you know that the superior man avoids suffering of any kind,

whether he himself is the cause, or an associate, or an enemy soldier?

[7] You take childish pleasure in having a reputation for courage among these men, while they say that I am the most cowardly and fear death most. After all, there is the evidence of your gleaming armour, without a dent or scratch upon it, which, they say, shows that you are invulnerable. But how would you react if one of the enemy came towards you wearing armour in such pristine condition? It would surely be a brave deed and something to admire if one of you got the better of such an encounter! So tell me, how is owning such armour any different from idling behind the fortress walls? I might add that as you use it, the term 'wall' has a different meaning than the one you intend, since you are unique in carrying around a virtual wall in the form of a body shield seven bull hides thick.

[8] As for me, I go without arms, and rather than attack the enemy's walls I walk right through them by dispatching the guards on duty with their very own weapons. I command as well as patrol, for you and the rest, and know what goes on in the enemy's camp as well as I do in our own. Nor do I send someone else to do reconnaissance for me. Like sea captains who personally attend to the safety of their crew, night and day, I look after your welfare and everyone else's besides.

[9] There is no danger I would avoid as beneath my dignity, provided I could do the enemy some injury by it. Even if I were bound to be seen, I would accept the risk and maintain my disguise. And if doing the enemy some mischief means assuming the part of a slave, beggar or thief, I would take on the mission regardless. It would be the same if nobody saw me. For success in war does not depend on impressions but on action, no matter if it be by day or night.

I have no weapons reserved for me especially when I challenge the enemy in the field. Whatever form of combat they choose I am always ready to meet them, whether I am matched against one or fighting with many.

[10] Unlike you, when I am exhausted from battle, I do not put into the hands of assistants my weapons of war. It is just when the enemy stands down at night that I set upon them,

taking with me the weapons likely to do most harm. Night has
never taken me out of action, the way it has often brought you
welcome relief from the fray. When you are snoring away, I am
working to keep you alive. Always I am making some trouble
for the enemy, with the use of those humble weapons – the
shabby clothes and self-imposed signs of a whipping – that permit you to sleep in security.

[11] You think yourself brave for having carried the body
and delivered it here. But suppose you could not have carried
it, and two men were needed; then they too might involve
themselves in our dispute about honour. My argument would
be the same one I use against you. But what would you say in
response to their challenge? Or wouldn't it bother you if there
were two to contend with, but feel shame in admitting that you
were more cowardly than one?[7]

[12] Don't you realize that the Trojans were concerned with
getting hold of Achilles' armour, not his dead body? The corpse
they meant to return; the armour they planned to consecrate as
a votive gift to the gods. Failing to make off with the dead body
of your enemy is no cause for shame in a soldier; refusing to
return it for burial is. Now, you brought back the body as soon
as you came across it; I, on the other hand, took the trouble to
deprive them of what would otherwise have been a source of
humiliation to us.

[13] You suffer from ambition and ignorance, two ills that
work at cross purposes. Ambition makes you eager for honours. But ignorance turns you against them. Your plight,
indeed, is shared by many. Because you are strong you think
you are brave, and don't recognize that physical strength is not
the same as being brave or wise in the conduct of war. And
people in a state of ignorance can suffer nothing worse.

[14] I imagine that if ever there arises a poet[8] who really
knows what counts for excellence in a soldier, he will represent
me as a clever, composed and resourceful combatant, a sacker
of cities who single-handedly brought about Troy's capture.
You, in my opinion, will have your character modelled after
dull asses or grazing oxen, practically inviting men to put you
in harness or tie you in chains.

DIOGENES

*Diogenes of Sinope established Cynicism as a practical philoso-
phy. Throughout its long history he remained the model by
which all later adherents defined themselves. Not that he was
beyond criticism; not only philosophical rivals but even later
Cynics displayed their school's characteristic* parrhêsia *in daring to challenge him on one point of doctrine or another.
Anecdotes of widely varying credibility dominate the tradition
concerning the man, but their cumulative influence in the ensu-
ing intellectual history of the movement is reason enough to
offer translations of even the more doubtful ones.*

7 Early life before exile (DL 6. 20–21)

Diogenes of Sinope, son of the banker Hicesias. According to
Diocles, he fled Sinope after his father, who managed the state
treasury, debased the coins. But Eubulides in his book on Diogenes says that Diogenes himself was responsible, and was
forced out of the city along with his father. Diogenes actually
confesses to the crime in his *Pordalus*. Others report that he
was a supervisor in his father's mint when workers there tried
to talk him into it, so he went to Delphi or the Delian oracle in
his own city to ask Apollo's advice. Apollo (the story goes)
gave him permission to alter the laws of the state but Diogenes
mistook his meaning, adulterated the coinage, and was caught.
According to some he was banished, while others say he took
fright and left the city of his own free will.

Another version has it that he debased the currency after his father had handed management of the treasury over to him. The father, they say, was thrown into prison and died; Diogenes fled the city and went to Delphi to ask – not if he should alter the currency, but what he should do to make a name for himself. And it was only then that he was given the oracle.

So he went to Athens, where he made the acquaintance of Antisthenes. Antisthenes tried to get rid of him, since he was not in the habit of taking students, but Diogenes won him over through sheer persistence. Once he was threatened with the staff and offered Antisthenes his head, saying, 'Go on, hit it, there is no wood hard enough to repel me as long as I find you have something to say.' From then on he became his disciple, and being an exile, he adapted to a lean and frugal life.

8 (Suid. 334)

'Know yourself' and 'Deface the currency': two Pythian proverbs. And the latter means, scorn common opinion and value truth over the moral coin of the masses.

9 (DL 6. 56)

Reminded once that he had defaced the currency, he responded, 'Well, that was at a time when I was a man much like you are now. But you will never be the man I've since become.' To another who brought up the same incident, he said there was a time when he also used to wet his bed.

10 (DL 6. 71)

Nothing in life, he would say, has any chance of success without self-discipline. With it, however, anything was possible. So why not choose to be happy by avoiding vain effort and focusing only on what nature demands, instead of making ourselves miserable with unnecessary exertion? You can even derive pleasure from despising pleasure once you have got used to it. Then pleasure becomes as distasteful an experience as being deprived of pleasure is for people who have not acquired self-discipline. That is what Diogenes said and what he did, defacing the coinage indeed by consulting nature and ignoring convention. He said his life had the stamp, as it were, of Heracles, since he valued nothing over freedom.

11 Association with Alexander the Great (Plutarch, *On the Fortune or Virtue of Alexander* 331F–332C)

When Alexander met with the great Diogenes in Corinth and spoke with him, he was so struck and amazed by the man's worth and singular way of life that, in thinking back on their conversation he would often say, 'If I were not Alexander, I would choose to be Diogenes.' By which he meant, 'I would gladly devote myself to a life of reason if I were not already putting philosophy into action'. Notice he did not say, 'If I were not a king I would be Alexander', or 'If I were not rich and an Argead'.[1] He did not prefer good fortune to wisdom, or value royal clothing and a crown above the Cynic cloak and satchel. In saying 'If I were not Alexander I would be Diogenes', he meant to imply 'If it were not my purpose to fuse Greek with barbarian, to traverse and civilize every continent, to explore the limits of land and sea and extend Macedon's borders to the edge of Ocean, to spread and disseminate Greece and its culture through Asia bringing peace and justice to every race, I would not sit idle and luxuriate in the privileges of power. I would instead contend with Diogenes in his simplicity. But as it is you must forgive me, Diogenes, if I emulate Heracles, take after Perseus, and follow in the footsteps of Dionysus, the god by whom my royal family was established and descends. I want to see Greeks again celebrating a victory dance in India, and reviving the Bacchic revels among the wild mountain peoples beyond the Caucasus. There too we have report of holy men called gymnosophists,[2] devoted to God and likewise inured to an ascetic way of life uniquely their own.

In frugality they outdo Diogenes since they manage without a pack and do not store food but gather and eat whatever grows fresh from the earth. For drink they have flowing rivers, while leaves and grass serve them for bedding. Through me they will get to know of Diogenes and Diogenes of them. Like Diogenes, I am also under an obligation to deface the currency, in my case by putting the stamp of Greek civilization on the barbarian.

12 (Plutarch, *Life of Alexander* 671D–E)

And now a general assembly of the Greeks was held at the Isthmus,[3] where a vote was passed to make an expedition against Persia. Alexander was proclaimed the leader. Many statesmen and philosophers came and congratulated Alexander, who had hoped to find Diogenes among them, since he happened to be in Corinth at the time. But when Diogenes took not the slightest notice of him and continued to spend his days outside Corinth in the Craneum, Alexander paid the man a visit himself. There he found him lounging in the sun. Diogenes stirred a bit when he saw his entourage approach and fixed his gaze on Alexander. The prince greeted him and put to him the question whether there was anything that he could do for him. 'Yes,' said the philosopher, 'shift a bit out of my sun.' Such pride and nobility, evinced by Diogenes' obvious scorn for him, is said to have made a great impression on Alexander. His followers laughed and made fun of him as they walked away, but Alexander for

his own part said, 'The fact is, if I were not Alexander, I would
like to be Diogenes.'

13 (Cicero, *TD* 5. 92)

Diogenes displayed the Cynic's independence and freedom of
speech in a most dramatic way when Alexander asked him if
there was anything he needed. 'Well, at the moment,' he said,
'I'd like you to move a little to one side.' Alexander, you see,
was preventing him from sunning himself. Diogenes himself
used to insist on the degree to which he outdid the king of Persia in his fortune and quality of life. He, after all, wanted
nothing, while the other could never get enough of anything.
And he had no desire for those pleasures that never satisfied the
king however much he indulged in them.

14 (DL 6. 60)

Alexander stood over Diogenes and introduced himself to the
philosopher thus: 'You see before you King Alexander the
Great.' 'Pleased to meet you,' the other replied, 'I am Diogenes
the Dog.'

15 (Seneca, *Benef.* 5. 6. 1)

Alexander, king of the Macedonians, used to boast that no one
had done people more favours than he . . . But Socrates could
justifiably make this claim, as could Diogenes, by whom Alexander was in every way surpassed. For all his pride, which
exceeded human limits, was Alexander not beaten as soon as
he met a man to whom he could give nothing, and from whom
he could take nothing away?

16 (Juvenal, *Satire* 14. 308–12)

The tub of the naked Cynic cannot burn; and if you break it he
will either have another one made tomorrow, or fix the old one
with leaden clamps. When Alexander saw its great occupant in
person, he could not help but feel how much happier the other
man was for needing nothing, when he wanted the whole world
for himself.

17 Relations with Plato (DL 6. 25–6)

At a rich banquet once, he caught sight of Plato reaching for
the olives. 'Why does the great philosopher,' he asked, 'who
journeyed to Sicily for the sake of the finer dishes here, not partake of them now?'[4] 'You have my word, Diogenes,' Plato
replied, 'in Sicily I also lived on simple fare like olives.' 'Then
why did you make the trip to Sicily?' Diogenes retorted. 'Wasn't
Attica bearing olives at the time?' Another time he was eating
dried figs when he bumped into Plato and offered him a share.
When Plato helped himself to whole handfuls he said, 'I said
share, not make disappear.'

Another time, when Plato was entertaining guests from
Dionysius, Diogenes walked over Plato's carpets and said, 'I
trample on Plato's superficiality.' Plato's comeback was, 'You
betray a great deal of pride in pretending not to be proud.'
Others report that what he said was, 'I walk over Plato's pride,'
and Plato replied, 'Yes, with pride of another sort, Diogenes.'
Diogenes once asked him for wine, then for dried figs; Plato
sent him a whole jar full. So he said, 'If you are asked how
many are two and two, do you say twenty? You neither give as
you are called upon nor answer as you are asked.' This latter
jibe was aimed at Plato's tendency to be long-winded.

18 (DL 6. 58)

On one occasion, when he was scolded for eating in public, he
replied, 'But it was precisely in public that I grew hungry.' Some
people also ascribe the following to him. They say that Plato
saw him scraping vegetables. Approaching him, he told him in
a confidential tone of voice that he wouldn't have to submit to
such work if he would only join Dionysius' entourage. To
which he answered, in just as discreet a manner, that he, Plato,
would not have to be part of Dionysius' entourage if he were
not too proud to scrape vegetables.

19 (DL 6. 41)

Once he stood stock still beneath a driving rain. Observers
took pity on him. But Plato happened by and told them to
move on if they really pitied him – an allusion to what Plato
took to be the man's perverse vanity.

20 (DL 6. 40)

Plato defined Man as a featherless biped. The definition was
generally well received. But Diogenes refuted it by plucking a
chicken, bringing it to Plato's Academy, plopping it down and
proclaiming, 'There's Plato's Man for you!'

21 (DL 6. 54)

On being asked what sort of man he took Diogenes to be, Plato
said 'Socrates with a screw loose'.

22 'Looking for a man' (DL 6. 41)

In the full light of day, a lighted lamp in hand, he used to go about saying, 'I'm looking for a man.'

23 (DL 6. 60)

He was returning from Olympia when he was asked if a great crowd of men was there. 'A great crowd, yes; a great crowd of men – no.'

24 Capture by pirates, sale and term of enslavement (DL 6. 74–5)

He was sold into slavery but dealt with his condition admirably. It happened on a voyage to Aegina; he was captured by pirates under the command of one Scirpalus and shipped to Crete where he was placed on the market. The auctioneer asked him what skills he possessed. 'I rule men,' he promptly responded. Pointing out a Corinthian buyer in a fancy purple robe by the name of Xeniades, he asked to be sold to him 'because he could use a master'. The sale was made and Xeniades returned with him to Corinth. There he not only gave him charge of his children and their education but entrusted him with the management of his entire estate. Diogenes so ordered things that Xeniades went around telling everyone that some spirit from heaven had been sent into his home.

Cleomenes in his *Treatise on Education* writes that friends of Diogenes offered to pay for his freedom. Diogenes, however, said that they were suffering under a well-meaning misapprehension. Lions, after all, were not the slaves of those who kept and fed them – just the reverse. For it is the mark of slaves to experience awe, the mark of wild animals to inspire men with that emotion.

25 (DL 6. 29–31)

In *The Sale of Diogenes* Menippus tells how, when he was captured and put up for sale, he was asked what he could do. 'Govern men,' he answered. He told the auctioneer to give notice in the event anyone wanted to acquire a master for himself. During the auction he was ordered to remain standing.[5] 'What difference does it make?' he said. 'After all, fish for sale are laid out for display in any old way.'

He said it was odd that we ring a cup or plate before buying it, but in the case of slaves rely on mere appearance. He told Xeniades, the person who bought him, that he, Diogenes, should be obeyed, even though he was the slave. After all, doctors and pilots who are slaves are also deferred to in their area of expertise. Eubulus, in his title *The Sale of Diogenes*, describes how he educated Xeniades' children. After their elementary studies he taught them to ride, to shoot with the bow, sling stones and hurl the javelin. When they were old enough to attend wrestling school, he told the school's master he did not intend them to become accomplished wrestlers, only to take part to the extent of acquiring a healthy glow and sound physique.

The boys committed to memory many passages from the poets and prose writers, as well as from Diogenes' own works. He taught them all manner of mnemonic devices. In the house he taught them to do their own chores, and to subsist on simple food and water. He kept their hair cropped short and their dress plain. They wore no undershirt, went barefoot, kept silent for the most part, and did not let their gaze wander when out walking in the streets. He also trained them to hunt.[6] The children for their part held him in great affection and often interceded with their parents on his behalf.

26 (Epictetus 4. 1. 114–18)

From Antisthenes Diogenes gained an understanding of how no one could really take away his freedom. This helps explain how he treated the pirates while in captivity. Did he address any of them as 'master'? And I don't just mean the word. It's not the terms of address that interest me, it's the attitude behind them. And how he laid into the pirates for not taking better care of their captives! When he was on the block, too, it was not a master he looked to get but someone of his own to govern.

And how did he act towards his new owner? He spoke right up, making comments on his dress and hairstyle, besides advising him how best to raise his boys. And why not? If the man had bought a physical trainer, would he have treated him as his slave or as his superior in matters of sport? What if he had bought a doctor or architect? In any field you name, it is only right that the person with experience take precedence over the layman. So whoever has acquired knowledge of the business of life as a whole should be deferred to as one's better.

27 (Philo, *All Good Men Are Free* 121–3)

The Cynic philosopher Diogenes was possessed of such poise and dignity that when he was taken prisoner by pirates who barely fed him enough to live, instead of letting circumstances get the better of him, or be cowed by his captors' brutality, he challenged them with the following argument. 'It is ridiculous, when pigs and sheep are provided with enough provender to make them sleek and fat before they're taken to market, to reduce the best of animals, man, to nothing but skin and bones by constant starvation. It only means you'll get less for us than you would otherwise.'

So he got a sufficiency of food. The day he was to be auctioned off with the other prisoners, he sat down and ate in a cheerful mood, taking care to distribute a share of his food

among his comrades. One of them, however, was quite overcome to the point where he could not speak for anxiety and
grief. Diogenes addressed the man thus: 'Try to stop brooding,
and take whatever is given. As Homer says,

> Even fair-haired Niobe thought of food again finally,
> She whose twelve children were slain in her palace,
> Six daughters and six sons still in the flower of youth.[7]

A motivated buyer soon questioned him as to what he knew.
'I know how to govern men,' he said with perfect frankness –
his inner soul, it seems, giving spontaneous expression to the
free, fine and royal elements in his nature.

28 Old age and death (DL 6. 79)

In his work, *On Men of the Same Name*, Demetrius reports
that Diogenes died in Corinth on the same day that Alexander
died in Babylon. Diogenes was an old man in the 113th
Olympiad.[8]

29 (Plutarch, *On the Ethics of Eating Meat* 995 C–D)

Diogenes dared to eat a raw octopus, just so that we could dispense with the cooking process when we prepare meat for
consumption. Before a large audience, he pulled his mantle
over his head and brought a piece of uncooked flesh to his
mouth. 'It is for your sake that I face this risk and run this mortal danger.' A glorious adventure, indeed, by God! Doesn't it
evoke the wars of the Pelopidae to free Thebes, isn't this philosopher's struggle with a raw octopus worth a place beside the
sacrifice that Harmodius and Aristogeiton made to liberate
Athens? Not to have to cook meat – a freedom that makes
human life resemble the lives of savage beasts![9]

30 (DL 6. 76–9)

By report he was nearly ninety when he died. Accounts differ as
to the cause. One has him seized by colic after eating raw octopus. In another version he held his breath until he passed
away . . . According to yet another tradition, he sustained a bad
bite to the foot while distributing octopus to a pack of dogs,
which eventually carried him off. But Antisthenes in his work
On Philosophers and Their Disciples reverts to the view that he
died of self-imposed suffocation. The story is that he was camp-
ing in the Craneum, the gymnasium outside Corinth, when his
friends arrived as usual one day and found him wrapped in his
mantle head to foot. They figured that he must be asleep,
although it was not like him to nap or doze in daylight hours.
Pulling the cloak aside, they found his lifeless body. The general
conclusion was that he had done it to take his leave of the world.

Supposedly, though, his followers then fell to arguing over
who should bury him. It even came to blows. The young men's
parents and estate managers had to intervene, until the decision
was made to bury the great man by the gate leading to the Isthmus. A pillar was placed on his burial mound, crowned with
the likeness of a dog carved from Parian marble. Later, citizens
of Corinth dedicated bronze statues on the site. On one of them
the following verses were inscribed:

> *Even this bronze will tarnish with time: but eternity itself cannot
> efface your name. For you alone pointed Man towards the path
> through life of greatest independence and least trouble or incon-
> venience.*

31 Writings (DL 6. 80)

Works assigned to Diogenes include a set of dialogues, known
collectively as *The Cephalion; Ichthyas;*[10] *The Jackdaw, The
Pordalus, The Athenian Populace, The Republic,* the *Treatise*

on Ethics, On Wealth, On Romantic Love, Theodorus, Hypsias, Aristarchus, On Death. A collection of letters under his name is also in circulation.

Seven tragedies have come down under his name: *Helen, Thyestes, Heracles, Achilles, Medea, Chrysippus* and *Oedipus.* But Sosicrates, in Book 1 of his *Successions,* as well as Satyrus in Book 4 of his *Lives,* claim that Diogenes wrote none of them. Satyrus is on record stating that Philiscus of Aegina, Diogenes' pupil, is their real author. And Sotion in Book 7 declares that the only authentic works of Diogenes are a dialogue *On Virtue,* one *On the Good,* on *Romantic Love,* one called *The Beggar, Tolmaeus, The Leopard, Cassander,* and *The Cephalion.* As for the *Aristarchus,* the *Sisyphus,* the *Ganymede, Chreiai,* and the collection of letters – those, he says, all came from the pen of Philiscus.

32 (DL 6. 72–3)

He sneered at high birth, honours and all such worldly distinctions, calling them camouflage for vice. The only genuine country consisted of the world as a whole.[11] He held that wives should be shared among men, and equated consensual sex with marriage. The sons of such unions were, in turn, sons of the entire state.

He saw nothing wrong in robbing temples. Nor, in his opinion, was it wrong to eat the flesh of any animal. He did not even look upon cannibalism as immoral, citing its practice among foreign nations.

33 (Philodemus, *On the Stoics* (part) [= *SSR* 5 B 126, lines 20–36])

Saying that there was no use for military arms in his republic, Zeno claims that Diogenes made a similar claim for his own republic.[12] Apparently Diogenes only gave expression to the idea in his *Republic.* In his book *On Things Not Necessary in*

Themselves, Zeno reports that Diogenes said that knucklebones ought to serve for money in his state. We find the same idea in the first book of his tract *Against Those Who Hold Opposed Ideas as to Wisdom*. In his book *On Life in Agreement with Nature* Chrysippus, citing that book, gives approval to the evil practices described in it. In *Honour and Pleasure* he many times refers to Diogenes' *Republic* and in glowing terms. In his work *On Justice*, Book Three, he takes up the subject of cannibalism . . . [unclear passage] In his tragedies *Atreus*, *Oedipus* and *Philiscus*, Diogenes registers as personal opinion many of the same vicious and unholy views promoted in his *Republic*.[13]

34 (Philodemus, *On the Stoics* (part) [= *SSR* 5 B 126, lines 46–85])

Let us now transcribe the noble sentiments of [Diogenes and Zeno the Stoic] in such a way as to get through it as quickly as possible. These two godly men believe it is right to trade our humanity in for a dog's life; to employ language that is frank and unrestrained; to masturbate in public; to wear a doubled cloak; to subject to scorn males who are in love with them and constrain by force those who do not welcome their advances . . . [They hold] that all children should be held in common . . . [One should] have sexual relations with one's sisters, mothers and other close relations, as well as brothers and sons. [One should] never miss an opportunity to take part in sexual activities, even if a degree of force is involved. Women will draw men on and induce them by any means possible to couple with them, and if they do not find a partner, they will go to the marketplace in search of someone to service them; and as occasion allows, they will have sexual relations with all and sundry, male or female. Married men should have relations with their slaves, and married women should leave their husband's bed and go off with whoever strikes their fancy. Women [should] wear the same clothes and share in the same activities as men without distinction; they [should] go to the stadium, and appear in the gymnasium naked ... and exercise with the men, concealing nothing ... [unclear passage] ... People should have their fathers killed and cease to acknowledge as their own any city or law that at present we respect. [They hold] that men, as they now are, are practically children, or mad, and should be treated as if they were sick ... They should consider all friends false and untrustworthy, as enemies of the gods and of themselves ...

So of the things now considered good or just, none, they maintain, is so by nature. People should be treated as if they were senseless and immature, confusing what is just with what in reality is unjust and shameful.

35 On the source and significance of the epithet 'dog' (DL 6. 60)

He was asked one day what he did to deserve the name 'dog'. 'I fawn on people who give me alms, I bark at them if they refuse me, and I snap at scoundrels.'

36 (DL 6. 61)

He used to flout convention by eating in full view of everyone, in the very heart of Athens' civic centre.[14] People took offence at this one day and stood around him, calling him 'dog'. 'It's you who are dogs,' he responded, 'standing around me, watching me eat.'

37 (DL 6. 69)

It was his habit to do everything in public, the functions of Demeter and Aphrodite alike.[15] He offered the following explanation. If there was nothing wrong with taking lunch, there was nothing wrong with taking lunch in the marketplace. But there is nothing wrong with taking lunch; therefore there is nothing wrong with doing it in the marketplace. Caught regularly masturbating in public, he would say, 'If only rubbing the stomach could alleviate hunger pains as easily.'

38 (Stobaeus 3. 13. 44)

Diogenes used to say, 'Other dogs bite enemies, I, by comparison, bite my friends, in a spirit of correction.'

39 (Themistius, *On Virtue*, p. 44, (ed. Sachau))

The Athenians called Diogenes 'the Dog' because he slept in fields, or in front of doorways when in town. Diogenes welcomed the name because he found it agreed with his habits. You know how Plato in the *Republic*[16] describes a dog's instincts: just by sight they learn in time to be on friendly, familiar terms with certain people. The philosopher, however, is endowed with reason, a faculty of discrimination superior to sight. With reason he learns to distinguish between friends and enemies so he can get closer to the former while chasing the others away. His aim in getting close to friends is not to bite them or let loose upon them a shower of abuse, but to improve their character by giving them honest advice. As to enemies, even his hostility serves to make them better by bringing their faults to light, exposing them, as it were, with the wound opened by his bite.

40 (Eudocia, *Violarium* (ed. Flach) 332, pp. 239, line 11–240, line 9)

He was called 'doglike' by analogy with real dogs. For dogs have a natural tendency to discriminate and protect. They discriminate between strangers, on the one hand, and people they know and are prepared to protect on the other. So Diogenes copied them and developed the same habits. He kept guard on the principles of philosophy, and learned to distinguish between people who were equipped to live by such principles and those who were not. Because of these talents it was only right that he should also enjoy other people's patronage and hospitality. For in his conversation he challenged the rich and famous – everyone in fact – to improve morally. And if he criticized or corrected people his style tended to be light and jesting, and was the more effective in consequence.

41 Diogenes' dress and frugal habits (*Anth. Pal.* 16. 333 (Antiphilus of Byzantium))

Satchel, cloak, a barley-cake soaked in water and squeezed tight, a staff to hold in front and lean on, and a ceramic mug – these are all the accessories essential to a Cynic philosopher's life. Anything else is superfluous. And even one of these turned out to be inessential. For seeing a ploughman taking a drink from his cupped hands, Diogenes addressed his mug thus: 'Why was I lugging you around with me all this time?'

42 (DL 6. 37)

His bowl, too, he got rid of when he likewise caught sight of a child who had broken her own and was using a concave piece of bread to scoop up a dish of lentils.

43 (DL 6. 22–3)

According to Theophrastus in his *Megarian Dialogue*, Diogenes discovered the means of dealing with circumstance by observing a mouse running about, with no need of a bed, no fear of the dark, and no desire for things commonly considered pleasant. He was the first, some say, to fold his cloak, since he needed to sleep in it too. He carried a pack in which he kept his food. He would use any place for any purpose, whether it be eating, sleeping or conversing. He also used to say that the Athenians had furnished him with living quarters, meaning the Stoa of Zeus and the procession storehouse.

The staff he first began to use for support following an illness. After that, however, it, and the satchel, were his constant accessories when he travelled, although he did without them in town. That is the testimony of Olympiodorus, an Athenian magistrate, of Polyeuctus the orator, and of Lysanius, son of Aeschrio. He wrote to someone to be on the lookout for a place for him to live. When the man was a long time about it, he took up quarters in the cask in the Metroön[17] of Athens, as he tells the story himself in his letters. In summer he would roll around in scorching sand; in winter he embraced marble statues covered in snow. He practised every sort of self-discipline.

44 (DL 6. 38)

He often said that all the woes of tragedy had been visited upon him. He was

> *A man without a home or country, lost to his native land,*
> *a beggar, a drifter, a starveling living hand to mouth.*[18]

But he claimed to oppose fate with courage, convention with nature and emotion with reason.

45 (DL 6. 35)

He said he modelled himself on conductors of the tragic choruses; they also encouraged the choristers to sing a little sharp, with the result that they ended up singing right on key.

46 (DL 6. 40)

Once he was questioned as to the best time to take lunch. 'Whenever you want, if you're rich,' he said; 'whenever you want not, if you are poor.'

47 (DL 6. 54)

Asked what kind of wine he preferred, 'Other people's,' he said.

48 (DL 6. 49)

He once begged money from a statue. Asked what he thought he was doing, he answered, 'Getting used to being refused.' When he begged – a practice he began owing to his poverty – he used to say, 'If you've given to others then give to me too; if you haven't, now's a good time to start.'

49 Diogenes' views on philosophy and training (DL 6. 63)

Asked what he had gained from philosophy, he answered, 'This, if nothing else: to be prepared for any contingency.'

50 (DL 6. 64)

A man once said to him, 'You know nothing, and yet profess to be a philosopher.' 'Aspiring after knowledge,' he said, 'already amounts to practising philosophy.'

51 (DL 6. 24)

He used to say that whenever he saw philosophers, doctors and pilots at work, he thought man the wisest of animals; but when he came upon dream interpreters and psychics and their clients, or people proud of wealth and reputation, he thought that no creature could be more stupid. He often repeated that to be equipped for life you needed either a sound mind or a sturdy noose.

52 (DL 6. 104)

The Cynics dispense with geometry, music and all such erudition. Once a man showed Diogenes a horoscope. 'That sort of thing is useful to keep you from being late for dinner,' is all he said.

53 (DL 6. 70–71)

Training, he said, was of two kinds, mental and physical. Physical training constantly produces thoughts and visions that promote in turn the kind of agility necessary for brave action. Both types of training needed the other to complete them; strength and physical fitness were among life's essentials too, and improved the mind no less than the body. He adduced proofs to show how quickly physical training led to moral virtue. You see in the case of common crafts and trades how their practitioners acquire exceptional manual dexterity. Musicians and athletes also make progress through devotion to their own discipline. Now, if they had extended such training to the mind, surely their efforts would not have failed or been in vain.

Nothing at all, he believed, could be accomplished without self-discipline; with it, conversely, anything could be done. Necessarily, then, people who apply themselves to natural pursuits are happy, while those who choose foolishly must be miserable.

54 On Society (DL 6. 37)

Diogenes deployed the following argument: everything belongs to the gods; wise men are friends of the gods; friends share everything in common; therefore everything belongs to wise men.

55 (DL 6. 72)

He said that everything belongs to wise men, propounding the same sort of argument we cited above: everything belongs to the gods; the gods are friends of wise men; friends share everything in common; therefore everything belongs to wise men.

With regard to the law, he held that it is impossible for there to be civic rule without it. He says, 'Without a city there is no advantage to being civilized; and the city is civilized. Without law there is no benefit in a city. Therefore, law is civilized.'

He would make fun of noble blood, fame and the like, calling them attractive disguises to camouflage vice. He said that the universe comprised the only correct constitution. He said that women should be shared in common, and refused to recognize the convention of marriage. In his view, there was nothing to prevent a man and a woman having sex together provided it was consensual. And for these reasons he held that sons should be common property of the state.

56 (DL 6. 63)

Asked where he was from, Diogenes answered, 'I am a citizen of the world.'

57 (DL 6. 50)

A tyrant wanted to know the best kind of bronze for statues. 'The kind from which Harmodius and Aristogeiton[19] are made.'

58 Diogenes' shamelessness and freedom of speech (DL 6. 69)

Asked what was man's most precious possession, he answered, 'Freedom of speech' ... It was his habit to do everything in public, the functions of Demeter and Aphrodite alike. He offered the following rationale. If there was nothing wrong with taking lunch, there was nothing wrong with taking it in the marketplace. But there is nothing wrong with taking lunch; therefore there is nothing wrong with doing it in the market-place. Caught regularly masturbating in public, he would say, 'If only rubbing the stomach could alleviate hunger pains so easily.'[20] Many other such antics are ascribed to him, too many to recount individually.

59 (DL 6. 24)

He was a great one for satirizing his contemporaries. He called Euclides' school drool,[21] Plato's instruction distraction, the tragic dramas sideshows for fools, and the orators lackeys of the mob.

60 (DL 6. 32)

He was once invited to a stately home where spitting was considered bad form. It happened, however, that he had to clear his throat of phlegm. So he discharged it into his host's face, with the excuse that no meaner place was available. (Other sources associate the anecdote with Aristippus.) Once he put out a general call for men. A crowd gathered, and he proceeded to hit out at them with his staff. 'I sent for men,' he said, 'not menials.' This is told by Hecato in the first book of his *Chreiai*.

61 (DL 6. 34)

He once caught sight of Demosthenes eating at a restaurant. Demosthenes withdrew to the back of the inn to avoid him. 'You're even more trapped inside the building now,' he said. When some non-Athenians expressed a wish to see Demosthenes, he stuck out his middle finger and said, 'There's your Athenian demagogue for you.'

62 (DL 6. 44)

Perdiccas[22] threatened to have him put to death if he refused to attend his court. 'That's nothing special,' he said, 'a spider or scorpion can do as much. I should have thought Perdiccas would insult me by saying that he could live quite happily without me.' Often he would deplore the fact that the gods had given men the means to live happily but this had been lost sight of by his desire for honey cakes, perfume and the like. Accordingly he told a man whose shoes were being put on by his slave, 'You won't be truly privileged until he wipes your nose for you too. But that will come when you lose use of your hands.'

63 (DL 6. 45)

He once saw temple officials arresting a man who stole a bowl belonging to the temple's treasurers. His remark: 'The professional thieves are leading off an amateur.' Another time he saw a teenager throwing stones at a gallows. 'Well done, my boy,' he said. 'You're certain to reach your target.' Another group of young men gathered around him and yelled, 'Watch out or he'll bite us.' To which he responded, 'Don't worry, lads, dogs don't eat weeds.' To someone who sashayed around in a lionskin, he said, 'Honour the costume of courage by never presuming to wear it.' He heard a man congratulate Callisthenes[23] on the favours he enjoyed as a member of Alexander's entourage. 'Pity him, rather,' he said, 'since he eats only when Alexander is hungry.'

64 (DL 6. 46)

In need of money, he told his friends he wasn't looking for pity but for payment. He masturbated in public once, and only said he wished it were as easy to relieve hunger by rubbing his stomach. Seeing a young man heading off to dinner with royalty, he dragged him away, put him in the custody of friends, and told them to protect him. When a young man, fashionably turned out, put a question to him, he said that he would not reply until he knew, after the youth exposed himself, whether he should address him in the masculine or feminine gender. To another who was playing a drinking game in the baths, he said, 'The better you play, the worse off you'll be.' At a dinner certain guests tossed bones his way as they might to a dog. He repaid them by pissing on them the way a dog might do.

65 (DL 6. 43)

At Olympia, when the herald proclaimed Dioxippus to be vic-
tor over men, Diogenes responded, 'No, he is victorious over
menials, *I* defeat men.' Still, the Athenians took him to their
collective heart. When some teenager broke his wine vat, they
gave him a flogging and Diogenes a replacement vat. According
to Dionysius the Stoic, he was brought captive to Philip after
Athens' defeat at Chaeronea. Asked who he was, he answered,
'A spy on your rapacity.' For this he was admired and released.

66 Various judgements on Diogenes and the Cynics (DL 10. 8, 119)

Epicurus branded the Cynics enemies of Greece ... In the
second chapter of his book on *Ways of Life* he says that no
enlightened person would choose the Cynic way, or take up
begging.

67 (Simplic., *comm. in Epict. enchir.* 2)

Rare are those moral and physical natures that can transition
from a life of vice to one of unimpeachable virtue – natures
such as distinguished Diogenes, Crates and Zeno.

68 (Simplic., *comm. in Epict. enchir.* 9)

What acts ill suited to men of honour does dire poverty drive
them to? Only when they were reduced to paupers did Diogenes, Crates and Zeno take up philosophy in earnest. And
only then did they begin to live the life nature intended man to

lead. When they traded in wealth for indigence they showed anyone with eyes to see that poverty holds hidden treasures.

69 (Cicero, *De off.* I. 148)

Rules relating to traditional moral principles and social standards are otiose because they are virtually laws in themselves. No one should make the mistake of thinking that, if Socrates or Aristippus ever violated these established norms, this gives them licence to do the same. They were indulged only because they were men of exceptional, even godlike, gifts. It follows that the Cynics' whole system of philosophy must be rejected, for it is incompatible with our innate sense of right and wrong. And without that there can be nothing good, nothing honourable.

70 (Sen., *Ad Lucil. epist.* 3. 8)

You ask after our friend Marcellinus and want to know what he has been up to. But he rarely visits me, for the simple reason that he is afraid to hear the truth – which he is in no danger of in any case. No one, you see, should be given advice that is not prepared to hear it. That is why it is often doubted whether Diogenes and the Cynics in general pursued a wise course in accosting people at random and being so blunt with them.

71 (Tatian, *Orat. ad Graec.* 25. 1)

What great and admirable things have your Greek philosophers accomplished? They leave one of their shoulders bare, they let their hair and beard grow to excessive lengths, along with their nails, which look like the claws of wild animals. They say they are completely self-sufficient; but in fact, like

Proteus, they need a leather worker to make their knapsack, a tailor for their cloak, and a carpenter to fashion their staff. They depend on the rich for food, as well as a cook to prepare it. You would-be dogs don't know god, so you have stooped to emulating the lives of irrational beasts. Bellowing your self-assured homilies in public, you are eloquent in praise of your own wisdom; but if your audience refuses to give you anything then you insult them, so that philosophy for you amounts to a tactic for making money.

72 (Lactantius, *Inst. epit.* 34. 4–6)

Diogenes, with his pack of dogs, who teaches that strict and superior brand of virtue that subjects everything to scorn, preferred to beg for his bread rather than make a living by engaging in honest trade or working private land. No doubt the life of a wise man ought to be an example to others. But if everyone adopted the wisdom of these men, what kind of state could there be? But perhaps from their number they could furnish us with a model of decent behaviour – these same Cynics who coupled with their partners in full view of the public. I don't know what virtue remains for them to defend once they have abolished all sense of shame.

73 (Augustine, *The City of God* 14. 20)

It is this which those canine or Cynic philosophers overlooked, when, ignoring mankind's modest instincts, they made the dirty and disgusting argument that, as sex in marriage is legitimate, so no shame should be attached to doing it in public, or any compunction felt about having sex in the middle of town or in any public square. Our innate sense of decency triumphed over this wild fancy. For though they say that Diogenes once dared to put his opinion into practice with the idea that his sect would

gain in stature if he did something whose boldness would forever be fixed in popular memory, his Cynic successors did not
follow his example. Shame had more influence with them,
making them blush as humans before their kind, than this wild
notion that humans should model their behaviour on that of
dogs. Hence I'm inclined to believe that even Diogenes, besides
others of whom this act is reported, only made pretence of
engaging in sex, partly hidden by a blanket that kept the public
from seeing what was really going on, than that they were able
to consummate the act while people were watching. For then,
at least, they were bold enough to pretend to be willing to lie
together, even if shame got the better of desire. And there are
still Cynic philosophers to be seen today; but they don't dare
do even this, knowing that, if they did, they would be spat
upon, not to say stoned, by the mob.

74 (Joann. Chrysost. *In Epist. I ad Corinth. homil.*
35. 4)

[The apostles performed acts of mercy from pure, selfless
motives.] Not so the Greek philosophers. As threats and enemies
to our common nature, they acted in a spirit of perversity.
[Crates], like any fool or madman, threw all his property into
the sea on no good grounds ... Everything they did they did
with a view to being admired. The apostles, in contrast, both
accepted what was given them and in turn gave so freely to the
poor that they endured a constant state of hunger ... Consider
their laws also, how sensible they were and without a trace of
vanity. 'Having food and shelter,' he said [I Tim. 6.8], 'let us
therefore be content.' Compare the man of Sinope, Diogenes,
who dressed in rags and lived in a barrel for no understandable
reason. And while he certainly amazed the masses, no one profited from this arrangement. Paul, in contrast, did not behave
like this since he did not want anyone's admiration. He wore
normal, decent clothes, lived in a house like most people, and
practised all the virtues without exception. The Dog sneered at

such behaviour, lived scandalously and shamed himself in public, driven by a mad passion for notoriety. For if anyone looks into the reason why he chose to live in a barrel, he must conclude that ostentation alone can account for it.

A collection of so-called Cynic Epistles has come down to us. They purport to be written by Diogenes, Antisthenes and other figures from antiquity who either professed Cynicism outright or subscribed to at least some of its values. They are not, however, considered genuine, that is, they were not actually composed by Diogenes et al., but probably are products, most of them, of the Augustan age. Samples from this collection are appended here, and in the chapter on Crates, because they are faithful to the spirit of the original Cynics and help attest to the unbroken history of the movement centuries after its founders had died.

75 (Diogenes, letter 30, Hercher)

To Hicetas

[1] I arrived in Athens, father, and heard that an associate of Socrates [Antisthenes] was teaching on the subject of happiness. So I sought him out. Just then he was saying that there were two, and only two, roads that lead to happiness. One was a short cut, the other a long way around. It was up to us which path to take. For the time being I listened quietly, but when we approached him after the lecture I asked if he would illustrate his meaning. He got up and took us to the centre of the city, then led us straight towards the Acropolis.

[2] When we grew near, he stopped and pointed out two particular roads to the top. One was short but steep and difficult, the other long, smooth and easy. 'Here are the roads to the summit,' he said, 'and they resemble the paths to happiness. Choose, each of you, which you prefer, and I will be your guide.' The

others, in fear of its steepness and difficulty, demurred at taking
the first road and asked him if they could please go by way of
the long and easy one. I, however, was up to the challenge and
chose the harder route. For the person pressing on towards
happiness must even be prepared to go through fire and sword.

[3] When I chose this way, he removed my cloak and tunic
and wrapped me in a mantle folded double. He hung a pack
from my shoulder, and put bread and porridge, a cup and a
bowl, inside. To the outside of it he attached an oil flask and
strigil. He also handed me a staff. I kitted myself out with this
equipment, and asked why he had folded my mantle double. 'To
prepare you for either condition – the heat of summer or winter's
cold.' 'But wouldn't the single one have done as well?' I asked.

[4] 'Not at all,' he said. 'It may be fine for summer, but in the
winter it means more chill than a person can withstand.' 'Well,
why have you put this pack on me?' 'So you can carry your house
around with you.' 'Why did you put a cup and bowl inside?'
'Because you need to drink and have some seasoning for your
food if there's no mustard about.' 'Why did you attach the oil flask
and strigil?' 'The one is useful for hard work, the other is to scrape
off dirt and oil.' 'And the staff – what is that for?' 'Security.' 'What
kind?' 'Against the poets – exactly what the gods used it for.'[24]

76 (Diogenes, letter 33, Hercher)

To Phanomachus

[1] I was sitting in the theatre, gluing together the pages of a
book when Alexander, the son of Philip, arrived. He came to a
stop right next to me, blocking my sunlight. I looked up, since
now I could not see where the pages joined, and recognized who
had joined me. At the same time he recognized me too, and
extended his hand in greeting. I returned his greeting and said
something to the following effect: 'It's no wonder that you are
invincible, lad, when you can perform deeds equal to the gods'
own. For just look, in coming here and standing opposite me

you've done the same thing as people describe the moon as doing when it passes directly in front of the sun, obscuring its light.'

[2] 'You're mocking me, Diogenes,' Alexander said. 'Why say so?' I replied. 'Can't you see that I am kept from my work because now I can't see, any more than if it were night-time? And though I have no interest at the moment in speaking with you, here we are speaking all the same.' 'King Alexander means nothing to you?' he asked. 'Not a jot,' I answered. 'I have nothing at stake or anything to lose in these wars of yours, unlike the Macedonians, Spartans and those barbarian races who need a king to rule over them.' 'But your poverty makes me of some potential use to you.' 'What poverty?' I asked. 'Yours,' he said, 'which makes you beg for all your needs.'

[3] 'Poverty does not consist in the want of money,' I answered, 'nor is begging to be deplored. Poverty consists in the desire to have everything, and through violent means if necessary – conditions that apply to you. Earth and springs are my allies in poverty, caves and animal fleece also. And not a single person is involved in war, on land or sea, because of it. We live our whole lives in peace and contentment. Neither land nor sea seems an ally of your army, however.

[4] But you ignore all this in aiming for heaven, not even giving Homer respect; he included the Aloadae and their downfall in his poem to warn against such ambition and to encourage self-control.'

As I warmed to my theme, a great sense of shame came over Alexander, and leaning over to one of his friends, he said, 'If I weren't already Alexander, I would want to be Diogenes.' Then he made me rise and began to lead me off, pleading with me to go on campaign with him, and only with difficulty was prevailed on to let me alone.

77 (Diogenes, letter 38, Hercher)

[1] When the games adjourned and you left me to go to Olympia, I stayed behind to watch the rest of the contest, since I am

exceptionally fond of shows. Some time was passed in the marketplace, with most of the crowd, and as I moved about, my attention was drawn to the merchants, then the poets, and sometimes to the philosophers or prophets. One fellow was giving a disquisition on the source of the sun's power. Most of his audience was persuaded, but I came forward and asked him, 'So how long has it been, philosopher, since you descended from the sky?' He had nothing to say in answer to that. The people standing around him drifted off, leaving him alone to begin putting models of the heavens back inside their box.

[2] Then I approached a prophet. He was seated in the middle, wearing a wreath bigger even than Apollo's, who invented the art of prophecy. Again, I came forward, and asked him, 'Are you a good or a bad prophet?' When he said he was good, I lifted my staff. 'Tell me, then, what am I going to do, hit you or not?' He reflected a moment, then said no. But hit him I did, with a laugh, raising uproar in the audience. 'Why the ruckus?' I asked. 'He turned out to be a bad prophet, and I hit him.'

[3] When the gallery deserted this man too, other people in the market broke up their conversations and began to follow me after word of the previous incidents got around. Some, trailing along, heard me discourse on the virtue of endurance, others saw actual displays of my endurance and austere style of life. As a result, some offered me money or jewellery, and many people invited me to dinner. Only from good people did I take, and then only what nature demands; scoundrels I ignored. If they knew they should be grateful for accepting from them once, I was ready to accept again, but otherwise not.

[4] I would scrutinize carefully even an offer of barley bread. If the person were likely to benefit, I took it, but accepted nothing from others, since I did not think it right to receive something from someone who got nothing in return. I did not dine with everyone, only with people who could profit from my company – people, for instance, who would like nothing better than to live like the kings of Persia.

Once I went to the home of a young man from a very wealthy family. I dined in a hall decorated on every side with gold and paintings. But such opulence had the unintended consequence of leaving no place where one could spit.[25]

[5] So, when something got stuck in my throat, I coughed and surveyed every corner of the room. Finding no place suitable, I spat on my host. Of course he attacked me for this, but in my defence I said: 'Look, so-and-so (I omit the man's name), why blame me instead of yourself? You've finished every inch of this hall, but with no concern for your own self-improvement you've made yourself the only place for spit to go. 'Presumably,' he said, 'you refer to my lack of education. But you won't have an opportunity to make that remark again. From now on I'm determined not to lag behind you a single step.' The next day he divided his property among his relatives, hoisted a backpack, doubled his cloak, and has been following me ever since.

That is what happened to me after we parted ways in Olympia.

78 (Diogenes, letter 47, Hercher)

It is best not to marry or raise children. Our race is weak; marriage and children only burden humankind with additional cares. People who choose to marry and raise children for support later regret it when they realize that both entail more trouble, trouble that might have been avoided in the first place. A person indifferent to material things declines to marry or produce children because he knows that he has enough resources on his own for a life of moderation.

'But life will become devoid of people. Who,' you ask, 'will take our place?'

Well, I wish that everyone would turn to philosophy and the world be purged of stupidity. As it is, though, it may be that only people of our persuasion will die out while the rest of the world, unconverted, will go on breeding. But if the human race were to die out, would that be any more lamentable than if wasps or flies became extinct? Such scruples only show the failure of people to see things for what they really are.

CRATES AND HIPPARCHIA

(fl. 326 BC)

As Diogenes' first pupil, it is not surprising that Crates occa-
sionally displays some of his master's abrasive manners and
acerbic wit. But what stands out in the tradition concerning him
are deeds of supererogatory good will, especially in restoring
peace to warring households. He is the most conspicuous repre-
sentative of the philanthropic strain in Cynicism. In the account
of his relations with Hipparchia we find the same pattern of
gruffness, alternating with and finally yielding to warmth and
intimacy. Their story is significant not only as highlighting the
more benign side of Cynicism but, in Hipparchia's case, demon-
strating the school's willingness to extend women the same
respect as men in every sense that mattered to them.

79 (DL 6. 85)

Then there was Crates of Thebes, the son of Ascondas, another
of the Dog's better known disciples. A certain Hippobotus,
however, alleges that he studied under Brison the Achaean, not
under Diogenes.

80 (DL 6. 87)

He came to prominence in the 113th Olympiad.[1]

81 (DL 6. 87–9)

According to Antisthenes[2] in his book *Successions of Greek Philosophers*, Crates was converted to Cynic philosophy when he witnessed the performance of a tragedy in which Telephus[3] was shown dressed in rags, carrying a satchel. He was moved to sell his property and distribute the sizeable proceeds (he came from a rich family) to the city at large. And so seriously did he commit to philosophy that he is memorialized in verses by the comic poet Philemon, who describes a person who aped his ways: 'In summer he wore a shaggy coat so as to be another Crates, and in winter dressed in rags.' Diocles relates how Diogenes himself induced him to sell his grazing lands, then toss the proceeds into the sea. He also says that he entertained Alexander for a time, much as Hipparchia had welcomed Philip, Alexander's father, into her home. He often had to use his Cynic staff to drive off relatives bent on recalling him to his old, conventional way of life. But he stuck to his purpose. Demetrius of Magnesia says that he gave a sum of money to a banker, asking him to divide it among his children should they adopt a conventional, bourgeois existence. But if they followed him into Cynicism the banker was to donate the money to the city, since as philosophers his children would have no need of it. Eratosthenes has a colourful story to the effect that he had a son by Hipparchia (of whom more later). After the boy, Pasicles, reached adulthood and had completed his military service, Crates escorted him to a house of prostitution. It was here, he said, that he had been introduced to sex himself. Adultery, he said, led to tragedy, murder or exile being the usual dénouement. Intrigues with prostitutes, on the other hand, were a matter for comedy, inducing madness through an orgy of drinking and spending.

82 (Apuleius, *Florida*)

[14] It was Diogenes' words, and others that spontaneously suggested themselves to him, which influenced Crates to at last rush off to the centre of the city and publicly renounce all he owned as so much filth and excess baggage, more hindrance than help. When his actions drew a crowd, he announced in a loud voice, 'Crates hereby grants Crates his freedom.' And from then until the day he died he not only lived alone, but remained scantily clad, free of property – and happy.

83 (Apuleius, *Florida*)

[22] Crates, the well-known disciple of Diogenes, was honoured at Athens by the men of his own day as though he had been a household god. No house was ever closed to him, no head of a family ever had a secret so great as to regard Crates as an untimely intruder. He was always welcome to help settle a quarrel or a lawsuit among relatives. The poets celebrate how, in the past, Hercules by his bravery subdued all the wild monsters and savage men of legend, ridding the world of them. Even so our philosopher proved Hercules' equal in overcoming anger, greed, envy, lust and all the monstrous vices of the human psyche. He rid them of all these sins, purified families and conquered vice. Like Hercules, too, he went half-naked and carried his own distinctive club; he even came from Thebes where men say Hercules was born. Even before becoming Crates, as he is now known, he was numbered among the city's leaders, from a prominent family whose house had many slaves and was conspicuous for its large, open court. His lands were rich and his clothing sumptuous. Later, however, he realized that the wealth he had inherited was no safeguard against life's realities nor was it something on which he could consistently rely, since nothing is certain and everything is subject to change, and all the riches in the world were of no consequence when it came to living honourably.

84 (DL 6. 85)

The following facetious lines are his:

> *I know a fair city, Pera⁴ by name, set in wine-dark vapour,*
> *beautiful and productive – dirty, too, and poor.*
> *It is no fit port of call for fool or parasite,*
> *Or any lecher who delights in the rumps of whores.*
> *But it produces thyme, garlic, figs and loaves*
> *Not things apt to start wars or incite men to combat.*
> *Nor do the people of Pera take up arms for money or fame.*

85 (DL 6. 86)

There is also his well-known commonplace book, containing the following sardonic advice: 'Pay the cook a hundred pounds.⁵ Give the doctor a pound. Reward flatterers with a small fortune; to friends who help you a mere thank you will suffice. Spend vast sums on whores. To philosophers you may give spare change.'

He was popularly known as 'the crasher' for his habit of inviting himself into people's homes and giving them the benefit of his advice. The following verses are his also: 'However much I know and understand I owe entirely to the Muses and to their benevolence. Whoever reaches for wealth and riches grasps at empty air.'

Two things, he said, he got from philosophy: a basket of lupins, and the habit of self-sufficiency. To him we owe this wry reflection: 'Love is cured by hunger or, failing that, by the passage of time. If neither of those works, there is always the noose.'

86 (Plutarch, *How to Tell a Flatterer from a Friend* 69 C–D)

It is said that Demetrius of Phalerum was exiled and residing in Thebes, living in disgrace and humble circumstances. He was not especially pleased one day to see the philosopher Crates making his way towards him, since he expected he would be treated to a sample of the candour and harsh words Cynics were notorious for. But Crates greeted him politely and consoled him on the subject of exile, saying that there was nothing shameful or trying about it. Instead, it released him from matters inherently hazardous and uncertain. He encouraged him to rely on himself and his own resources of character. Feeling better and more optimistic Demetrius told his friends, 'Now I regret those duties and concerns that kept me from making the acquaintance of a man like that sooner.'

87 (DL 7. 2–4)

[2] Zeno[6] was a pupil of Crates, as stated above . . . As to how he came to know Crates, on a voyage from Phoenicia with a load of purple dye, his ship was forced to make a landing in Peiraeus. (This was when he was around thirty.) He made his way into town and settled himself in a bookshop. As he began to read the second book of Xenophon's *Memorabilia*, he was so delighted that he asked where men like Socrates and his kind were to be found. Just then Crates entered the shop. The owner pointed him out to Zeno and said, 'Follow him.' From that moment he became his pupil, in most respects showing a marked aptitude for philosophy, but too modest to emulate the Cynics in their effrontery . . . For a time, then, he associated with Crates, and when Zeno published his *Republic*, some people joked that he had written it on the Dog's tail.

88 ([Demetrius of Phalerum], *On Style* 170)

Even men of refinement will make jokes in the appropriate setting, for example at parties or symposia. It can also serve to
satirize extravagance . . . as in Crates' poetry, or his seriocomic
piece in praise of lentils, supposing it were read in the company
of hedonists or gourmands. This is the Cynic style to be found
in most of their compositions. Such light-hearted works make
frequent use of anecdotes and citations.

89 (DL 6. 96–8)

[96] Hipparchia[7] came under the Cynics' spell. She was capti-
vated by Crates' talk and behaviour. The wealth, birth and
personal charm of conventional suitors had no appeal for her;
Crates was her all in all. She even threatened her parents with
suicide if they would not allow her to marry him. At their urging, Crates did everything he could to put the girl off, but
without success. He finally planted himself in front of her and
removed his clothes. 'Here is your husband,' he said, 'and here
is all he owns. So consider carefully, because you cannot be my
partner unless you are prepared to adopt my ways.'

[97] The girl made her choice in his favour. Assuming Cynic
attire, she went around with him in public, even accompanying
him to private dinners. In fact, this is how she came to be present at a party given by one Lysimachus. Theodorus, the
notorious atheist, was also present, and she posed the following sophism to him. 'Anything Theodorus is allowed,
Hipparchia should be allowed to do also. Now if Theodorus
hits himself he commits no crime. Neither does Hipparchia do
wrong, then, in hitting Theodorus.' At a loss to refute the argument, Theodorus tried separating her from the source of her
brashness, the Cynic double cloak. Hipparchia, however,
showed no signs of a woman's alarm or timidity. [98] Later he

quoted at her lines from the *Bacchae* of Euripides: 'Is this she who abandoned the web and woman's work?' 'Yes,' Hipparchia promptly came back, 'it is I. But don't suppose for a moment that I regret the time I spend improving my mind instead of squatting by a loom.'

90 (*Anth. Pal.* 7. 413, Antipater of Sidon)

Instead of the role of a fashionably dressed woman, I, Hipparchia, chose the Cynics' uniquely demanding way of life. I don't care for shawls secured with clasps, high-heeled leather shoes, or fancy fillets to hold my hair in place. Supplied with barley meal, supported by my staff, with my doubled cloak that serves for dress by day, at night as bedding on the rocky ground, I outdo Atalanta of Arcadia, inasmuch as wisdom outclasses a gift for nimbly negotiating mountain terrain.

From the letters of Crates. On the so-called Cynic epistles, see the introduction to the selection of Diogenes' letters in the Diogenes chapter.

91 (Letter 2, Hercher)

To his followers

Don't ask just anyone for food, and don't take from everyone what they offer; it isn't reasonable that virtue should depend on vice. Only beg and accept your bread from people schooled in philosophy. Then you will be not so much begging as asking to be paid, and won't seem to be demanding what by rights belongs to you already.

92 (Letter 4, Hercher)

To Hermaiscus

Whether you like to or not, acquire the habit of working hard, then you won't have to work hard. Idleness does not make work easy, it ensures that work will be hard.

93 (Letter 5, Hercher)

To his followers

Law is good, but philosophy is better. Law uses force against wrong action, philosophy uses persuasion to show us *why* an action is wrong. It is superior to the same degree that acting willingly is preferable to acting under compulsion. Which is why I say study philosophy and stay out of government. Knowing how people are taught good behaviour is a finer thing than knowing how to keep them from breaking the law.

94 (Letter 16, Hercher)

To his followers

Cynic philosophy derives from Diogenes. A Cynic works hard in the service of that philosophy, and it is a style of philosophy which is short and to the point. So don't fight shy of the Cynic label, or of the Cynic pack and heavy coat. They are the gear of the gods, and a quick way to identify yourself to people of honest character. If you were good you would not be annoyed at being called bad, but would simply laugh it off; so now don't be offended if practising philosophy without frills is called 'behaving like a dog', and you personally are called a dog, and Cynicism is described as 'philosophy for dogs'. All that is mere opinion. And to be a slave of opinion, good or bad, especially in the matter of names – 'mere shadows,' as they say – is to be subject to the lowest form of slavery. So try to ignore such trivial stuff.

95 (Letter 19, Hercher)

To Patrocles

Don't call Odysseus the father of Cynic philosophy – Odysseus, who was the most self-indulgent man in his company and valued pleasure above everything – just because he once assumed a Cynic form of dress. Clothes don't make the Cynic, but the other way around. Such was not the case with Odysseus. He was continually overcome by sleep and hunger, always sighed over the life of ease, accomplished nothing without Athena's help, or by sheer good luck, begged from everyone, even the very poor, and was just as indiscriminate in what he took as from whom he took it.

Reserve, instead, that honour for Diogenes, who wore the Cynic outfit not once but throughout his entire life. He was capable of hard work, and indifferent to pleasure. He did not so much beg as ask to be paid – and never from the poor. Anything but the bare necessities of life he abjured and so could rely on his own resources. He never counted on people's pity for favours, he commanded their respect, and depended on reason, not duplicity and a bow, to gain his ends. Courage he showed not just at the moment of death, but in the constant exercise of virtue. And unlike Odysseus, Diogenes is a realistic role model. He converted many from vice to virtue while he lived, and continues to do so with the words he left behind.

96 (Letter 28, Hercher)

To Hipparchia

Women are not naturally the weaker sex. Look at the Amazons; they were as physically tough as any man. So think on them and don't fall short of their example. You certainly won't persuade *me* that you are fragile when backs are turned. And since you agreed to share with me, your husband, the rigour and poverty of the Cynic lifestyle, and showed such early promise, it would be a shame if you were to lose heart now and turn back halfway down the road.

97 (Letter 29, Hercher)

To Hipparchia

It is not because we are completely insensitive that people first called our philosophy 'doglike'. Rather, it is that we bravely defy pain and popular opinion when most people can't. That is the real reason why the label 'dog' was first attached to us. So persist in being a Cynic with us. You are no weaker by nature, any more than bitches are weaker than male dogs. Female liberation will then be justified on grounds of nature, since it is acknowledged that slavery in general, if not based on proven inferiority, exists by mere convention.

98 (Letter 30, Hercher)

To Hipparchia

I am returning the shirt that you sewed and sent to me. We live a life of hardship and such things are not allowed us. I also want to discourage you from such work and the considerable effort that went into it if you meant to prove to conventional society that you have a wife's traditional devotion towards her husband. Now, if I had married you for that reason, of course you would be acting properly and your devotion would be very evident to me in this. But since I married you for the sake of philosophy – to which you yourself are committed – renounce such pursuits and aim to benefit the human race as a whole. This is what you were taught both by me and by Diogenes.

BION

Reading Bion we can see how, as a school of philosophy, Cynicism graced with a capital 'c' evolved, or devolved, into the modern, lower-case adjective 'cynical'. What sentiments survive under his name give no hint of a reforming spirit; they are closest, perhaps, to the world-weary epigrams of La Rochefoucauld or the Nietzsche of Human, All Too Human. *But his literary talent and influence show that he was not a pessimist with nothing to contribute but a talent for curmudgeonly humour. He is one of the Cynics' most gifted writers, especially in the invention of apposite metaphor, as evidenced in the fragments below and in the examples credited to him by Teles.*

99 (DL 4. 46–53)

[46] Bion was by birth a citizen of Borysthenes. Who his parents were, and what his circumstances were like before he turned philosopher, he personally described to Antigonus in plain and honest terms. For when Antigonus put to him the line from Homer: *'Who among men are you, and from where? What is your city and who are your parents?'*[1] Bion, knowing that the king had already heard unflattering things about him, replied, 'My father was a freedman who wiped his nose on his sleeve – which is to say, he was a dealer in salt fish – and a native of Borysthenes. He was a man of no distinction unless you count the marks on his face, tokens of his master's cruelty. As for my mother, she was exactly the sort of woman you

would expect a man like my father to marry – they met in a whorehouse. Then the whole lot of us were sold into slavery when my father engaged in a bit of embezzling. My relative youth and good looks helped me find an owner in the form of an orator, who left me everything when he died.

[47] 'I burnt his books, scratched together all I could, came to Athens and took up the study of philosophy. And now you know all about my glorious family background and social circumstances. So it's time Persaeus and Philonides² stopped telling stories about me and you judged me for yourself.'

To be frank, Bion was in many respects a shifty character and wily sophist. He provided the enemies of philosophy with plenty of ammunition. On occasion he could act superior and indulge in arrogant behaviour. But he left behind many memoirs and useful sayings. As an example, when he was faulted for not trying to win over a young man, he said, 'You can't get hold of soft cheese with a hook.'

[48] Being once asked who suffers most from anxiety, he replied, 'Whoever is most ambitious to succeed.' Asked if it was wise to marry, he answered, 'If your wife is ugly you'll be swearing, if she's pretty you'll be sharing.'³

He called old age life's harbour from troubles; everyone, after all, takes refuge there. Fame he called the mother of misery; beauty, he said, only benefited others; and money was the glue that held society together. A spendthrift had gone through his entire patrimony, his lands included. 'The earth devoured Amphiaraus,' Bion said to him, 'but you have succeeded in devouring the earth.' In his view, not being able to bear with misfortune was a misfortune in itself.

[49] He often said that it was better to share one's youth and beauty with others than to take pleasure in the charms of someone else, because the latter habit spelled the ruin of not just the body but the soul. He even criticized Socrates, saying that if he was drawn to Alcibiades but abstained from sex with him he was a fool; and if he was not attracted to him then there was nothing remarkable in his restraint.

The journey to Hades, he used to say, was an easy one; men did it with their eyes closed. He criticized Alcibiades because as a boy he drew husbands away from their wives, and as a young man stole wives away from their husbands. When the Athenians were absorbed in the practice of rhetoric, he taught philosophy at Rhodes. To someone who faulted him for this, he replied, 'I have a supply of barley; am I then to try and trade in wheat?'

[50] He would say that a worse punishment for the Danaids⁴ in Hades would have been to make their vessels sound instead of full of holes and leaky. To a chatty young man who pestered him for favours, he said, 'I will oblige you but only if you send friends to plead your case so that I won't have to deal with you face to face anymore.' He once found himself in the company of criminals on a ship overtaken by pirates. 'If we are recognized, we are done for,' the others said. 'And I am done for if I am not,' Bion responded. Self-satisfaction he called an obstacle to progress. There was a rich man who worried over every penny. 'He does not own a fortune,' he observed, 'his fortune owns him.' Also: 'Misers of this sort watch over their property as if it were their own, but it may as well belong to others for all the good it does them.'⁵ And, 'Young men have courage enough, but knowing when to pick one's battles only comes with age.'

[51] He said that good sense surpassed the other virtues as much as sight excels the other senses. And we should not malign old age considering we all hope to reach it. A notorious misanthrope had a particularly black look one day. 'I don't know whether you have met with bad luck,' he said to him, 'or a neighbour with good.' According to him, low birth was inimical to free speech, 'Because it humbles a man, however bold he is by nature.'⁶

Know well the characters of your friends, he urged, to avoid the reputation of keeping company with low-lifes, or miss the chance to associate with people worthy of your time. When he first studied philosophy, he studied the doctrines of the Academy, even while he was attending Crates' lectures. Then he devoted himself to the Cynic discipline, putting on the cloak and satchel; for how better to achieve the ideal of serenity and self-possession? For a time he subscribed to the views of Theodorus the atheist, seduced by the mass of sophistic arguments

that filled his lectures. After his Theodorean phase he attended
the talks of Theophrastus the Peripatetic.

He was flamboyant and very sarcastic, often referring to
things by their vulgar names. Eratosthenes, we are told, said
that he was the first to dress philosophy in flowery robes,
because he brought all the various literary styles to bear in its
exposition. [52] He also had a gift for parody; here is one
example:

> O gentle Archytas, musician-born, great in your own estimation,
> and more skilled than any man in playing the high string that
> calls men to battle.[7]

[53] He had nothing but scorn for music and mathematics. He
lived extravagantly, and for this reason he would move from
one city to another, sometimes contriving to make a great show.
Thus at Rhodes he persuaded the sailors to put on students'
garb and follow in his train. And when, attended by them, he
made his way into the gymnasium, all eyes turned towards
him. It was his custom also to adopt certain young men for the
gratification of his appetite and in order to be protected by
their goodwill. He was quite the egotist and attached great
importance to the maxim that 'friends share everything in
common'.

Hence it happened that not a single pupil out of all who
attended his lectures became his disciple. And yet there were
some who followed his lead in shamelessness. [54] Betion, for
instance, one of his intimates, is said to have once addressed
Menedemus in these words: 'For my part, Menedemus, I pass
the night with Bion, and don't think I am any the worse for it.'
In private conversation he would often promote fiercely atheis-
tic views, the fruits of his association with Theodorus.
Afterwards, when he fell ill (so it was said by the people of
Chalcis where he died), he was persuaded to wear an amulet
and to repent of his blasphemies against religion. With no one
to care for him, his suffering was appalling until Antigonus sent
him two attendants. And Favorinus in his *Miscellaneous History* reports that the king himself joined his cortège in a litter.

100 (Plutarch, *On the Delays of Divine Vengeance* 561C)

To Bion it seemed even more ridiculous for god to visit punishment on an offender's children for their own crimes than for a doctor to administer medicine to a child or grandchild to cure their father's or grandfather's ills.

101 (Seneca, *Benef.* 7. 7. 1)

Bion is able to prove by argument at one time that everyone is sacrilegious, at another that no one is. When he is in a mood for casting all men down the Tarpeian rock, he says, 'Whosoever touches that which belongs to the gods, and consumes it or converts it to his own uses, is sacrilegious; but all things belong to the gods, so that whatever thing anyone touches belongs to them to whom everything belongs; whoever, therefore, touches anything is sacrilegious.' Again, when he bids men break open temples and pillage the Capitol without fear of the wrath of heaven, he declares that no one can be sacrilegious; because, whatever a man takes away, he takes from one place that belongs to the gods to another place belonging to the gods.

102 (*Gnom. Paris.* 320)

According to Bion, literary critics who try and trace Ulysses' wanderings fail to notice where they themselves go wrong; they are not aware how their minds get lost in studies as tortuous as they are trivial.

103 (Stob. 2. 1. 20)

But astronomers he thought the most ridiculous, because they overlook fish lying at their feet on the seashore but claim to find them in the sky.

104 ([Plutarch] *On the Education of Children* 10 C–D)

It was a clever saying of Bion the philosopher, that just as Penelope's suitors, being denied access to her, consorted instead with her maidservants, so people who are not able to attain to philosophy waste their lives pursuing other, meaner types of learning.

105 (Stob. 4. 21b. 23)

To those who claimed that beauty had great power, Bion replied, 'Alas, it is a power that hangs by a hair.'

106 (Sen., *On Tranquillity of Mind* 15. 4)

Just consider one by one the causes of our happiness and sadness and you will see the truth of Bion's remark, that human affairs all resemble their beginnings, that our lives are no more solemn or significant than our conception, and that born from nothingness to nothingness we return.

107 (*Codex florent. of John Damasc.*, 2. 13. 97)

Following Hesiod, Bion used to say that there were three classes of student, composed of gold, silver, and bronze.[8] The gold students pay something and take something away, the silver ones pay but learn nothing, while the students made of bronze get something from their classes but pay nothing in return.

108 (Gnomol. Vat., 157)

Asked why he did not put his own teachings into practice, he replied, 'Vials containing the most effective remedies get no benefit from them either.'

109 (Plutarch, On Progress towards Virtue, 82 E)

Bion would tell his friends that they could feel confident that they were making moral progress when they reacted to abuse no differently than if they had been addressed as follows:

> Stranger, you look not like a bad or foolish fellow;[9]
> or
> Well met, sir, greetings, and may the gods grant you happiness.[10]

110 (Cic., TD 3. 62)

It is to the notion that the deceased deserve an extravagant show of grief that we owe all these various, grotesque forms of lamentation: womanish tearing of the cheeks, beating ourselves about the head, thighs and chest, general neglect of our appearance. Thus Agamemnon in both Homer and Accius is made to 'tear his uncombed hair in anguish'. Which prompted Bion to remark drily that it was a foolish king who supposed that baldness would alleviate his sorrow.

ONESICRITUS

(c. 380–c. 305 BC)

Onesicritus was a Greek Cynic and historian who participated in Alexander's expedition until its termination in India. The account he left of the campaign is unreliable in details, marred, among other things, by a tendency to interpret the exotic cultures of the East in terms of Cynic categories of thought and discipline. Still, he maintained enough objectivity in his description of the Indian 'gymnosophists' (literally 'naked wise men', as the Greeks called them: the ancient Brahmans or rishis) to serve as a valuable source for knowledge of the contemporary representatives of this ancient tradition, if we allow for the distortions inherent in his tendency to cast their culture in terms with which he was familiar.

111 (DL 6. 84)

One tradition has it that Onesicritus came from Aegina, but Demetrius of Magnesia says that he was a native of Astypalaea. He was another of Diogenes' more distinguished students. His career to a certain extent parallels that of Xenophon, who went on campaign with Cyrus, while Onesicritus accompanied Alexander. And Xenophon wrote the *Cyropaedia*, while Onesicritus has described Alexander's education in the same adoring manner and in a similar literary style. Because he is so obviously derivative, however, he is considered second-rate.

112 (Plutarch, *On the Fortune or Virtue of
Alexander* 1. 10, 331E)

That Alexander made Onesicritus, Diogenes' pupil, chief pilot
of his fleet, is attested in many sources.

113 (Plutarch, *Life of Alexander* 65. 1 seq.)

[1] To the gymnosophists, Indian philosophers of wide repute
who live as hermits in the quiet and solitude of the forest, Alexander sent Onesicritus to arrange a meeting. Now, Onesicritus
was a philosopher in Diogenes the Cynic's circle.

[2] He reports that Calanus very rudely and abruptly ordered
him to strip to the skin and attend to his teaching, or he would
not converse with him even if it were not Alexander but Zeus
himself who had sent him as an envoy. But Dandamis, he says,
was of a milder disposition, and after listening at length to
descriptions of Socrates, Pythagoras, and Diogenes, he said
that they impressed him as honourable men, although they
seemed a bit too ready to conform to society's unwritten laws
in conducting their lives.

[3] Others, however, say that Dandamis only opened his
mouth to ask why Alexander had journeyed such a long way
there. Calanus, nevertheless, was persuaded by Taxiles to pay
Alexander a visit. His real name was Sphines, but because he
greeted those whom he met with 'Cale', a common form of
greeting in the Indian language, he earned the nickname Calanus among the Greeks. It was he, we are told, who gave
Alexander a figurative lesson in how best to govern. [4] At the
king's feet he threw down a dry and shrivelled ox-hide. Stepping on one edge, he held that particular part of the ox-hide
down. But the rest of the stiff old piece of leather lifted in the
air. Making a circuit of the thing, he showed that the outcome
was always the same. Finally, he stood in the centre with the
result that the whole skin remained flat and flush against

the ground. The demonstration was meant to show that Alexander was well advised to concentrate his forces in the centre of his empire and not venture too far from it.[1]

114 (Strabo 15. 1. 64–5)

[64] Onesicritus says that he conversed with one of the gymnosophists, Calanus, who marched with the king as far as Persia. His death conformed to the custom of his people, on top of a funeral pyre. Calanus was lying on rocks when he made his acquaintance. Onesicritus says he went up and greeted the man, explaining that he had been delegated by Alexander to learn the gymnosophists' philosophy, then return with a full report. So if they had no objection to sharing their wisdom he stood ready to hear it. Calanus, however, took one look at the cloak, broad hat and tall boots that Onesicritus wore and laughed in his face. 'In the beginning the world teemed with wheat and barley. Now it is mostly made of dirt. Once fountains yielded an abundance of water, milk – even honey, wine and olive oil.[2] But excess and self-indulgence only made men insolent. In disgust at this state of affairs Zeus took away these blessings and subjected man to a life of labour. When self-restraint and the other virtues developed, then opportunities for a good life reappeared. But greed and arrogance,' he said, 'are once again threatening man's existence, and at present there is renewed risk of widespread devastation.'

[65] After these words of warning, Calanus told Onesicritus that if he wished to be schooled in their philosophy he would have to shed his clothes, lie naked on the rocks beside him, and listen to him lecture. While thinking the proposition over, Onesicritus says that Mandanis, the oldest and wisest of their number, faulted Calanus for ordering his guest around so, especially after he had just denounced high-handedness in others. Mandanis then invited Onesicritus to spend some time with him. He began by complimenting Alexander on his intellectual curiosity, especially as he had such a large empire to govern; he

was the only philosopher in arms he ever knew. Nothing could be better than if men of intelligence and breeding had the means to persuade the willing, and force the unwilling, to behave more like civilized human beings. But he asked Onesicritus' indulgence if he took little of value away from their talk. The three translators through whom they were communicating knew well enough the equivalent words in either language, but were no more able than most to understand the substance of his philosophy; one might as well look to extract clean water from mud.

At any rate, the gist of his teaching was that the best philosophy aimed to free the soul from considerations of pleasure and pain. Pain should not be confused with stress or physical hardship. We are naturally averse to pain. But the ascetic practices to which they subjected their bodies served to sharpen their minds, so that they were better able to settle differences among themselves and become trusted advisers in matters both public and private. In fact, he would advise Taxiles[3] to ask Alexander to become his guest. If Alexander was the better man, he would be improved by associating with him; if the opposite were true then it was Alexander who stood to gain from their friendship.

Mandanis then asked if such issues were also discussed among the Greeks. Onesicritus cited Pythagoras as holding similar doctrines (besides, like the Indians, promoting abstention from meat).[4] He also named Socrates and Diogenes as two other philosophers with ideas comparable to the Indians' own, adding that he personally had studied with Diogenes. Mandanis' considered opinion was that the Greeks were sensible in most respects, but wrong to defer to custom over nature. Why else were they ashamed to live, like he did, without clothes and other inessentials? Even in the case of shelter, after all, the best house is the one requiring the least maintenance.

Onesicritus gave further details relating to the gymnosophists' life. They interest themselves in many natural phenomena, like portents, rains, droughts and disease. When they travel to a city they scatter among different markets. If they happen to meet with someone supplied with figs or grapes they are provided with a share for free. If they run across a person carrying oil, a little will be poured on them and rubbed in. The homes of the well-to-do are always open to them, even the women's quarters. They enter freely and are welcome to a share of the food and conversation. Chronic disease or disability to them is the source of the greatest shame. Anyone suspecting that he is so afflicted will contrive his own death by fire. Building a pyre, he anoints himself with oil, seats himself on the top of the pile, gives the order that it be lit, then remains perfectly still until he dies.[5]

DEMETRIUS

Compared with the case of Demonax, the historicity of
Demetrius is well established. Tacitus and Lucian also mention
him, although all the testimony below is culled from the writings of the Roman Stoic Seneca (c. 4 BC–AD 65), a personal
friend and admirer. Seneca emphasizes two things about
Demetrius, one of the first Cynics to come to prominence in
Rome: his disdain for wealth and luxury, and the consistency
with which he applied the Stoic-Cynic principles that most philosophers (Seneca included) were better known for paying lip
service to, either in speeches or written compositions. Any
reader of Juvenal or Petronius knows that extravagance and
the pursuit of riches were besetting vices of the early Roman
Empire. Demetrius also represented a flesh-and-blood exem-
plum of the moral values Seneca and others espoused, and
exempla (living paradigms) of the traditional virtues carried
more weight with the Romans than formal arguments in their
favour. In praising Demetrius, Seneca dissociates him from
Cynicism's more controversial features, such as acts of a shameless or antisocial nature, acts that Romans, again compared
with Greeks, were less disposed to tolerate.

115 (Sen., Benef. 7. 1. 3–7. 2. 1)

[3] Demetrius the Cynic, a great man, in my view – among the
greatest, in fact – makes a good point when he says that it is
best to adhere to a mere handful of philosophical principles,

but to hold them close and practise them continually. Knowledge of a great many precepts, if they are not second nature, is not as efficacious. [4] Or, as he puts it, 'The successful wrestler is not the one who knows all the holds and positions of the sport – most of which he will never get to use on an opponent – but one who has steadily practised and mastered a handful, and focuses on the right moment to deploy them. It does not matter how many grips he knows, only that he knows enough to guarantee victory.'

In our own training, likewise, there are many points that are interesting but few that are crucial. [5] You may have no notion of the law that governs the ebb and flow of ocean tides, why every seventh year marks a new stage in a human life,[1] why the columns of a stoa, when viewed from a distance, are not proportional in width but narrow at either end until the intervening spaces seem to disappear; what accounts for the simultaneous birth of twins if they are conceived separately, or whether they are products of a single sexual act or of two; what accounts for their different destinies[2] if they are born together and why their lives can differ so much when so little time elapses between their births. You will not lose much by being ignorant of matters of no personal importance to you – matters, in fact, that no one understands. Truth is complicated and profoundly obscure.

[6] But we cannot charge Nature with spite on that account, since the only things hard to learn are the ones whose sole benefit lies in the sense of gratification involved in the process of their discovery. She has put in plain view and within easy reach whatever will improve us or make us happier.

[7] The soul that has come to despise the accidents of fortune, to rise above fear and not zealously crave riches without end, but has learned to look for wealth within itself; that has banished fear of gods and men, knowing that from another man there is not much, and from god nothing at all to fear; that scorns those specious worldly goods that always entail trouble and complication – that soul is advanced to the point where it can see that death is not the source of any sorrow, but the end of many.

If your soul is devoted to virtue and you think that any way she leads is smooth; if you as a social animal born to serve the common interest view the world as the shared home of humanity and can bare your conscience to the gods and, from self-respect, always live as if your acts were publicly on display – then you are a person standing on solid ground, under a clear sky, protected from the storms of fortune. You have attained to knowledge of everything vital and essential. Anything more is matter for diversion in one's leisure hours. Once it has found safe harbour, the soul is free to study topics that enhance one's personal refinement instead of one's moral strength.

[7. 2. 1] These are the doctrines that my friend Demetrius says we must grab hold of with both hands if we are to progress in philosophy. They are the principles we must never let go of but must cling to and incorporate, so that by daily reflection on them we reach the point where their moral influence becomes second nature. In any situation where they are relevant, their presence in our soul must at once make clear what is right and wrong.

116 (Sen., *Benef.* 7. 8. 2–7. 11. 2)

[2] I will not cite Socrates, Chrysippus, Zeno, or other standard paradigms – great men, to be sure, but perhaps too great in the popular imagination because envy sets no limits to the praise of our predecessors. A little while ago, however, I brought up the name of Demetrius. I think that nature produced such a contemporary to show that there was still someone who could not be corrupted by us nor we be corrected[3] by him. He is a man of perfect wisdom, even if he demurs, and devoted to his principles. And he is eloquent, more remarkable perhaps for vigour than for elegance or fluency. But his style befits one dealing, as he does, with matters of great weight. He speaks from the heart, *ex tempore*, but at the same time in an orderly and coherent fashion.

[3] I am convinced that he was endowed by providence with such a stainless life and with such powers of persuasion that our age should not lack for either a model of behaviour or a powerful moral critic. If Demetrius were offered unlimited riches by some god on condition that he kept it all to himself, my view is that he would decline the offer and say:

[7. 9. 1] 'I really cannot chain myself to such a treasure chest, and drag myself down, free and unencumbered as I am now, to the slime at the bottom of the sea. Why offer me what proves the bane of all existence? Even if I were to bestow it all I would not accept it, seeing it includes much that it would not suit me to give away. I prefer to keep in view before me that which dazzles the eyes of nations and kings; I want to inspect at leisure the things you are ready to pay for with your life and blood.

[2] 'First spread out before me the rewards of a life devoted to luxury, arranged in a row, if you like or, better yet, stacked in a heap. I see a tortoise beautified with exquisite designs, and the shells of other foul and slothful creatures bought for an enormous price whose subtle colours, for which they are valued, are enhanced by the application of dyes rivalling nature's own. I see tables fashioned out of wood worth a senator's fortune, the more prized examples featuring a greater share of knots produced by the tree in its original gnarled and twisted state.

[3] 'Here I see crystal bowls, whose value is increased in proportion to their fragility; for the pleasure of fools is heightened by the risk that by rights should dampen it. I see cups carved from semi-precious stone: no doubt men would pay too little for their luxury unless, when they toast each other, they had jewels to hold the wine – wine that they will eventually throw up. [4] I see pearls, and not single ones designed for each ear; for ears now have been trained to hold up under the weight of whole clusters of pearls. They come in pairs, and above each pair another one is appended. Female vanity has so infected men that two or three fortunes dangling from either ear are needed to sate it.

[5] 'I see silk garments – if you can call "garments" sheer

sheets of fabric that do nothing to protect a woman's body, much less her dignity. Dressed in one of these shifts she will be hard pressed to insist that she isn't simply naked. These outfits are fetched at enormous cost from barely civilized tribes. Our wives can hardly show more of their bodies to their lovers in the bedroom than they do, wearing such apparel, in the street.

[7. 10. 1] 'And how is conventional greed for money holding up? So many things exceed it now in the popular imagination. All the goods I mentioned are more highly prized. So I want to examine the two main precious metals – the things for which our greed drives us to excavate deeply underground.

[2] 'But just consider, the earth is the source of everything possibly beneficial to us. Gold and silver, however, it interred, concealed and buried deep beneath its cumulative weight almost as though it recognized that these minerals were harmful and likely to bring general trouble to mankind. I note that iron is also recovered from the same subterranean murk as silver and gold, lest we lack the raw material to kill one another or to reward the agents of such slaughter.[4] But there's no denying iron's practical use.

[3] 'The value of other things, however, is based on delusion, in which the eye and mind conspire equally. Here I see bonds, deeds and securities – simulacra of genuine wealth, dreams invented by greed to deceive a mind that basks in empty hope. What are these things anyway? Loans, debt-books, interest – they are names for things that don't exist in nature, invented to serve man's materialistic values.

[4] 'I could complain that nature did not bury gold and silver nearly deep enough, that she did not lay a weight upon them too heavy to be removed. But what can I say with respect to these bills of yours, these accounts, these billable hours, this barbarous rate of interest? They are conscious evils that stem from our character – evils that cannot be seen or held in the hand – but evils nevertheless that aim to change avaricious dreams into reality.

[5] 'I pity the person whose chief delight is the inventory of his estate, of the vast tracts of lands tended by prisoners of war, the huge herds that require whole kingdoms and provinces to

feed, the army of slaves outnumbering uncivilized tribes, the private palaces that exceed some cities in extent.

[6] 'Because when he has made a review of his wealth and, taking careful note of investments and expenditures, is filled with pride, then let him compare what he owns with what he still desires: then suddenly he feels poor. Leave me in peace to enjoy my innate wealth. The kingdom of philosophy I know: it is great, it is secure. It is mine in the sense that it belongs to everyone.'

[11. 1] So Demetrius only laughed and declined Caligula's offer of two hundred thousand in cash. To him it was not even worth boasting that he had refused such a sum. My god, what a contemptible character the emperor betrayed in trying to compliment, much less corrupt, Demetrius with such a proposition.

117 (Sen., *Letter to Lucilius* 20. 8–9)

[8] Limit your needs, so that you will not run short. And helping you to achieve that end will be the burden, the substance of this letter – which I come to now.

[9] You may disapprove, but once more I call on Epicurus to deliver on that promise. 'Your advice will be more effective delivered from a plain cot or dressed in simple rags. That way they are not just words, they carry spontaneous conviction.' Personally, I give more credence to what our friend Demetrius says because he himself sleeps without even a cloak to cover him, much less rugs to rest upon. He is not only a guide, but a witness, to the truth.

118 (Sen., *Letter to Lucilius* 62. 3)

Though he wears barely enough to cover him, I prefer to go about in the company of Demetrius, whom I regard as the finest of men, rather than with people tricked out in purple robes.

I hold him in high esteem and I benefit from our association. And why not? In his character I cannot discover a single fault. We cannot have everything. On the contrary, there is nothing we cannot survive without. The quickest road to wealth is to learn to despise it. Our friend Demetrius, however, lives not merely as if he holds all goods in contempt, but as if he has put them in the possession of others.

119 (Sen., *Letter to Lucilius* 67. 14)

Apropos, I think of Demetrius and his comparison of an easy life untouched by fortune's ups and downs to the Dead Sea. If you have nothing to rouse or stir you to action, nothing to test your character by way of challenges or attack – if you recline in a constant state of inertia – that, he says, is not peace, it is a coma.

120 (Sen., *Letter to Lucilius* 91. 19)

Fear exists by consensus. Your fear of death is like your fear of malicious gossip. But what is more stupid than a person afraid of what other people say? Our friend Demetrius is inclined to put it neatly: 'The talk of fools to me is like the sound of farts. For what difference is it to me whether their rumblings issue from above or below?'

121 (Sen., *Prov.* 3. 3)

Among his many admirable sayings, our friend Demetrius recently added another, which still rings in my ears: 'Nothing seems to be more unfortunate than a man who has never had to face misfortune.' For he has never had the chance to test himself. Though all his prayers seemed answered, the gods had formed a poor opinion of him even before his prayers had been formulated.

122 (Sen., *On the Happy Life*, 18. 3)

What I consistently praise is not the life that I lead, but the one that I know I should be leading. I admire and follow virtue, even if I remain a long way behind and only pursue her with a halting gait. Can I really expect malice to spare anything, when even Cato and Rutilius were subject to their share? Should anybody care if critics call him too rich, when they judge Demetrius the Cynic insufficiently impoverished? Here is a man of the greatest austerity, who struggles with all the desires of nature, and is poorer than other Cynics in that he has not only rid himself of property but even the desire for it. And this very man people say is not poor enough. Well, you see: like me he does not profess to know virtue but is conscious of lacking it.[5]

DIO CHRYSOSTOM

Dio Chrysostom was a native of Bithynia who travelled to Rome c. AD 75 to advance his career. He fell foul of the Emperor Domitian because of his outspokenness, and was exiled from Rome and barred from his native Bithynia. During his term of banishment he adopted the Cynic regimen almost by default, owing to his reduced material circumstances. This proved to be something of a blessing in disguise because of his facility as an orator with a background in Cynic-Stoic discourse. When he was allowed home around the year 97, he turned his hand to the composition of speeches, including Orations 6 and 8 translated below. They promote such characteristic Cynic values as self-sufficiency (autarkeia), training (askêsis), and freedom of speech (parrhêsia). Diogenes of Sinope features prominently as a model in all these programmatic speeches – which are believed to be partially intended for the ears of the Emperor Nerva, Domitian's successor, who promised (and adopted) a less oppressive, more tolerant posture towards philosophers and their idiosyncratic values.

123 Oration 6

[1] Diogenes relocated to Greece after he was exiled from his native city of Sinope. Here he divided his time between Corinth and Athens. In doing so he said he was imitating the very King of Persia, who wintered in Babylon and Susa with occasional trips to Bactra, spent the spring in the more temperate parts of

Asia, and passed his summers in Median Ecbatana, whose climate is always cool and whose summer resembles Babylon's winter.

[2] Diogenes likewise relocated with the seasons. Unlike the Peloponnese or Thessaly, Attica has no tall mountains or major rivers. Its soil is poor and its climate dry; rain is infrequent and does not collect. And the sea surrounds it on nearly every side, which accounts for its name,[1] since Attica is practically one continuous shoreline.

[3] The city is low-lying and faces south, as shown by boats making for Peiraeus from Sunium, which depend on a southerly wind to reach port. It follows that the winters in Attica are mild. In Corinth, by contrast, the summer is breezy owing to the great number of gulfs indenting the coast and the winds that regularly blow off them. The town also lies in the shade of Acrocorinth and inclines towards Lechaeum and the north.

[4] In Diogenes' view these cities were far more beautiful than either Babylon or Ecbatana. He felt that the Craneum[2] in Corinth and the acropolis in Athens with its Propylaea excelled any Persian monuments, which had only their greater size to recommend them. Even as to that, Athens was nearly twenty-five miles in circumference now that Peiraeus and the circuit walls, encompassing tracts of land uninhabited in ancient times, had been incorporated. So Athens was now fully half Babylon's area – if, indeed, we can credit hearsay about the latter city's proportions.[3]

[5] And although he did not set much store by these things, he believed that Athens excelled in the standard of its statues and paintings, its gold, silver and bronze works, its coinage, furnishings and the condition of its buildings.

[6] The king also faced a long trip between residences. His summers and winters were pretty much spent on the road. Diogenes, on the other hand, could leave Corinth, put up for the night at Megara and easily be in Athens the following day, either by passing through Eleusis, or by way of Salamis – a shorter route with no barren stretches in between. [7] So he used to say half in jest[4] that he had the advantage of the king as far as living arrangements were concerned. Yet he had a serious

aim: to make those who envied the Persian's king's wealth and his celebrated fortune see that his life was nothing like as enviable as they imagined it to be. For aspects of it served no useful purpose, and the rest was within reach of even the very poor.

[8] In fact, Diogenes was not neglectful of his body,[5] as ignorant people alleged. When they saw him fasting or living outdoors in the cold, they reckoned he was contemptuous of health and of life itself. In fact such privations are healthier than stuffing oneself, keeping to one's house, and never enduring hot or cold. [9] When he did warm himself by a fire, or indulge his appetite, his pleasure was that much greater.

Most of all he enjoyed the change of season. He was cheered by the first sign of summer that took the edge off winter's chill. But he was not sorry to see summer end as it meant relief from the blazing heat. By gradually exposing and inuring himself to the extremes of either season he arrived at the point where he could face either without discomfort.

[10] He rarely had recourse to fire, shade, or shelter to counteract the weather's effects. The ordinary run of people can light a fire any time, are well supplied with clothes, and have a roof above their heads. At the first hint of cold they immediately seek protection from the open air. The upshot is that their bodies are too frail to cope with winter's rigour. [11] And because their house provides them with unlimited shade in summer, and they can drink as much chilled wine as they like, they never experience the full effects of the sun, never know true thirst and, like the women of the house, live life as virtual prisoners. Their bodies are weak and sluggish, their souls lost in a nearly constant state of drunken torpor.

Boredom compels them to invent unwholesome dishes, then to take spa treatments to combat the unwelcome side effects of such a diet. In the space of a single day they often want both breeze and a heavy cloak, heat as well as ice to offset the heat and – what's most absurd – [12] they hanker for hunger as well as thirst. Addicted to sex, they nevertheless derive no pleasure from it since they do not wait until the urge arises in its own good time. The upshot is that the pleasures they pursue are joyless and disappointing in their consummation.

Diogenes, however, waited until he was hungry and thirsty before settling down to eat; he thought hunger acted as food's most piquant and satisfying sauce.[6] He used to devour a barley cake with better appetite than others dined on the rarest foodstuffs, and drank clear water from a stream with more pleasure than others do their vintage Thasian wine.

[13] He found it funny that thirsty people would pass by a spring in pursuit of Chian or Lesbian wine at any price; they were far dumber than cattle, which never pass a spring or clear stream when they are thirsty, or scorn to eat their fill of grass and tender leaves when they are hungry.

[14] He said that in every city the finest and most cultivated houses were open to him, meaning the temples and gymnasia. As for clothes, a single garment sufficed him all year round, [15] since he had learned to tolerate any climate.

He always went barefoot since our feet, according to him, were no more delicate than our eyes or faces. These were naturally sensitive but grew resistant to the cold through continual exposure. For men could walk around with their feet protected but hardly with their eyes covered. Those with a great many material possessions, he used to say, were like newborn babies because they were in constant need of swaddling clothes.

[16] The business that produced the most drama in human lives, and the most expense – the thing responsible for the destruction of many states and the sad ruin of many nations – this cost him nothing either in terms of effort or expense. [17] Which is to say, he did not have to go anywhere for sex. As he jokingly put it, Aphrodite made herself available to him everywhere, and for free. It was the poets' own lechery that was behind the malicious epithet 'all-golden' that they routinely applied to her. Since many scoffed at this boast, he masturbated in public before a crowd of witnesses, saying that, if more people were like him, Troy would have never fallen and Priam, king of Phrygia and Zeus' son, would not have been slaughtered on Zeus' altar.

[18] The Achaeans had been foolish enough to believe that even dead men needed a woman. This resulted in the slaughter of Polyxena on Achilles' tomb. Diogenes said that fish showed

themselves smarter than men in a way, because when they needed to ejaculate they simply went forth and rubbed up against something hard. [19] He thought it was odd that people did not like to have their arms, their legs, or any other body part rubbed – certainly not if they had to pay for it (however rich they were). But when it came to that one particular body part they were prepared to spend small fortunes; some even risked their lives.

[20] He invented a facetious myth to the effect that the solo form of sex was invented by Pan. He fell in love with Echo and wandered the mountains day and night, but she continued to elude him. Finally Hermes, his father, took pity on him and taught him the trick of self-gratification. From then on, Pan was freed of his torment. And, Diogenes added, it was from Pan that shepherds learned proficiency in the same practice.

[21] With such irreverent humour he rattled a smug and ingenuous public. But sophists especially were the butt of his satire. They not only believed that they knew more than anyone else, they insisted on being recognized for it.

In his view, humans, because of their vulnerability, had a harder time of it than beasts. [22] The beasts, after all, drank only water and ate uncultivated plants, and got through the year without the protection of so much as a blanket. They never went indoors, had no need of fire, and yet most, unless they were slaughtered for food, lived to the natural limit of their lives. All alike were strong and healthy without recourse to drugs or doctors.

[23] Humans, by contrast, clung desperately to life by resorting to various means of cheating death; and all the same few managed to reach old age. They lived with a host of complaints the majority of which don't even have a name. [24] Since earth does not produce medicinal plants to cure them all they are forced to submit to cautery and the knife.

Chiron, Asclepius and the sons of Asclepius,[7] for all their powers of healing, could not offset the ill effects of their patients' pleasant vices; [25] seers with their prophecies and priests with their rituals were equally worthless. Men crowded into the cities for mutual defence against outsiders, but then turned on each other and committed the foulest crimes, as if that were their real motive for congregating.

The reason, in his opinion, why Zeus in the myth punishes Prometheus[8] for sharing his discovery of fire was that this marked the beginning of mankind's weakness and love of luxury. For Zeus certainly did not hate men or wish to deny them any benefit.

[26] Some objected that man was not meant to live like the beasts because, unlike them, his skin was soft and lacked wool, fur or feathers. [27] Nor was he protected by a sturdy hide. Diogenes countered that if men were weak it was owing to their lifestyle. They do their best to avoid the sun as well as the cold; the smoothness of the human body was nothing to do with it. Look at frogs, he said, and any number of other animals that are even softer than man and have no hair at all. [28] Frogs not only live outdoors, they survive the winter in freezing water.

He also pointed out that the eyes and face of man have no need of protection. It was a general rule that animals were not to be found in places where they could not survive. How else could the first humans have managed before the advent of fire, houses, clothes or agriculture?

The fact is, all man's ingenuity and advances in technology were at best mixed blessings in the lives of later generations. [29] For man did not use his intelligence in the service of justice or bravery, only pleasure. And in this single-minded pursuit their lives actually became less pleasant and more oppressive; their devotion to self-interest brought them to dreadful ends.[9] [30] This is why Prometheus is said to have been justly bound to a rock while an eagle tore at his liver. So whatever cost a lot in terms of time, trouble and money, these things Diogenes rejected because, as he was able to show, they hurt whoever used them. [31] But if there were resources that helped the body to withstand hunger or cold naturally, or alleviate desire, he was perfectly willing to employ them. In fact, he favoured Athens and Corinth because their climate was healthy and they were fertile all year round. He took care to have a sufficiency of food and clothing. But he would have nothing to do with

politics, lawsuits, rivalries, wars or factions. Above all he modelled himself on the gods. Homer, after all, said that their life
alone was trouble-free. This implied that man's was harsh and
difficult.

[32] Even the beasts had better sense than men, according to
him. Storks flee summer's heat for a cooler climate, and remain
there as long as conditions permit. They then give way to winter and leave en masse. Cranes, on the other hand, withstand
winter well. So they regularly show up in the autumn[10] to glean
seed from the fields. [33] Deer and hares descend from the
mountains to winter in plains and valleys conveniently protected from the wind. In the hot season, however, they retreat
to the woods and regions far to the north.

[34] When he noticed that most people were beset by troubles their whole life and constantly in conflict; that they had so
many problems that they did not have a moment's peace, even
during the Panhellenic games when a general truce was
declared; that crimes were committed just to stay alive; that
there was widespread panic lest men lack the so-called necessities of life; that great plans and efforts were made to ensure
that children inherit large sums of money – when he saw all
this, he marvelled that he alone was free because he abstained
from such behaviour, yet no one appreciated how uniquely
blessed he was.

[35] Taking everything into account, he believed that he was
actually unfair to himself by inviting comparison with the Persian king. The difference between them was great. In fact, of all
men the king was most to be pitied. With all his riches he lived
in fear of ruin. He dreaded illness but could not deny himself
the causes behind it. And he was terrified of death, which he
was certain many were plotting against him, including his own
sons and brothers.

[36] The result was that the finest dishes afforded him no
pleasure and wine brought him no relief from his concerns.
Not a day passed but he imagined himself involved in some
disaster. When he was sober he longed to be drunk as an escape
from his troubles; and when he was drunk he despaired because
he had made himself vulnerable and weak.

[37] Again, when he was awake he prayed for sleep so he could forget his fears, but he was no sooner asleep than nightmares made him leap out of bed as if he were under lethal attack. Neither the golden plane tree[11] nor the castles of Semiramis nor the walls of Babylon could help. [38] Strangest of all, though, he entrusted his life to armed guards despite being afraid of armed men.[12] And he had everyone who came into his presence searched for weapons, while at the same time surrounding himself with people armed to the teeth.

For protection he ran back and forth between an armed escort and unarmed attendants. Bodyguards defended him from the mob, eunuchs kept him safe from the bodyguards. He had no one he could trust or anywhere he could go to enjoy even a single untroubled day. [39] He had misgivings about everything he ate or drank and kept professional tasters, like so many lookouts posted along a road overrun by a hostile force. Nor were his family, even his wife and children, above suspicion. Yet hard and heavy as it was to be king, he never gave a thought to abdicating, even had such a thing been possible.

[40] Now, whatever straits a person is in, he can take comfort in the thought that it all might eventually end. The prisoner hopes some day to be freed, the exile might return home, the patient believes in the chance of recovery until his dying breath. Not so the king: practically anything is his for the asking, except release from his position. Anyone who has experienced the death of a loved one can be certain that in time his grief will end. For a king, however, anxieties always grow. His life expectancy is short to begin with. [41] If he does attain old age he finds it more than commonly difficult, unlike the horse in the fable.[13] The number of people with a grievance against him has increased and so, consequently, has the number of his enemies. And his infirmities make it impossible for him to defend himself.

Now, most misfortunes are more frightening in anticipation than painful in reality, and this includes poverty, exile, imprisonment and the loss of legal rights. Remove the fear of death, and there is nothing left to be anxious about. Death in itself does not cause its victims suffering; death is nothing other than the cessation of all suffering. [42] Fear of death, on the other hand, involves so much emotional pain that many people choose to pre-empt it. There are those, for instance, on a storm-tossed ship, who will take their own life rather than wait for the ship to sink. Others do the same thing when surrounded by the enemy, even knowing that they can suffer nothing worse at the enemy's hands. [43] And this same fear is never absent from a monarch's life, night or day. Condemned criminals at least have a date fixed for their execution. But a king doesn't know when death will come – it may be tomorrow, it may be today. No period of time, however small, is exempt. Whether eating, sacrificing, drinking or sleeping, fear of death is a king's constant companion.

[44] If they venture on romance, the thought of death still haunts them, even during the act of love, no matter how great the degree of passion. Perhaps, they think, their own lovers are out to get them. I conclude that they only know happiness when they are actually killed, as only then does this appalling torment end.

[45] What's most absurd, though, is that other men realize when their situation is hopeless, so that they do not suffer long when the option of suicide is available to them. But monarchs mistake the great complications of their life for blessings, influenced, I suppose, by the views of people who have no knowledge of kingship at first hand. And god saw to it that they stay wedded to this illusion so that they put up with this anguish.

[46] Again, for successful people, life is sweeter, and death, on that account, more grievous. [47] The less fortunate seem to find life harder to bear and almost welcome death. Kings have the worst of both worlds, since their existence is even less pleasant than that of people who long to die, and yet they are afraid of death as though they could pass their life in no greater state of bliss. [48] Since pleasures are naturally more appreciated when they are infrequent, and gradually lose their appeal for people who have uninterrupted access to them; and since bad circumstances are made worse for never letting up, we might almost say that the king's experience of both is such that he rarely finds relief from pain and is rarely responsive to pleasure.

[49] Besides, they distrust the power of the rich as well as the poor man's desire for riches. They don't get credit for the favours they do their subjects, who never think them enough. And subjects whose petitions are flatly denied hate them most of all.

[50] The most detested person is he who has the most ill-gotten gains. Therefore no one is more detested than a tyrant. Add to which, he has to bestow favours on his court or he will be soon replaced. But it isn't easy to gratify regularly the wishes of a large court without depriving others. The people he robs are therefore his enemies, while his beneficiaries suspect his motives and look to get rid of him soon. Matters at a distance scare him because he cannot examine them closely, while things nearby he fears precisely because of their proximity. From people at a distance he looks for war, from those close at hand, betrayal.

[51] Peace is undesirable because he fears his subjects' idle hands, and war because he is forced to trouble them for money and recruits. Consequently, he longs for peace in wartime, and when peace arrives, at once he casts about for a pretext to make war. [52] In boon times he fears the public's insolence, their resentment in times of need. It is not safe to go abroad or stay at home, to appear in public or live in seclusion, even to venture where he may do so securely: treason and treachery seem to menace him on every side.

[53] Each king is acquainted with fatal conspiracies involving monarchs of the past, and imagines that now they all are aimed at him; he is as terrified as if he personally were fated to die all those historical deaths. He must keep a constant check on the impulse to whirl around and look behind him, from shame and fear alike. [54] For the more apparent a prince's fear, the more emboldened conspirators become from scorn of his timidity. He lives like someone narrowly confined, with swords hanging above his head and others arranged in a circle around him, positioned mere inches from his skin.

[55] These swords, indeed, are poised in such a way that Tantalus in Hades has it far easier, dreading the rock, they say, that totters overhead. Tantalus, at least, no longer has death in

prospect. The tyrant has to endure in this life what is ascribed to Tantalus in the next.

[56] Tyrants of a single city or a small nation may possibly run away from their responsibility and make a life for themselves in hiding. But they are not welcome anywhere, are objects of suspicion, and readily turned over to those they have offended. Rulers of many cities or nations, or of whole continents like the Persian king, however, cannot escape their condition, even if by the grace of some god they are allowed to see how miserable it is. [57] So it would seem their life is never safe; even turned into bronze or iron they could be smashed or melted down and their memory thus effaced.

[58] Speak to them boldly and you rouse anger and resentment with your candour, while deference and humility only make them suspicious. Deal with them honestly and they think they are being insulted, approach them humbly and they think they are being tricked. They take criticism much worse than others, being tyrants after all; but praise they don't like because they doubt its sincerity. [59] Where the greatest benefit of all is concerned, a tyrant is the most impoverished, because he can never hope to know real warmth and friendship. Keepers of savage lions will sooner feel affection for those brutes than tyrants will be loved by their sycophants and petitioners.

[60] I, however, (Diogenes continued) go wherever I like at night, and during the day am not afraid to travel alone – through the heart of an army, if necessary, without protection of the herald's staff. I even pass through gangs of thieves because I have no enemy, public or private, who stands to gain by confronting me. If the entire world's gold, silver or bronze should disappear I would not be in the least affected.

[61] And if an earthquake toppled all the houses, as happened in Sparta once, and all the sheep were killed, so that no wool was available in which to dress warmly; if poverty afflicted Attica as well as Boeotia, Thessaly and the Peloponnese, as it is said to have done in the past, I will be none the poorer nor any the worse. [62] How much more naked will I be than I am now? How much more homeless? For food I am content with apples, millet, barley, vetches, common pulses,

roasted acorns and cornel berries, all of which Homer says Circe fed the companions of Odysseus, and on which even the largest animals manage to subsist.

124 Oration 8, On Virtue

[1] After he was exiled from his native Sinope and reduced to poverty, Diogenes went to Athens. He found many of Socrates' associates there, including Plato, Aristippus, Antisthenes and Euclides of Megara. Xenophon was away on campaign with Cyrus.

The others he soon grew tired of, but he enjoyed Antisthenes' company, not so much for the man's character as his philosophy. He thought there was much of truth to admire in it and it was best adapted to help mankind. [2] Antisthenes himself seemed much more easy-going by comparison with what he taught. In mockery, Diogenes used to call him a trumpet, which cannot hear itself no matter how loud it blasts. Antisthenes put up with his scorn because he valued Diogenes' honesty.

[3] But in return for being called a trumpet, he liked to say that Diogenes resembled a wasp, the buzz of whose wings was soft but whose sting was sharp. He was charmed by the man's candour, like horsemen with a fiery mount, who put up with the animal's difficult side for the sake of its courage and stamina, and come to despise horses that are slow and docile. [4] Sometimes he provoked him, other times he tried to calm him down. In this he was like musicians who tune their instruments, taking care never to wind the strings so tight they snap.

When Antisthenes died, Diogenes moved to Corinth. He did not think enough of the other philosophers in Athens to remain there. He lived in Corinth without renting a house or staying with a friend. Instead he camped in the Craneum. [5] He knew that the city attracted a great crowd of people owing to its harbours, its central location – and its supply of prostitutes. So he reasoned that, just as a good doctor goes where there are the most people to heal, a philosopher belongs where there are the most reprobates, to expose their folly and correct their mistakes.

[6] When the time for the Isthmian games arrived, he made his way there along with everyone else. He saw the festivals as an opportunity to study people's wants and interests. He liked to find out why they had travelled to the games and what things they took pride in. Like many another visitor he made his services available to the public. [7] He thought it strange, though, that if he said he could fix teeth, everyone needing a tooth pulled would seek him out; if he claimed to be an eye doctor, everyone with an eye complaint would show up at his door; and the same if he knew a cure for a bad spleen, gout, or the common cold.

[8] But because he professed to heal his followers of ignorance, vice and a disordered life, no one paid him any mind or asked to be treated, even if they stood to gain by it financially. Apparently they were less concerned about their moral than their physical health. They thought it was worse to suffer from an enlarged spleen or a rotten tooth than from a soul that was benighted, stupid, cowardly, rash, licentious, slavish, mean – depraved, in short, in every imaginable way.

[9] In due course, the area around Poseidon's temple was full of worthless orators by turns bawling their lectures and deriding their competition; self-styled pundits could be heard arguing among themselves; a great many speech-writers read out their tedious speeches; poets in plenty recited verses to an appreciative mob; magicians worked their magic, astrologers told fortunes; lawyers were out in force perverting the law; and there was no lack of peddlers hawking whatever it is each happened to bring. [10] Soon Diogenes attracted an audience too – no Corinthians, however, since they did not think they stood to benefit from someone they saw every day already. His audience consisted of foreigners. But even they exchanged only a few words before moving on, for fear of being shown up. [11] Seeing this, Diogenes likened himself to Spartan hounds:[14] lots of people would pet them when they were shown at the festivals, but few were ready to buy, because they could not completely tame them.

Someone asked him if he was on hand as one of the spectators. 'No,' he replied, 'as a contestant.' The other man laughed and wanted to know who his opponents were.

[12] With a characteristic glare he said, 'The toughest and hardest to defeat: no Greek can look them in the eye. They don't box, they don't wrestle or run, they don't throw the javelin, hurl the discus, or compete in the long jump.' 'Who are they, then?' [13] 'Hardships – impossible to cope with for people soft and gone to seed, people who feast all day and snore away the night. They yield to skinny, wraithlike figures whose waists are as pinched as wasps. [14] I mean, you surely don't think these potbellies are good for anything? Unless it is to purify the community[15] of its collective guilt by being led around the city before being thrust beyond its borders. Or maybe they ought to be killed, quartered and eaten, the way we do with large game fish. Or boiled in brine and rendered for their fat, the way natives of Pontus extract pig's lard with which to anoint themselves. Because, in my opinion, these men are less endowed with a soul than pigs.

[15] 'A real man thinks hardships are his worthiest opponents. He enjoys grappling with them day and night – and not for the benefit of a sprig of parsley, like goats, or for a branch of olive or pine.[16] He aims for virtue and happiness all his life, not just when the Eleans or the Corinthians, or the Thessalian assembly make proclamation of the games. [16] Fearing none of them, he never begs to be allowed to draw a different opponent. Instead he welcomes all of them in turn – battling cold and hunger, enduring thirst, never yielding even if the whip, the sword, or fire is applied. Hunger, exile, social stigma and the like are matters of indifference; the philosopher makes sport of them as children play with dice or multicoloured balls.

[17] 'To cowards, of course, such challengers seem terrifying and unbearable. But stand up to them and you will find that they are the weak and timid ones. In this they much resemble dogs that will chase and bite you, even tackle you and tear you to pieces if you try running from them. If you show them you are not afraid, however, they will cower and slink away, and in time even show you affection.

[18] 'But most men live in mortal terror of these opponents. They never look them in the face and make a clear-eyed assessment. Skilled boxers, by anticipating their opponent, will win, sustaining barely any hurt to themselves. But let them back away in fear and they expose themselves to a brutal beating. Similarly, if we face down our troubles and deal with them directly we deprive them of their power over us. But if we retreat from them or waver, they grow greater in our imagination. [19] You can see the same thing in the case of fire: attack it aggressively and the blaze is at once extinguished; treat it timidly and you end up badly burned – like children playing with fire who try to put it out with their tongue. And the adversaries I'm talking about fight with no holds barred – punching, choking, slashing, even killing on occasion.

[20] 'There is another, even harder struggle than the one against painful circumstances. This is the one fought against pleasure – a greater contest and more hazardous. It is not a straightforward trial of strength; pleasure uses cunning and seductive means to gain the upper hand. This is no straightforward fight of the kind Homer describes:

> Battle was now joined fiercely around the ships . . .
> With halberd and keen battle-axe
> They fought, and broadswords double-edged.[17]

[21] No, it is no fair fight; pleasure uses tricks and powerful charms to achieve her ends. She operates the way Homer says Circe drugged the companions of Odysseus, turning them into pigs, wolves or any number of other beasts. Such is this thing called pleasure; she has not one trick but many up her sleeve to corrupt men through sight, sound, smell, touch and taste. [22] She makes food, drink and sex her allies too, and practises equally on people sleeping or awake. You cannot just set a watch for the night and then sleep safely, as in normal warfare. [23] It is just then that she is most aggressive, enslaving and enfeebling us with the lure of sleep itself, or sending crude and insidious dreams that evoke the memory of pleasure again.

'Now pain derives from, and mainly affects, the sense of

touch. [24] Pleasure, on the other hand, gains access by way of all five senses. And whereas pain should be faced and engaged, we should avoid pleasure as far as possible and have only incidental dealings with her. The strongest man, one might say, is the man who can keep furthest from pleasure, because one cannot be intimate, or even acquainted, with her for any length of time without becoming entirely her slave.

[25] 'When pleasure with her charms gains possession of the soul, the rest of Circe's effects soon follow. With one touch of her magic wand she drives her captives into a kind of pen and there they live out the rest of their lives as wolves or pigs. [26] She also spawns all manner of deadly snakes and other creeping things, her faithful familiars, who, though devoted to pleasure, involve a world of pain and disease. For once she has got control of her victims, she betrays them by abandoning them to the cruellest suffering.

[27] 'This is the contest between pain and pleasure that I stake my life on. Yet none of you sorry lot give me the least regard. You care only for these worthless runners, dancers and jumpers. Yet, after all, they didn't take any notice of Heracles' labours either.[18] There were athletes even then to occupy people's attention: Zetes, Calaïs, Peleus, and other such runners and wrestlers. Others they would admire for their wealth or beauty, as for instance Jason and Cinyras.

[28] 'They also say that Pelops had an ivory shoulder – as if a man could have any use for an ivory shoulder (or a gold one, for that matter), or for eyes of emerald or diamond. As for what his soul was like, this they did not care to explore. They pitied Heracles for his toils and troubles, and said he was the most unfortunate man. Which is why they called them 'labours', as if a life devoted to good works were laborious. [29] But now that he's dead they heap him with honours, worship him as a god, and say that he has Hebe for his wife. Everyone prays to him for good fortune – this man who himself was supposedly most unfortunate.

[30] 'Further, they have an idea that Eurystheus controlled him and ordered him about – Eurystheus, whom no one respected and no one ever sacrificed or prayed to. Heracles,

however, made the circuit of all Europe and Asia, and did not look a bit like today's athletes. How far could he have got if he had carried that much weight, eaten that much meat, or needed that much sleep? No, he was as alert and agile as a lion, keen of eye and ear, heedless of hot and cold, having no use for heavy coats, beds or blankets, dressed in a dirty skin, with an air of hunger about him, meting out justice to good and bad alike.[19]

[31] 'Diomedes the Thracian fed strangers as well as his own subjects to his large team of wild mares, while he sat in state, dressed in royal finery and drinking all day. Because of this Heracles hit him with his club and smashed him as if he were an ancient pot. Geryones had huge herds of cattle and was the richest and most arrogant king in the west. Heracles slew him along with his brothers and drove his cattle off.

[32] 'Busiris did nothing all day but eat, exercise and boast about his wrestling. Heracles lifted and dashed him to the ground, bursting him open like a bloated leather bag. He loosened the girdle of the Amazon Hippolyte, who led him on and tried to win him with her beauty. But after sleeping with her he promptly departed, showing that he would never let beauty get the better of him, or ignore his duties for a woman's sake.

[33] 'He found Prometheus, whom I take to be a sort of sophist, being corrupted by popular opinion, since his liver would swell[20] and expand when he was praised but wither under the weight of criticism. He took pity on him and scared off the eagle that plagued him, ending his pride and excessive ambition and leaving him whole. And none of these exploits did Eurystheus any good. [34] If he gave him the golden apples of the Hesperides that he managed to retrieve, it was because he had no use for them, and neither did they. Eurystheus was welcome to them for all the good golden apples can do anyone.

'When finally he grew slower and weaker, unwilling to reconcile himself to old age and attacked, I suppose, by some debility, he made the best end a man could make, building a pyre of the driest wood available and demonstrating how little he was affected by the fire's heat.

[35] 'But first he cleaned out the dung from the Augean stables, the accumulation of many years, to show that he was not above tending to low and undignified tasks. He thought it was no less his duty to oppose and combat popular opinion than beasts and wicked men.'

[36] A large audience listened to this speech of Diogenes with great appreciation. But then thinking, I suppose, of Heracles' lack of pretension, he stopped speaking, squatted, and performed an unseemly act. At which the mob turned on him and called him crazy, while the sophists on hand booed him loudly – like a chorus of frogs who don't see the snake in the water.

TELES

The eight extracts preserved and translated below (seven, if IVA and B were originally parts of a single composition) cannot be regarded as literary productions of any great distinction, in terms of either style or content. But, as explained in the Introduction, this may be attributable, at least in part, to the details of their transmission. And they are among the fullest treatments to survive of such characteristic Cynic themes as poverty, exile and self-reliance. They are also valuable for enhancing our knowledge of Bion whom Teles cites frequently.

125 On Appearance and Reality

[3] Some say it is better to appear just than to be just in reality. Now, appearing good is not better than being good, is it?

'Of course not.'

So are actors judged good by appearing to perform well on the stage or by actually being good actors?

'By being good actors.'

And musicians – is it appearance or reality that earns them acclaim?

'Reality.'

Generally speaking, then, are we better off being good, or merely giving that impression?

'By being good.'

What about living a good life? The means that lead to this end must be better than those that do not. Therefore being good must be better than the appearance, because the just man is good, not the one who only seems to be just. And does the same principle apply to other things we value? Would you rather practise good deeds or make a mere show of it? To have good things or only look as though you did? Would you prefer to see, for example, or only appear to see? [4] To be healthy or only have a semblance of health? To have riches and friends, or be content with giving that impression?

Again, in the case of the goods of the soul, would it be enough to project the appearance of intelligence in lieu of the reality? Would you be content to seem happy but not experience true happiness? To be confident, fearless and courageous, or only pretend as though you were? And to return to the matter of justice, would you rather be possessed of the authentic virtue or its counterfeit?

'Actually, I would sooner appear, than be, courageous.'

But isn't a courageous man, unlike one who only seems courageous, also fearless and self-confident?

'Yes, but I will be honoured all the same.'

Indeed you will, and be placed in the front line of battle. The lottery will be fixed to guarantee your name is drawn when combat is to be settled by a duel, and others will take great pleasure in your fate just as the Greeks did with Ajax.[1] Then what do you expect will happen to you – a coward in crisis? If you're captured, your reputation for courage will ensure that you're put in manacles and handcuffs. No one will trust you; you will be locked up, and if you're subject to torture, be prepared for the worst. If you admit the truth you won't be believed but assumed to be making light of the whole situation because of your reputation for fortitude. Then you will be flayed, tortured, and finally roasted alive.

Now look what you'll have to endure in return for coming off as tough and courageous. But you affect those virtues the way politicians do, and keep your true nature concealed.

126 On Self-Sufficiency

[5] Just as a good actor should perform well any role the play-wright assigns him, so a good man should play well whatever role fortune assigns him. As Bion says, fortune, like a play-wright, sometimes casts us in a leading role, sometimes a supporting one; sometimes makes us king, other times a beggar. So if you are a supporting player, you should not aspire to play the lead part or you will only create confusion.

[6] One person says: 'You are a good ruler, while I make a fit subject. You rule over many, as a tutor I only have charge of this one boy here. You are rich and give generously of your wealth, and I am glad to accept a share of it – not in the spirit of a slave or an inferior, nor bitter that fate has put me in the position of having to depend on other people's charity. You have many possessions, I have few, but we both can make equally wise use of them. For it is not expensive articles that sustain us (he continues), nor do they work to our advantage. A few, inexpensive things are sufficient, provided we exercise sense and self-control in making use of them.'

Bion goes on to say that if inanimate things had our own capacity for reason and speech, they well might address us the way a slave seeking asylum at an altar customarily defends himself to his master: [7] 'What can you accuse me of? Have I stolen from you? Don't I do everything you tell me to do, and regularly give you a share of my earnings?' And Poverty with as much right could say to someone who complains of being poor: 'What do you have against me? Do I deny you goods such as justice, courage or self-discipline? Or deprive you of life's essentials? Aren't there plenty of vegetables alongside any road, and plenty of water from natural springs? Do I bar you from access to the whole Earth with its abundance of grass and leaves for bedding? Is it really impossible to find happiness with me? Don't you see old women gossiping happily away as they gnaw on a fragment of barley cake? Don't I give you a simple, inexpensive relish – namely, a healthy appetite? Doesn't a hungry man enjoy his food the most and suffer least from the lack of

expensive spices? And whoever is thirsty – don't they derive the
most pleasure from drink and express satisfaction with whatever is available? [8] Do they hunger for pastries or thirst for
Chian wine? It is only self-indulgence that inspires a taste for
luxury goods. Don't I also give you free shelter – the baths in
winter, in summer the temples? As Diogenes said, "What house
can compare with my corner of the Parthenon, so elegant and
airy?"'

If Poverty were to speak to you that way, what answer could
you make? Personally, I wouldn't know what to say. But we
tend to blame anything other than our own sullen and petulant
nature – be it old age, poverty, or someone we happened to
meet, or maybe just the weather, the season, or locale. So Diogenes says he heard Vice aptly accusing herself: *No one else
brought this upon me, I alone am responsible.*[2] [9] In their confusion, however, people hold circumstances, never themselves,
to blame. As Bion says by way of analogy: 'It's like trying to
capture a wild animal: if you grab a snake by the middle you
are going to get bitten. But take hold of it by the neck and it
cannot hurt you. It's the same with the conditions of life: handle them one way and you make yourself vulnerable. But deal
with them like Socrates and you will be beyond harm's reach.
Approach them in another spirit and you will be miserable –
owing to your own character and mistaken values, however,
not because of your situation.

[10] So don't try to alter circumstances, adapt to them as
they are. Look at sailors.[3] They do not try to change the wind
and sea; they learn to cope with them in their various moods.
The weather is fair, the sea calm: they bring the oars into service. The wind is with them; now they hoist full sail. The wind
is against them; the sails are reefed and allowed to go slack.
You should be just as attentive to conditions, just as ready to
adjust. You've grown old, bid farewell to the things of your
youth. And if you are sick, don't try to lift and shoulder loads
that only a person in their prime could handle. Do as Diogenes
did: he was unwell on one occasion when someone gave him a
shove and put him in a headlock. Instead of engaging the man
in a wrestling match, he took a stand before him, showed him

his penis, and said, 'Try, sir, to wrestle me to the ground by applying pressure to *this*.' [11] Or say you are in financial straits: do not dream of the rich man's lifestyle. Adapt as you would to the weather: when it's fair you dress lightly, in the cold you bundle up. Finances call for similar flexibility: if you are doing well, you can afford to spend freely, in hard times you have to cut back. We can't be satisfied with what we have, though, when we spend lavishly on frills, look upon work as a hardship, and think that death is the greatest misfortune. But learn to scorn pleasure, to respect hard work, ignore reputation, good or bad, and not to fear death, and you will be able to do anything you want, and gladly too.

[12] As I say, then, I do not see how circumstances themselves present any problem – not old age, not exile, not poverty. As Xenophon aptly observed, 'I can show you two brothers who have inherited equal shares. One is in constant need, the other lives in comfort. It's obvious that money cannot account for the difference; there must be another explanation.' And if I show you two old men, two poor men, and two men in exile, where in each case one is calm and content, while the other is in despair, isn't it likewise evident that some factor other than old age, exile or poverty is at work?

Do you know the story of what Diogenes did with the man who complained that Athens was an expensive city? [13] He took and led him first to the perfumer and asked how much a half-pint of myrrh cost. 'A mina,' the merchant said. 'You're right,' he roared, 'this city is expensive.' Then he accompanied him to the butcher and asked the price of calves' feet. 'Three drachmas.' 'The city is expensive indeed,' he shouted. Next it was on to fine wools. 'How much for a sheep?' 'A mina.' 'No doubt about it,' he declared, 'this is an expensive city.' But then they headed to the lupin market. 'How much for a quart?' 'A copper.' 'Why, this city is cheap!' he cried. Then it was off to price dried figs: 'two coppers'. And the myrtle? 'Two coppers.' 'This city is cheap!' he exclaimed again. So you see, a city is not simply expensive or inexpensive, it is a matter of one's habits. Live one way and it costs dearly, live simply and it is affordable. The same applies to the state of things in life: adopt a spirit of accommodation and it will seem free and easy; otherwise it is bound to seem hard.

[14] 'But poverty still seems to be somehow painful and harsh; and I would be more inclined to praise someone who contentedly bore old age in poverty than one who did so blessed with wealth.'

What exactly is painful or harsh about poverty? Weren't Crates and Diogenes poor? But they had an easy existence regardless because they cast off pride, did not scruple to beg, and found the strength to live simply and inexpensively. You have no money, only debts? [15] 'Gather mussels, beans and the like,' Crates said, 'and in time you will set up a trophy to celebrate your triumph over poverty.' Why, after all, should we admire someone who contentedly bears old age in poverty more than one who does so blessed with wealth? Ideally, of course, we would pay wealth and poverty no attention at all. But in fact we see plenty of rich people who handle their wealth along with old age peevishly, and who seem as unhappy as those who grumble and whine about being poor. The latter class of person would not know how to be free and generous with money if they had it, any more than the former could manage without. Character makes all the difference: whoever can make use of great resources wisely can likewise cope with few.

If at all possible, a man of little means should remain in this world; but if his situation is insupportable he can easily leave, as if departing a festival. As Bion says, 'Just as we are evicted by the landlord who does not receive the rent, and who removes the door, the furniture and chokes up the well, [16] so I am being evicted from my body when nature, my landlady, takes away the use of my eyes, ears, hands and feet. And I do not try and stall for time; I exit life as if I were excusing myself from a party, with no feelings of bitterness or regret. When the hour comes, step on board the boat.' Just as a good actor performs the prologue, central acts and dénouement equally well, the good man should acquit himself well in youth, in middle age, and in the years approaching death. When my cloak becomes too old and worn for practical use, I get rid of it. Similarly I will not stall or cling to life; when I no longer enjoy it I will bid it goodbye.

[17] It was much the same with Socrates. He could have escaped prison had he wished. When the jury initially imposed a fine by way of punishment, he proposed an alternative: that he be repaid for his actions with free meals in the town hall. And although he was given three days' reprieve before his execution, rather than watch and wait until the sun disappeared behind the mountains on the third and final day, he swallowed the poison on day one, in good spirits, according to Plato, and with no change in colour or expression. He drained the cup of its hemlock quite carefree and content. Then flinging out the last drop, he said, [18] 'And that's for the handsome Alcibiades.' (Note the characteristic blend of seriousness and play.) As for us, we cannot even witness the death of another without being shaken. But on the point of death Socrates fell into such a deep sleep that it was only with difficulty that someone was able to rouse him. Whereas I suppose that if one of us succumbed to sleep . . .[4]

Socrates bore patiently with his wife's shrewish nature. Even her yelling did not upset him. Critobulus was moved to ask how he could stand to live with her. Socrates answered with a question of his own: 'How do you put up with the geese around your house?' 'How do they concern me?' Critobulus replied. 'Exactly. My wife is of no greater concern, I pay as much attention to her as I would to a goose.' On another occasion he was entertaining Alcibiades when she came in and knocked the table over. [19] Instead of yelling or complaining about her outlandish behaviour, he simply collected what had fallen to the floor and gave orders that Alcibiades be served again. Alcibiades, however, had covered his head in embarrassment and was sitting in silence, in no mood now to eat. 'Let's go outside, then,' Socrates said, 'Xanthippe seems to be giving us indigestion.'

A few days later he was a guest himself in Alcibiades' home when a giant bird flew in and knocked over a dish. Socrates sat with his head covered in shame and wouldn't touch his food. The other laughed and asked whether Socrates refused to eat because a bird had flown in and caused a mess. 'Of course,' he answered. 'The other day when Xanthippe upended the table you lost your appetite. So do you think that I could eat now that a bird has done the same thing? Or do you think there is any difference between my wife and a cackling fowl?' [20] 'But,' said Alcibiades, 'if a pig had caused the accident, you would not be put out?' 'Correct; but a swine of a wife would have been a different matter . . .' (Evidence again of the man's droll humour.)

127 On Exile[5]

[21] In answer to those who claim that exile reduces a person's worth, we could cite technical skill as a counter-example. A person can no more lose the capacity for acting or playing the flute by having to perform in a foreign city than their capacity for rational thought is diminished thereby. If anyone believes that exile is undesirable for some other reason, let him take it up with Stilpo,[6] whom I have quoted before:

[22] 'What do you mean?' he says. 'What goods – whether they pertain to the soul, the body or property – does exile take away from us? Common sense, moral decency, kindness – docs exile deprive you of these?'

'No.'

'What about courage, justice, and the other moral virtues?'

'No again.'

'And surely you are no worse off from the physical point of view. Aren't health, strength, keen eyesight and sharp hearing the same when one is abroad, sometimes even better?'

'True enough.'

'And does exile always entail the loss of material wealth? Haven't you heard of many people who are better off financially for being condemned to exile? You remember Phoenix:[7]

> To Peleus I came . . .
> Who enriched me and furnished me with a large retinue.[8]

[23] Themistocles[9] himself said to his son, "It would have been our undoing, my boy, if we had not been undone."'

There are plenty of similar cases. What do we lose by exile, then, or what problems does it create? Personally I don't see them. On the contrary, in many respects we get in our own way, becoming virtual aliens in our native town.

But people say that exiles are never among the ruling elite, tend to be distrusted, and do not enjoy freedom of speech. On the contrary, some exiles command garrisons in the king's service; some have entire nations in their charge; others are honoured with sizeable gifts and pensions. Think about Lycinus:[10] expelled from Italy, he was entrusted by Antigonus with command of a garrison over Athens, and though this was our own country we had to obey him. To cite other contemporary examples: what about Hippomedon[11] the Spartan – isn't he a governor now in Thrace serving Ptolemy? Don't Chremonides and Glaucus, Athenians both, share a table and the benefit of their combined wisdom with Ptolemy? Finally, wasn't Chremonides[12] sent on a mission of great importance, entrusted with much money and full authority to bring Ptolemy's plans to fruition?

'But exiles can no longer be a political force in their native city.'

[24] Well, neither can women, who for the most part keep to the house. Children don't rule either, neither do these young men here, nor people past their prime. But you don't hear them complain; that would show weakness. What is the difference between being a ruler and a private citizen? The ruler commands many people, people in the best years of their life as well. As a private citizen and teacher I rule over a mere handful of immature boys. Oh, and I rule myself as well. But the same expertise is needed to manage the masses, or rule just one, to serve in public or run a household, in a foreign city or in the country of one's birth. And the same powers of judgement apply to good public leadership or the successful management of one's private affairs. So what is the difference if I exercise control only in personal matters and not in the public square?

'But you are barred from entering your homeland, even to visit.'

[25] Well, I'm also barred from entering the Thesmophorion,[13] while the temple of Ares is closed to women, and there

are other sacred precincts to which we are denied admittance.
But it would be considered foolish to object. Sometimes I cannot even enter the gymnasium; so off I go to the bath where I
am able to oil myself and exercise just like I normally do in the
gymnasium. My policy with regard to my homeland is the same:
judging myself unwelcome I took up residence somewhere else.
And just as I can change ships and have an equally good voyage, so I can transfer to another city and be just as content.
There is certainly nothing to regret or be ashamed of in emigrat-
ing, as long as you do not take up with a bad crowd in your new
environment. If there is any disgrace, it belongs to those who
banished me, since I had led a just and exemplary life. Philemon
made a clever remark in this connection. After meeting with
success in a legal action, he was confronted by witnesses to the
proceeding. 'How lucky for you, Philemon,' they said. 'You say
that because you saw how it chanced to turn out,' he replied.
'But I congratulate myself on being fair and honest always.'

[26] 'But is it not an arrant outrage to be exiled by inferior
men?'

Would you prefer the sentence be imposed by the city's elite?
Isn't this what your complaint amounts to? For honourable
men do not pass such a sentence unjustly or without good reason; they would not be accounted honest otherwise.

'But to lose to such men in private and public ballots – isn't
this a kind of dishonour?'

Certainly not yours. It is the men who vote for and elect
such men whose reputation suffers. It was as though they were
to dismiss the best doctor in the city and in his place put a drug-
gist to supervise public health. Would you say that the shame
and misfortune pertain more to the doctor in the case or to
those responsible for the appointment?

'Fine, but to have served your city honestly and diligently,
only to find it thankless and corrupt – how is this not cause for
regret?'

On the contrary, it is a blessing in disguise, as you must admit
if you agree that it is an advantage to discover a friend's true
character which you were ignorant of before. Wouldn't you
be grateful to learn that your wife was mean and underhand if

you did not know it previously? Or if you learned that a slave was a thief and a runaway, so that you could take the proper precautions? If you are made to realize that your native city is thankless and corrupt, then, should you take it hard or consider it a stroke of luck?

[27] 'But still it seems to me a fine thing to dwell in the same place where you were born and raised.'

Just as it would be to dwell in the house in which you were born and raised even if it were rotten, crumbling, and falling down around your ears? Or to continue to sail the same boat you have relied on since your youth, even if it were no more than a dinghy and you burst your sides rowing it, when you might easily switch to a galley equipped with twenty oars, involving much less strain to yourself? People look down on natives of Kythera, Mykonos or Belbina;[14] but they continue to say that it is a fine thing to live out your life where you were born and raised. And though most cities are in decline and their populations corrupt, one's hometown (they say) is inherently valued and important.

[28] But many people also hold the status of metic[15] in derision and like to quote the line, 'You, metic, you are no native son and yet you hold this city enslaved.'[16] You admire Cadmus, the founder of Thebes, but look down on me because I am not a full citizen. And we honour Heracles as the greatest of heroes and still regard metics as of lower status. Yet Heracles was chased out of Thebes and took up residence in Argos. Such incidents do not detract from one's reputation in the eyes of the Spartans. Whoever adopts their rigid way of life and sticks to it is honoured as a peer, even if he is a foreigner or a helot's son. But whoever departs from their code of conduct, even the king's son, is relegated to the rank of helot, and the disgraced party has no standing in the state.

[29] 'But to be denied burial where one was born – how is that not a dishonour?'

How can it be, when it often happens to the best of men? Or, for that matter, how can anything that is possible for the worst men be an honour? People commend Socrates because he criticized Athens for saying, 'The generals, on whom the Athenians pride themselves, have been buried outside the city limits, while the scum of the democracy are interred in public graves.' Yet burial in foreign ground is disgraceful, while in public graves it is an honour? And, after all, what does it matter? There's a witty remark attributed to an exile from Athens. By way of insult someone said to him, 'You won't even be buried at home, but in Megarian soil, like those Athenians who die under a sacrilegious curse.' 'Yes,' he replied, 'in Megarian soil – just like those Megarians judged at the time of their death to be pure and pious.' So what's the difference? [30H] As Aristippus said, 'No matter where you start, the route to Hades is always the same length and in the same direction.'

But let's take a step back. Why should you care whether you are buried at all? As Bion remarked, anxiety over burial has furnished material for many tragic dramas. There is, for instance, Polyneices' dying wish:

> Bury me, mother, and you, my sister,
> In my native ground, and reconcile the angry citizens,
> So as to have this much share of my family's city to call my own,
> Though I have otherwise brought our ruling house to ruin.[17]

Even if burial within the city's walls is refused and you are laid to rest in exotic lands, why worry? Or does Charon's ferry only run between Hades and Thebes?

> But to lie beneath a mound of one's native soil is an
> excellent thing.[18]

[31] Is it really so bad if no mound is built over your bones, and you are tossed out unburied? What odds does it make if you are cremated, exposed to be eaten by dogs or ravens, or consumed underground by worms?

> Close my eyes fast with your own hand, mother.[19]

But should she not 'close your eyes fast' and you should die with open eyes and open mouth – again, what about this is so terrible? Victims of war and shipwreck are denied this rite. These conventions of ours seem like so much foolishness. We are reluctant to touch or look upon the dead. But other races[20] embalm and keep their dead inside the house as a mark of respect and form of protection, so dissimilar are their practices from our own.

128 IVA – A Comparison of Poverty and Wealth[21]

[33] 'The way I see it, acquiring wealth serves to protect us from shortage and scarcity.'

Really? Don't you see many people obviously possessed of great wealth who are prevented from enjoying it because they are miserly and mean? They are like Priam, who declined even to sit upon the throne –

> [34] *Although there was a crowd in the hall*
> *He sat on the ground regardless*
> *Wallowing in filth.*[22]

Many people of means are kept from appreciating and making use of their advantages because they love money too much. Vermin get a greater share of the provisions stored in their house. They are like Laertes on the outskirts of his landed estates, attended only by an old female slave who sees that he eats and drinks just enough to survive. He has exiled himself to the country, denying himself every pleasure and withering away while the suitors <lay waste to his son Odysseus' birthright.> Or like Tantalus who, in the poet's telling, stood in a pool, trying as hard as he could to grab the fruit hanging on the branches above,

> [35] *But whenever the old man made the effort*
> *The wind carried the fruit towards the dark clouds and*
> *out of reach.*[23]

while the pool itself dried up as soon he made to drink from it.

In the same way cheapness and moodiness serve to scatter some people's supply of wine, food and fruit – not indeed to the clouds – but to various markets and taverns, while they personally don't share in any of it, however much they might want to.

If the man receives an invitation to dinner he is inordinately pleased. But for all his resources he declines to return the favour because of his stinginess. If he is made to feel unwelcome at somebody's home, he regards that man as his enemy. But if, by his temperament, he ensured that the door would be closed to him, at no time will it dawn on him that his worst enemy is himself.

The first Cynics, in my opinion, discussed these matters with wit and acuity. Whatever does not cure a person of greed, cheapness and arrogance will not cure him of hardship and need. [36] Now, wealth in any form fails in this regard, since it does not improve one's character. Conversely, an honest person is not changed for the worse if from prosperity they are reduced to privation. And coming into money will sooner alter a person's skin colour, height or appearance than it will change his character. As long as he remains greedy, cheap, crabby and over-cautious, he will experience scarcity and need.

'And just how do they come to experience the lack of things they own?'

Well, as Bion himself asked, how do bankers lose money when they have such a lot of it? It's because it is not really theirs, they only have it for safe-keeping. These people act as if the same applies to them. And if someone should entrust you with something on a temporary basis, it both does and does not belong to you, since you are not entitled to make use of it. The daughters of Phorcys furnish a fitting analogy. In legend they stored away a single eye that belonged to each of them equally. Since they couldn't see a thing in front of them – <and refused to share> – they bumped into walls and fell into ditches and mudholes. Still they kept the eye in storage, [37] until Perseus <came and> simply took it from them.

What is the difference between not having food, and having food you cannot eat – fish and doves, for instance, <if you happen to be Syrian,> dog meat if you are an Egyptian, or a human skull if you are Greek? All are in the same category as someone

with no food at all. So what benefit does possession of such
food confer? Fine, you have money. But you gain nothing by it
because you are mean and over-cautious. Apropos of this, the
old Cynics aptly distinguished between having money and
hoarding it. Those who really have it make use of it, while
others hoard it, neither spending it on themselves nor sharing it
with others. [38] When a king or some other dignitary puts his
property under seal, access to it is forbidden. In the same way
a miser or Scrooge effectively puts his belongings under lock
and key, depriving himself of their enjoyment and making
himself virtually poor in the process. Their lust for money
and material goods is as great as ever, but since they cannot
have their cake and eat it too, they refuse themselves the use or
enjoyment of the wealth that they've sequestered.

· Crates was once asked what he stood to gain by turning
philosopher. 'You will be able to open your wallet, withdraw a
sum, and spend it freely without guilt, instead of shuffling your
feet, as you do now, halting and flinching as if you suffered from
palsy. If you find the wallet full, fine; if you find that it's empty,
you won't be put out. If you decide to buy something, you will
do it with a free conscience; if you are short on funds, you won't
miss them but will manage with whatever you have. You will
not hanker for what you do not own, nor [39] be disappointed
with whatever comes your way.'

If you want to deliver yourself or another from shortage and
scarcity, amassing money is not the solution. It is, as Bion says,
like trying to quench the thirst of a person suffering from
dropsy not by attacking the sickness itself, but by leading him
to springs and whole rivers. The victim will drink to bursting
before finding relief. In the same way, our man can never get
enough as long as he remains greedy, concerned about keeping
up appearances, and superstitious as well.[24]

[40] So if you want to spare your son the experience of
shortage and scarcity, don't send him to Ptolemy to seek his
fortune. He will only return having added arrogance to his
problems and you will have accomplished nothing. Send him to
Crates instead. He knows how to transform the greedy and
self-indulgent into open-handed and unaffected young men.

Even the great Metrocles reportedly said that when he studied with Theophrastus and Xenocrates, even though many food parcels from home were sent to him, he lived in constant fear of starvation and was always destitute and in need. But when he switched to Crates, he found that even without help from home he was able to feed not only himself but others too. For in the former case he simply had to have new shoes, a wool overcoat, a throng of slaves and spacious quarters. At the common table he required white bread, gourmet treats, [41] sweet wine and choice entertainment, to suit the style to which he was accustomed; because among the Academics and Peripatetics maintaining such a way of life is considered de rigueur. There was none of this with Crates, however. His habits grew modest, so that he was content with a rough mantle, barley bread and greens. Nor did he miss his old, privileged state or find any fault with the new one.

To protect against the cold, most of us look for a heavier coat. But he folded his cloak in two, and so went around as if wearing two. If he needed to be rubbed down with oil he would go to the baths and anoint himself with second-hand scrapings. On occasion he went to the furnace of a bronze foundry where he would fry sprats, drizzle a little oil on them, sit himself down and make a meal. In summer he would pass the night in temples, during the winter he took shelter in the baths. Where before he felt poor and deprived, now he lacked for nothing. What he had was sufficient and slaves were no longer necessary. As Diogenes said, 'It would be odd if Manes can live without Diogenes, but Diogenes cannot live without Manes.'

But once you have spoiled <your son> and made him insolent, prodigal, vain, [42] superstitious and greedy, any money you give him will be money gone to waste. As the verse of Philemon aptly says, 'You will acquire another fortune, not a new character.'

And as long as his character remains the same, he will never be satisfied or content. His tastes and desires will be so numerous and extravagant that he will be in a continual state of shortage and lack. 'Corrupt men are never content.'[25]

As a child he yearns for adolescence; in adolescence he wants to put aside the short cloak of his teenage years; when he reaches maturity he looks forward to the comforts of old age. 'My life is unlivable now: campaigning, public service, affairs of state – I have no time for myself.' Soon enough old age is upon him and he is nostalgic for the pleasures of youth.

> Youth is always dear to me but old age weighs on me
> heavier than Mount Aetna.[26]

[43] And a child's life seems a paradise in retrospect.

Or let us imagine that he is a slave. He longs to be free – this will guarantee his happiness. But no sooner does he gain his freedom than he wants to own his own slave. And if he gets one he immediately wants another; for as the saying goes, 'One swallow does not make a spring.' Then it's a home, a plot of land, Athenian citizenship, public office, kingship, until, like Alexander, he wants to be immortal. And if he realizes that, next, I suppose, he'll want to be Zeus!

How is such a person not destitute? Or how much money does he need to be quit of such desires? Even kings, with all the territory they control and revenues they receive, never feel it's enough, so that they break into tombs, rob sanctuaries, and unjustly exile the richest of their subjects in order to take possession of their estates. For they imagine that kingship entails a great many needs. But they are neither inclined to give up their power nor limit their spending. So they are forced to take measures they would sooner forgo.

[44] If we could overcome these impulses, we would have enough and more to serve our purposes. As Crates cleverly put it,

> You don't know the capacity of the satchel –
> A quart of lupins and a free and easy existence.

Indeed, it is no small thing to be free of care courtesy of a satchel, lupins, vegetables and water – to be done, too, with flattery and subservience.[27]

129 IVB – A Comparison of Poverty and Wealth[28]

[45H] 'Poverty is a disadvantage, wealth an advantage in the pursuit of philosophy.'

On the contrary, how many people do you know who are kept from study because of need as opposed to wealth? Surely you must see that it is mainly the poor who take up philosophy, while the rich, due to their circumstances, use any excuse not to apply themselves to learning. As Theognis aptly says, 'Many more people have been ruined by having too much than by having too little.'[29]

How can you possibly say that poverty is as much a barrier to philosophy as wealth? [46H] Look around you: poverty makes people tough, riches have an enfeebling effect. When someone can satisfy all his desires easily, having enough money to support a life of luxury, there's no pleasure they will not succumb to. Again, look how the rich, with all their distractions, have no time to spare for study.

But a poor man finds in philosophy a purpose and vocation. Zeno reports that Crates was sitting in a shoemaker's shop, reading Aristotle's *Protrepticus*, an exhortation to philosophy addressed to Themison, king of Cyprus. In it Aristotle writes that Themison had every advantage a philosopher could desire. He had enough money saved so that he could devote himself to study; and being king meant his reputation would not suffer for associating with philosophers.[30] Philiscus, the shoe-maker, kept at his sewing but eavesdropped on the reading all the while. So Crates said, 'Philiscus, I think I'll write my own *Exhortation to Philosophy* and address it to you, seeing as you have more of what it takes to be a philosopher than the man to whom Aristotle dedicated his book.'

Or take your ordinary slave: [48H] he supports himself and gives his master a share. The free man, meanwhile, has to struggle to maintain his lavish lifestyle. And since he is free of such concerns, a poor man seems to me a more promising pupil for having nothing. In the present war,[31] for instance, he has only himself to worry about, while a rich man must spare thought for others. The lines Sophocles gives Oedipus are apposite:

> Your anguish is for yourselves alone;
> I grieve not just for me, but for you and the entire city.[32]

Yet in spite of this evidence poor people still consider themselves unhappy. They also say that the rich are more respected in their communities than the poor. Apparently they have never heard of Aristides,[33] [48] the poorest man in Athens as well as the most revered. When the Athenians wished to collect tribute from their allies, the choice fell on him to organize it, knowing that no one would do so more equitably. And Callias, despite being the richest Athenian, was appointed Aristides' assistant, not, you'll note, the other way around. They also say that Aristides was more ashamed for having to associate with Callias and his riches than Callias was embarrassed by Aristides' poverty.

What about Lysander of Sparta? Never has there been a man more praised or revered. Yet this is the man who could not even furnish his daughters with a proper dowry when he married them off.

There's really no telling how many others have likewise earned more respect than men of greater means. It seems to me characteristic of Euripides to praise Eteocles by describing him as young and destitute, then add 'But in the city of Argos no one enjoyed more influence or honour.'[34]

130 V – That Pleasure is Not the Goal of Life

[49] If one were to use abundance of pleasure as the standard of a happy life, no one, Crates said, would prove happy. If you want to review the various stages of our life, you will find that pain and suffering predominate, and by no small measure. First of all, we spend half our life asleep, experiencing no pain [50] but no pleasure either. The years of infant training are fraught with difficulties: the child is hungry and the nurse tries to make

him sleep; he's thirsty, but she gives him a bath; he wants to
sleep, she disturbs his rest by shaking a rattle.

If the child survives the nurse, he is handed over to his tutor,
gymnastic coach, grammar teacher, music teacher and drawing
instructor.

He grows older. Now come instructors in arithmetic, geometry and horseback riding – and each one subjects him to a
whipping. He's awakened at dawn and doesn't have a moment
to himself.

Then he reaches adolescence. Now he lives in fear of the
principal, sports trainer, drill sergeant and gymnasium director.
By all these he is beaten, closely supervised and dragged around
by the neck.

He's outgrown his youth and now is twenty years old. Still
he lives in fear and apprehension of his gymnasium director
and ranking officer. Some youths his age stand guard when
necessary, others lose sleep taking their own turn on watch.
Still others are called to a life onboard ship.

He becomes a man in the prime of life. He serves in the
army, goes on embassies for the state, holds public office, commands troops, sponsors the arts, presides at public games. Now
the life he lived as a boy only fills him with nostalgia.

So he passes his heyday and nears old age. Again he submits to
being cared for like a child and mourns his vanished youth: [51]
'My youth was dear to me, while old age weighs on me heavier
than Mt. Aetna.'[35] In sum, I cannot see how anyone can be said to
live a happy life if we use its quota of pleasure as the standard.

131 VI – On Circumstances

[52] Fortune is like a poet who creates all manner of roles.
Some people are shipwrecks, some are poor, some are exiles,
some are illustrious, others are obscure. A good man will find
a way to play well the role assigned him, whatever it happens
to be. You have been shipwrecked, play the shipwreck well.
Once prosperous, now you are poor; so play the poor man

well, 'resilient in circumstances good or bad'.[36] Adapt to the clothing fortune dresses you in, to the food she serves you, to whatever duties she has you perform. [53] Imitate Laertes, 'With an old slave woman, who saw to his food and drink.' [37] He slept on the ground on a pallet, 'His humble bed strewn with fallen leaves.'[38]

Such conditions suffice for a calm and healthy life. If you prefer a life of luxury, of course they will not do; but 'The good does not lie in filling one's belly to repletion.'[39]

Nor is it found in fashionable clothes or the softness of a sumptuous bed. As Euripides well said, 'Self-indulgence compels us to search out means for many different kinds of food,'[40] and not only food, but scents and pleasant sounds. But do not look for luxury when matters stand opposed. Be like sailors attending to the wind and other conditions. If the conditions are favourable, make use of them; otherwise hold off. Or like soldiers – if you have a horse you serve in the cavalry, if you have the requisite armour you join the hoplites; [54] and if you have neither, then you fight light-armed. And in that case, when the enemy bears down on you, hurling their weapons, you retreat to camp, since you are inadequately equipped to face them. In life too we are sometimes embroiled in war, with poverty, say, or bad health. Cut back to one meal a day, learn to manage on one's own, to make do with one threadbare cloak – and there's always the option of suicide as a last resort.

132 VII – On Freedom from Passion

[55] One sometimes calls a pomegranate seedless, or describes someone as having no neck or chest. With similar hyperbole, it seems, we characterize some people as being devoid of fear or sorrow.

Using the same examples, of a pomegranate that is said to be 'seedless', or a man said to lack a neck or chest – is it in the same sense that we also call certain people free of blame or envy? As the epithet 'without a chest' really implies having a chest of a particular kind, so 'senseless' and 'brainless' are applied to people whose mind or intellect is of a certain calibre. 'Without a chest' connotes a narrow chest, 'senseless' and 'brainless' are not intended literally but hint at some deficiency in a person's wits. Or is it vain to insist on such distinctions?

The blameless person is innocent, [56] someone with no envy or resentment is free of these vices, someone who minds their own business or seldom complains is above such behaviour. But is the so-called carefree or fearless individual really unacquainted with feelings of sadness and fear? Because in that case someone genuinely happy will likewise know nothing of passion or distress. How can a person experiencing pain, fear or grief enjoy life; and if he does not enjoy life, how can he be happy? Or if he is touched by grief, how can fear, anger, pity and dismay not follow in their turn? For when adverse conditions evoke such feelings, we are upset; and if we anticipate them we experience anxiety and fear. We pity those who, in our judgement, unfairly face such prospects; and feel anger, mistrust and indignation when a person's own bad choices are to blame. When we see our enemies doing well we are moved by envy and resentment; when we hear that they have met with some misfortune we are apt to gloat.

How, then, can we be sad and not feel some other emotion besides? And if we are prey to every emotion, how can we be free from passion?

But free from passion is exactly what the happy man should be, so that he is not affected by the loss of a child or friend – [57] even by the expectation of his very own death. Don't those people who face death without courage or dignity strike us as cowards? Isn't the model of a brave and manly death provided by Socrates, who betrayed no fear or agitation? Or are you of the view that more upsetting than our own death is the death of a friend? Do we love and prize ourselves in equal measure?

On the one hand we admire the girl who, on the point of death, says to her mother,

'But you, dear parent, should not allow tears to stain your cheek.'[41] At the same time a woman who heeds such advice is barely considered human. But then the women of Sparta are everywhere admired for their emotional strength. On learning that her son was saved by fleeing the enemy, one wrote to him in terms quite unlike those an Athenian mother would have used – [58] 'Well done, my child, you have saved yourself for me!' – but rather, 'An evil report has been spread about you; either remove it or keep out of my sight.' In other words, 'Go hang yourself!' Another received official word that her son had died in the line of battle. 'How?' she wanted to know. 'Like a hero,' she was told. 'Bravo,' she replied, 'that is just why I brought you into the world, to serve and safeguard Sparta.' She did not weep or carry on; she only expressed pride on learning that he had acquitted himself honourably in the field.

Then there was that other Spartan woman, how proud she was! Her sons deserted and presented themselves before her. 'Why have you come running to me?' she asked. 'Do you intend to crawl back to where you originally crawled out?' And with that she lifted her skirt and exposed herself. Can you see any of our own women[42] doing that? [59] They would be happy to see their sons safely returned. But not the women of Sparta: they would gladly receive news that a son of theirs had died bravely. Hence the Spartan funerary inscription:

> *Do not account life or death good,*
> *But to live or die well – this is what is good.*

It is irrational, and pointless besides, to sit down when a friend has died, crying, moaning, and allowing ourselves to fall apart in the process. It would better suit a philosopher to express sadness and remorse to the bereaved before he has died, as a way of reminding them that their friend is a man and therefore born to die. As Stilpo says, it is irrational to neglect the living for the dead. An orchard farmer does not chop down the others when a single tree withers and dies. Instead he takes that much better care of them, [60] to try and compensate for the one he has lost.

It is the same with respect to parts of the body. If someone loses an eye, it would be absurd for him to insist that the other be put out too. Or if he has a clubfoot, to have the other disabled; or after a single tooth is pulled, to extract the rest as

well. Such reasoning would be evidence of an unbalanced
mind.

If your son or wife dies, is it reasonable, while you remain
among the living, to neglect your own well-being and let your
affairs go downhill? If a friend incurred the same loss you
would console him and urge him to bear with it bravely, like a
man. But in the face of such misfortune,[43] you think it is actually incumbent upon you to make a great, instead of a moderate,
show of grief. Again, if it happens to someone else, your duty,
as you see it, is to help relieve that person's sense of loss and
moderate its expression. He should not think life unlivable, but
learn to take a positive view of what now seems only tragic.
When he thinks, for instance, 'A friend is gone,' he should
reflect, by way of compensation, 'Yes, because I was lucky
enough to have one.' You consider yourself miserable because
your friend has died, but fail to appreciate how lucky you are
that he lived. Now that he has passed, you are inconsolable
because you have been deprived of a friend's favours; [61] why
not congratulate yourself on having enjoyed them while he was
with you?

'Yes, but he will exist no longer.'

Nor did he exist ten thousand years ago, nor in Trojan times,
nor, in fact, in your grandparents' age. Yet this causes you no
upset, only the idea that he will not exist in the future.

'Well, that is because I am now denied the benefits of his
friendship.'

And you yourself are released from the support you used to
give your child during his lifetime, as well as the hardships and
expenses you incurred in the interest of your friend. To quote
Socrates, as one can never be sure whether marrying a beautiful
woman will bring more joy or pain, having friends and children involves the same uncertainty.[44]

Moreover, you are deprived of the rewards of his friendship
whenever he is travelling, on military campaign, on a diplo-
matic mission, off fulfilling a sacred vow, or when he is sick or
grown old. And if you chafe at his absence on all such occasions, what will you leave old women to grumble about? You
cannot reasonably have it both ways: expect your friend to

serve his turn in the army or leave the city on public business –
duties which he himself consents to [62] and you would be
among the first to blame him for evading – and at the same
time be vexed at his absence. As the pilot caught in a storm
said, 'Whatever happens, Poseidon, be sure that this ship will
at least remain on an even keel.' In the same spirit, a good man
might say, 'Do your worst, Fortune. At all events you'll find in
me a man not short of spirit.'

LUCIAN

His piece on the Cynic philosopher Demonax reflects little of Lucian's comic invention. Chreiai of no great pungency make up the better part of the encomium; other sections clearly reflect the influence of the tradition concerning Crates, particularly as regards his peace-making skills. It is still an important witness to the vitality of Cynicism within the greater Roman empire in the second century AD, and to the respect it commanded, even among satirists like Lucian, despite the disapproval of Cicero and other Romans who were among the first to make the school's acquaintance.

The description of the life (and death) of Peregrinus engages in full Lucian's satiric talents. His subject's parricide, his career as a confidence trickster, including a stint as an opportunistic Christian preying on the charity of Christian communities, and finally the account of his sensational end, make compulsive reading for prurient reasons alone. The manner of his voluntary death on top of a funeral pyre was undoubtedly suggested to Peregrinus by reading Onesicritus and his account of the Indian practice of ritual suicide by fire (see section 114).

133 Demonax

[1] It seems that even our own day was to have its share of men notable for physical strength, and for a philosophical cast of mind. For the first I refer to the Boeotian Sostratus, whom the Greeks called (and really believed to be) Heracles; and for the

second, to the philosopher Demonax, whom I saw and admired
for myself and in whose company I spent a fair amount of time.
About Sostratus I have written elsewhere. In that book I
described his exceptional size and strength as well as his open-
air life on Mt Parnassus. He slept under the stars, ate what
food the mountain furnished, and did deeds worthy of his
namesake, Heracles, involving the slaying of bandits as well as
building roads and bridges in places previously inaccessible.[1]

[2] There are two good reasons to turn my attention now to
Demonax: so that he may be remembered by men of my own
generation and so that in the next generation youth of promise
and a philosophical bent might have someone besides men of
the past to model themselves after. I now present a paradigm
from their own day to follow. He was the best of all the philosophers I have known personally.

[3] He was Cypriot by birth, from a family not undistin-
guished for wealth or position. But he thought he was born for
better things – for the best, in fact – and so he undertook to study
philosophy. He did not do this at the urging of his predecessors
Agathoboulos, Demetrius or Epictetus, although he associated
with all of them as well as with Timocrates of Heraclea, a sophist as accomplished in rhetoric as he was in philosophy.

Nevertheless, it was not, as I say, at their instigation that he
turned to philosophy; from childhood on he was driven by an
instinct for fair pursuits and a passion for that field of study in
particular. He despised worldly success and devoted himself
entirely to freedom and the frank expression of ideas. Until the
end, his life was upright, sound and morally unimpeachable,
furnishing proof of the keenness of his own mind and philosophy's inherent worth. [4] Nor did he come to the subject
unprepared. He read the poets from an early age and knew
most of them by heart. He studied rhetoric. When it came to
learning the doctrines of the various philosophical schools, he
learned them by heart. He trained his body to be tough. Above
all he practised to be self-reliant. So when he realized, with
advancing age, that he would have to depend on others, he
deliberately took his own life, leaving behind a formidable
reputation among the noblest of Greeks.

[5] He did not adhere to a single school of thought. Instead he chose what was best from among many, and never gave an indication of favouring one more than others. Perhaps it was Socrates he most closely resembled. If he seemed to emulate Diogenes in his dress and informal lifestyle, he did not go to extremes in order to be admired or gawked at by passers-by. He lived like everyone else, was down-to-earth, and not the least bit affected in his private or public life.

[6] He did not assume Socrates' ironic style. His conversation brimmed with Attic wit, so that people went away neither despising him nor abashed by jibes born of a superior attitude. All kinds of people were happier, better behaved, brighter and more hopeful for associating with him.

[7] He was never known to raise his voice, to get worked up or excited, even if he felt called upon to take a person to task. If he hated sins, he forgave sinners, taking his example from physicians, who heal the disease but do not blame the patient. He believed that to err was human, but to correct mistakes was the job of god (or a godlike human being).

[8] Leading such a life, naturally he wanted nothing for himself, but always did the right thing by his friends. He liked to remind fortune's favourites that their elevation depended on fleeting and counterfeit goods. Whoever was taking poverty hard – or sickness, exile, or old age – he would brighten with a joke. He would also point out that their troubles would soon end to be replaced by eternal freedom and forgetfulness of everything good or bad.

[9] He cared enough to reconcile feuding relatives as well as estranged husbands and their wives.[2] There were even times when he talked reason to excited mobs, and prevailed on them to put the interests of their city first.

[10] This, then, was the style of his philosophy – cheerful, bright and humane. Only the death or illness of a friend could upset him since he considered friendship mankind's dearest gift. He was friendly with everyone and, if you were a man, he looked upon you as a brother. Though there were some whose company he preferred more than others, he only avoided people who, in his opinion, were beyond hope of improvement. And

all his behaviour seemed blessed by the Graces and by Aphrodite herself, so that, to use the phrase of the comic poet,
'Persuasion seemed to live upon his lips.'[3]

[11] In Athens, therefore, he came to be looked upon as a
superior being by magistrates and the whole city. Initially, it is
true, he incurred some of the same hostility Socrates had met
with for his direct expression and unconventional ways. Your
Anytuses and Meletuses attacked him with the same accusa-
tions levelled at Socrates – that he had never been seen to make
public sacrifice, and that he was the only person among them
not to be initiated into the Eleusinian Mysteries.[4]

His response was to put on a garland and a clean cloak and
manfully enter the Assembly, where he defended himself with
his usual good humour, but also with an uncharacteristic touch
of tartness. 'Do not be angry with me,' he said, 'if I haven't in
the past sacrificed to Athena; I did not imagine she needed anything from *me*.'[5] As to not joining them in the Mysteries, he
challenged them with the following dilemma:[6] 'If the Mysteries
were foul, I could not keep silent but would dissuade non-
initiates from participation; and if they were good – well, then
I would tell everyone about them out of general benevolence.'

The result was that the Athenians, who were listening to him
with stones in their hands, immediately calmed down. And
their attitude towards him grew from respect, to reverence,
finally to veneration, though he had opened his speech on a
rather sardonic note: 'Athenians, I come before you dressed in
a garland. Sacrifice me, then, as you did Socrates, since the
omens in his case were none too auspicious.'

[12] Now I want to give a sampling of his witty and well-
timed remarks.[7] What he said to Favorinus is a good place to
start. Favorinus had heard from someone that Demonax was
deriding his lectures, particularly their sing-song quality, for
being low, effeminate and inappropriate for philosophy. So he
hunted him down and asked him who he thought he was to be
making fun of him. 'Someone who's not easy to fool,' Demonax
answered. Favorinus pressed him by asking what he had that
qualified him for philosophy. 'Balls,' the other said.

[13] On another occasion Favorinus again approached him

to ask what school of philosophy he espoused. 'Who told you I was a philosopher?' he answered, and gave a little laugh as he walked away. 'What are you laughing at?' Favorinus wanted to know. 'I just thought it was funny that you of all people judged philosophers by their beard[8] when you don't have one yourself.'

[14] A sophist from Sidon who was popular at Athens was once boasting how he was at home in any philosophy. I will quote him directly: 'If Aristotle calls me to the Lyceum, I will go; if Plato calls me to the Academy I will answer his call; if Zeno calls on me, I will serve in his Stoa; if Pythagoras calls me, I will take his oath of silence.' Demonax stood up in the audience and shouted, 'Hey, I think I hear Pythagoras calling your name.'

[15] Another time a certain Python, a good-looking little chit from one of Macedon's better families, was baiting him and challenging him to solve a captious puzzle in logic. 'It's certainly hard,' he said, 'just the way you like it.' Incensed at this double entendre, the boy threatened him with, 'I will soon show you what a man is.' 'Are you going to point out your lover?' Demonax said in response.

[16] There was the time when he ridiculed a champion of the Olympic games for appearing in public in a flowery robe. The athlete hit him on the head with a rock. Blood flowed freely, and witnesses to the event were all as angry as if they had been struck themselves. They shouted their demand that a magistrate be notified. 'Don't call a magistrate,' he said, 'just a doctor.'

[17] Another time he found a gold ring on the ground while out walking. He posted a notice in the public square that its owner could come and collect it, provided he knew its weight, stone and design. A pretty young boy claimed it, but got all the details wrong. So Demonax said, 'Go and guard your own ring, boy, you can't have lost this one.'[9]

[18] A Roman senator in Athens introduced his son to him. The boy was very attractive, but weak and effeminate. 'My son salutes you,' the man said. 'And a fine-looking lad he is, too,' Demonax replied, 'worthy of his father and a dead ringer for his mother.'

[19] There was a Cynic philosopher who practised his trade in a bearskin. To Demonax he was never Honoratus (his real name), only 'Arcesilaus'.[10]

Someone once asked him for his definition of happiness. He answered that only a free man was happy. [20] The other objected that many men were free. Demonax said that he only considered a person free if they were free of both hope and desire. 'And how is that possible?' the other came back. 'Nearly everyone is subject to those emotions.' 'But,' Demonax said, 'scrutinize human affairs, and you will find nothing there deserving of hope or desire, since pains and pleasures in any case will both be extinguished.'

[21] Peregrinus Proteus took him to task for joking around and poking fun at people. 'Demonax,' he said, 'you're no dog.' 'Peregrinus,' he answered, 'you're no human being.'

[22] A scientist was once giving a discourse on the upside-downers[11]. Demonax took him outside, led him to a well, pointed to the man's reflection, and asked, 'So is that what the Antipodes look like?'

[23] Another time, a magician went around saying he had powerful spells to induce anyone to give him anything he wanted. Demonax said to him, 'That's not so great. Even I can do the same thing. If you care to follow me to the baker's you will see me make her hand over some bread using a simple charm and one little token.' He meant, of course, that money was the equal of any talisman.

[24] Then there was the time the great Herodes Atticus[12] held a public memorial for Polydeuces, who had died in early manhood. Herodes had the boy's chariot drawn up, just as if he were about to take his seat as usual, and a place laid for him at table. Demonax approached and said, 'I come with a letter from Polydeuces for you.' Herodes was delighted that he seemed to be entering into the spirit of the occasion along with the other company. 'And what does Polydeuces want?' he said. 'He blames you,' was the reply, 'for not joining him forthwith.'

[25] A man had shut himself up in the dark in mourning for his dead son. Demonax gained admittance by claiming to be a magician who could raise the boy's ghost for him; all the man

had to do was chant the name of three people who had never had occasion to mourn. He thought and thought but got nowhere – I presume he couldn't come up with a single name. So Demonax said to him, 'Do you think that you're the only one to suffer unbearably, when you don't find even one person who hasn't experienced grief?'

[26] He also used to tease people who affected rare or archaic words in their conversation. To take one example, he happened to ask someone a question, and was answered in the style of the Athens of old. 'I asked you a question in the present,' he said, 'and you reply as if we were still in the Bronze Age.'

[27] One of his friends happened to suggest that they go together to the Asclepeion to say a prayer for his disabled son. 'Asclepius himself must be afflicted with deafness,' Demonax answered, 'if you don't think he can hear us from here.'

[28] Once he saw two philosophers engaged in a really pointless debate, one posing strange questions, the other giving irrelevant answers. 'Friends,' he said, 'doesn't it seem as if one of these men is milking a billy goat, and the other is collecting the milk in a sieve?'

[29] Agathocles, the Peripatetic philosopher, was congratulating himself on being the best and only logician around. 'Look, Agathocles,' Demonax said, 'if you are the best logician you can't be the only one, and if you are the only one, you are not just the best but the worst.'

[30] Cethegus, the ex-consul, said and did many stupid things while passing through Greece on his way to Asia to serve as legate to his father. Noting this, a friend of Demonax called him a big waste of space. 'He isn't a big anything,' Demonax replied.

[31] Then there was the time he saw Apollonius the philosopher setting forth with his entourage; he had been called to Rome to serve as tutor to the emperor. 'There goes Apollonius[13] and his Argonauts,' he remarked.

[32] He was once asked whether he believed in the immortality of the soul.[14] 'I do,' he came back, 'inasmuch as I believe everything to be immortal.'

[33] Apropos of Herodes, he used to say that Plato must have been right to claim that we don't have a single soul.[15] 'Whoever invites Regilla and Polydeuces[16] to dinner as if they were still living can't be the same man who makes those clever speeches.'

[34] He even dared on one occasion, after hearing the proclamation announcing the Mysteries, to challenge the Athenians on their exclusion of foreigners from the rites. 'After all, it was a Thracian, Eumolpus, who established them in the first place.'

[35] Once he was planning a winter voyage, and a friend asked whether he wasn't afraid that the boat would capsize and he would become food for fishes. 'It would be ungrateful of me,' he said, 'to begrudge the fish this one meal, when I have eaten so many of them myself.'

[36] He urged a speaker who had made a poor showing to keep practising and rehearsing. 'But I'm always declaiming to myself,' the other said. 'It's no wonder you perform so badly, then,' Demonax responded, 'having such a bad audience.'

[37] He once came upon a fortune-teller plying his trade in public for a fee. 'I cannot see how you justify charging for your services,' Demonax said. 'If you claim that you can change the future, then whatever you charge is too little; and if everything happens as god decides, then what is the point of prophecy?'

[38] An elderly but well-preserved gentleman gave him a demonstration of armed combat against a post. 'What do you think of my fighting?' he wanted to know. 'Capital,' came the answer, 'provided your opponent is made of wood.'

[39] He was particularly adept at fielding trick questions. In an effort to embarrass him, he once was asked, 'If I burned one hundred pounds of wood, how many pounds of smoke would that amount to?' 'Weigh the ashes,' Demonax said, 'and the difference will all be smoke.'

[40] A certain boor named Polybius, given to malapropisms, said to him, 'The emperor has honoured me with Roman citizenry.' 'If only he could have made you Greek instead of Roman,' he responded.

[41] He saw an aristocrat preening over the width of the purple stripe in his wool cloak. Taking hold of it, Demonax

bent down and whispered in the man's ear, 'A sheep wore this before you, and was a sheep for all that.'

[42] Another time, at the baths, a man called him a coward because he hesitated before stepping into the piping hot water. 'Tell me,' he said, 'was I supposed to endure this for my country's sake?'

[43] Once he was asked what he thought Hades was like. 'Just hold on a bit,' he said, 'and I'll send you word from there.'

[44] A bad poet named Admetus announced that he had composed a one-line epitaph, and by the terms of his will intended to have it engraved on his tombstone. It won't do any harm, I suppose, to quote it: 'O Earth, you may have Admetus' shell, Admetus himself is gone to god.' Demonax snorted and said, 'That's so good, Admetus, I wish it were inscribed already.'

[45] Someone asked him about discoloration on his legs of a kind old people often have. He smiled and said, 'Charon bit me.'

[46] Then there was the Spartan he saw beating his slave.[17] 'Stop putting him on a social par with you,' he told him.

[47] A woman named Danaë was in a dispute with her brother. 'Take the case to court,' he said. 'You may share her name, but you are not Acrisius' daughter.'[18]

[48] He waged his greatest crusade against philosophers interested less in the truth than in creating an effect. To give one illustration: a Cynic philosopher loudly proclaimed himself a follower of Antisthenes, Crates and Diogenes, and had the cloak and pouch to prove it. But he carried a cudgel (*hyperon*) instead of a staff. 'Don't lie,' he said, 'you really follow Hyperides.'

[49] When he found many athletes biting their opponents in violation of the rules of the ring, he commented, 'No wonder their fans refer to today's athletes as "lions".'

[50] It was a caustic *bon mot* he directed at the proconsul. The man was one of those in the habit of removing their body hair with pitch-plasters. A Cynic got up on a rock and began to harangue him for this allegedly effeminate practice. Exasperated, the man threatened to have the Cynic thrashed or even exiled. Demonax happened along and pleaded for mercy on his behalf, since such licence was traditionally accorded the

Cynics. 'I will let him off this time,' the man said, 'but if he tries it again, what should his punishment be?' 'Have his body hair removed,' came the answer.

[51] Someone entrusted by the emperor with the command of legions and the governorship of a large province asked him how best to rule. 'Calmly, talking little, listening much.'

[52] On being asked whether even he ate honey cakes, he said, 'Why of course, did you imagine that bees built their honeycombs for fools?'

[53] Seeing a statue in the Painted Stoa with one arm broken off, he observed, 'It's about time the Athenians honoured Kynegeiros[19] with a bronze effigy.'

[54] Then there was his remark upon noticing that Rufinus the Cypriot – I refer to the lame disciple of Aristotle – spent much of his time in the covered walkways of the Lyceum. 'No one is more out of their depth than a lame Peripatetic.'

[55] He had a devastating comeback for Epictetus, who told him roughly that he ought to take a wife and start a family, since this too befits a philosopher – to leave to nature someone to take his place: 'Why not give me one of your own daughters,[20] then, Epictetus?'

[56] It's also worth noting what he said to Herminus the Aristotelian. The man was a scoundrel and guilty of any number of crimes, yet was forever talking up Aristotle and the ten Categories. 'Herminus, you deserve ten prosecutions (*catêgoriae*) of your own.'

[57] In competition with Corinth, the Athenians were debating whether they should institute gladiatorial games of their own. 'Don't approve the measure,' he told the Assembly, 'unless you first pull down the Altar of Pity.'[21]

[58] At Olympia he declined a statue the Eleans had voted for in his honour, saying, 'Don't do it; it might be taken as a rebuke to your ancestors for failing to erect statues of either Socrates or Diogenes.'

[59] I once heard him make the following remark to a legal expert. 'I'm afraid that laws may do no good at all, whether they are written with good men in mind, or bad. The former don't need them, and the latter are not improved by them.'

[60] He liked to quote one line of Homer in particular: *Hero and coward both meet the same end.*[22]

[61] He even expressed admiration for Thersites as a kind of Cynic demagogue.

[62] Once he was asked who his favourite philosopher was. 'I admire them all,' he answered, 'but I honour Socrates, revere Diogenes, and love Aristippus.'

[63] He lived to be nearly a hundred, without sickness or pain, troubling no one for favours, helpful to his friends, and without an enemy in the world. So great was the affection that the Athenians and the rest of Greece felt for him that magistrates would stand up whenever he walked by while everyone else fell silent.

By the end, in extreme old age, he was welcome as a matter of course anywhere he went, to share a meal or be put up for the night. To his hosts the event was like a divine visitation; they thought a good spirit had entered their home. Bread-sellers tugged on his sleeve as he walked past, each competing for the honour of giving him bread for free, and considered it a piece of good luck to have it accepted. Children would bring him gifts of fruit and call him 'father'.

[64] On one occasion he had only to enter the Assembly and the Athenians, who had turned on each other, were reduced to silence. Seeing that they were ashamed, he turned and walked out without having to say a word.

[65] When he realized that he could no longer look after himself, he quoted the tag the heralds use to close athletic contests:

> *Here end the games that have the fairest prizes,*
> *And now it's time for us to say goodbye.*

Then he abstained from food and departed life as cheerfully as he had behaved towards everyone he met.

[66] Shortly before death he was asked what his wishes were regarding funeral arrangements. 'Don't trouble yourself, the stench will ensure that I get buried.'

[67] 'But,' the other objected, 'isn't it wrong that the body of a great man should be exposed as food for birds and dogs?'

'On the contrary,' he said, 'it's the part of a great man, even in death, to be of service to the living.'

Nevertheless, the Athenians gave him a grand public funeral and announced a prolonged period of mourning. The stone seat where he used to rest when tired became a shrine that they bowed to and decked with garlands; they felt that the stone itself was hallowed by association. Absolutely everyone attended the funeral, especially the philosophers; indeed, it was they who conveyed the body to its resting place.

This is but a fraction of what I could report about Demonax, enough, though, to allow readers to judge for themselves the great man's qualities.

134 On the Death of Peregrinus

[1] Lucian to Cronius, greetings

Poor Peregrinus, or Proteus, as he was pleased to call himself, has done exactly what Proteus in Homer did. After turning into everything imaginable to attract attention, and assuming all sorts of shapes, at last he has turned into fire; so great, it seems, was the love of renown that possessed him. And now your excellent friend has been reduced to ashes after the fashion of Empedocles, except that the latter at least tried to avoid publicity when he threw himself into the volcano, while this gentleman waited for the Panhellenic festival, which draws the greatest crowds, and leapt into it in front of all those witnesses after constructing a very large pyre. He even addressed the Greeks on the subject a few days before his act of derring-do.

[2] I imagine I see you laughing at the old man's drivelling senility. I can even hear you shouting your likely reactions: 'What stupidity! What perverted pride!' – and similar phrases that so bizarre a demonstration is bound to elicit. Only you are doing this at a distance, in the security of your home. I said it right by the fire and even earlier in a crowd of listeners, some of whom – the crazy old man's supporters – were stirred to anger. Others, however, were moved to laugh along with me.

However, I narrowly missed getting torn limb from limb by the Cynics in the audience, as Actaeon was by his dogs or his cousin Pentheus by the Maenads.

[3] The whole setting of the drama was as follows. You know, of course, what that artist was like and what grand spectacles he put on throughout his life, such as Sophocles and Aeschylus never produced. As for my part, as soon as I came to Elis, in going up by way of the gymnasium, I overheard a Cynic bawling out their usual material in a loud, harsh voice: exhortations to virtue alternating with insults directed at everyone indiscriminately. Then the man turned to the subject of Proteus, and I will try as best as I can to reproduce his words exactly. You will recognize the style at once, of course, as you have often stood by while his kind ranted and raved.

[4] 'By the earth, the sun, the rivers, the sea, by our patron god Hercules, who here dares call Proteus a glutton for glory – Proteus, the man who was imprisoned in Syria, who bestowed five thousand talents on his native city, and who was banished from Rome? Who outshines the sun and rivals Olympian Zeus himself? Because he is determined to take his leave of the world by way of fire, are there people who put it down to love of fame and attention? Didn't Heracles die this way, and Asclepius too? And what of Dionysus, consumed by lightning? Didn't Empedocles end by leaping into an active volcano?'

[5] When Theagenes – for that was this thunderer's name – said this, I asked the man beside me the meaning of this talk about fire, and what Proteus had to do with Heracles and Empedocles. 'Pretty soon,' he told me, 'Proteus is going to turn himself to toast at the Olympic festival.' 'How,' said I, 'and whatever for?' He tried to explain, but with the Cynic still at full volume it was impossible to hear anything more. So I turned my attention back to him, and he emptied the rest of his diatribe over our heads, producing a series of incredibly inflated claims on Proteus' behalf. Neither Diogenes, nor Diogenes' teacher Antisthenes – not even Socrates – could stand comparison with him; Zeus, he said, was his only competition. Finally, though, he declared them about equal, then proceeded to his peroration.

[6]'These are the two noblest masterpieces that the world has seen – Proteus and Olympian Zeus.[23] Of the one, the creator and artist was Pheidias; of the other, Nature. But now this paragon is about to depart the company of men to join the gods, carried aloft by flames, and leaving the rest of us desolate.' After this discourse, now drenched in sweat, he wept in a manner that could only evoke laughter in his audience, and tore at his hair (taking care not to pull very hard). Finally he was led away sobbing by some of the Cynics, while they made a show of consoling him.

[7] After him, another man[24] mounted the podium before the audience had scattered and immediately poured libations on the sacrificial offerings that were still ablaze. At first he laughed a long time, obviously in a spirit of genuine mirth. Then he began something like this. 'Since that pitiful Theagenes put a stop to his contemptible speech with the tears of Heraclitus, I will do just the opposite and begin with the laughter of Democritus.' And again he succumbed to a prolonged fit of laughter, so that most of the audience was moved to join in.

[8] Then, shifting mood, he said, 'What else can we do but laugh, forced to listen to such ridiculous pronouncements and watch old men doing everything short of public acrobatics just to make a measly name for themselves? And just so you know what this "paragon" who is about to be incinerated is really like, give me your attention, because I have observed his character and tracked his career from the start. And others from his native city and otherwise in a position to know him well have also supplied me with details concerning him.

[9] 'This masterpiece of nature, this Polycleitan ideal, as soon as he reached adolescence, was taken in adultery in Armenia and soundly thrashed. At last he managed to jump from the roof and make his escape, but not before a radish had been thrust up his anus.[25] Then he corrupted a handsome boy. But by paying the boy's parents, who were poor, 3,000 drachmas, he succeeded in escaping arrest and arraignment by the governor of Asia.

[10] 'All this and more I guess I should omit mentioning, since he was still unshaped clay, and this ideal and masterpiece

of nature had not yet received the final touches. What he did to his father, however, you all deserve to know if you don't already – how he strangled the man, exasperated that he had lived past sixty. Then, when the business threatened to become a public scandal, he adopted a life of exile, constantly moving from one city to the next.

[11] 'It was then that he absorbed the sublime wisdom of the Christians, by associating with their priests and scribes in Palestine. And I can tell you that in short order he made them all look like children. Prophet, cult leader, head of the synagogue – he was everything at once. He also expounded their books, commented on them, and wrote many a volume himself. They revered him as a god, accepted his legal pronouncements, and made him their leader – second only, of course, to the man who was crucified in Palestine and introduced the world to this strange new cult.

[12] 'Then Proteus was arrested for this as well and tossed into prison, a distinction that actually contributed in no small measure to his later career, not to mention his established reputation as a fraud and publicity hound. Well, while he was in custody, the Christians, who thought the situation calamitous, did everything in their power to free him. When this proved impossible, they showed their unstinting devotion to him in every way conceivable. Orphans and aged widows could be seen waiting by the prison every day at dawn. Their officials bribed the guards to be allowed to sneak in at night and sleep in his company. Fancy meals were smuggled in, there were group readings from their sacred texts, and the great man Peregrinus – for he still went by that name – began to be called by another name, "the new Socrates".

[13] 'People even came from the cities of Asia, brought by the Christians at their shared expense, to help support and encourage the man. It is amazing how quickly they organize such efforts on behalf of their kind; in no time they lavish their all. So it was in the case of Peregrinus. Much money came to him from them when they learned of his incarceration, and by his plight he managed to obtain a small windfall. These poor deluded souls are first of all convinced that they are immortal

and will live forever, which explains why they do not fear death and why most are even ready to sacrifice themselves voluntarily. Added to which, their first law-giver taught them that they are all brothers as soon as they commit the collective crime of repudiating the Greek gods, worshipping that crucified sophist himself and living by his commandments. They despise all worldly goods and consider them common property. And all such doctrines they accept on faith alone. So if any fraud or impostor, quick to see his main chance, gets in among them, his fortune is as good as made; it's like taking candy from a baby.

[14] 'However, Peregrinus was freed by the then governor of Syria, a man partial to philosophy. Aware that Peregrinus was possessed and would welcome death if it ensured his name, he denied him this satisfaction and set him free, not even deigning to flog him as is usual in such cases. When he returned to Parium, he found that his father's murder was still a hot issue and that many clamoured to have him put on trial. Most of his property had been confiscated during his absence. Only his farms remained, valued at fifteen talents or so; for the entire estate which the old man left behind amounted perhaps to thirty talents. Theagenes was talking nonsense as usual when he said it was worth five thousand. The whole city of Parium, with its five neighbouring villages thrown in, men, cattle – the lot – could not fetch so much.

[15] 'The charge, however, was still a hot topic. It did not seem long before someone would appear against him. The commoners were especially angry, mourning a good old man (as he was called by those who had personally known him), so wickedly slain. But observe the plan our clever Proteus devised to deal with this and evade danger. Appearing before the assembly of the Parians – he wore his hair long now, wore the Cynic satchel and the Cynics' dirty cloak, had the Cynic staff in hand, and was in general turned out in a way calculated to have the most dramatic effect – thus arrayed, he announced that he was leaving to the state all the property that his sainted father had handed down to him. When the common people, living in poverty and desperate for handouts, received the news, they shouted as one, "The only true philosopher! The only true

patriot! The one and only rival of Diogenes and Crates!" His enemies were reduced to silence, and if anyone so much as alluded to the murder they were immediately pelted with stones.

[16] 'He left home then for the second time, to wander about. He had the Christians pay for his expenses. Under their sponsorship he lacked for nothing. And he lived off their charity for quite some time. But then he offended against their commandments as well. He was caught, I believe, eating food that is forbidden them,[26] and was no longer welcome among them. In desperation he felt he had no choice but to go back on his word and beg his city to restore his inheritance. Accordingly he appealed to the emperor to have it returned. But the city sent representatives to oppose his petition, and the status quo was preserved. Since he had been under no compulsion when he decided to make the bequest, he would have to live with the decision.

[17] 'Excursion number three took him to Egypt, to Agathobulus, specifically. There he withstood that amazing ascetic regimen that involved shaving one half of his head, smearing his face with mud, and masturbating in public before a crowd of witnesses to prove his so-called "indifference". Besides that, he gave and received blows on the backside with a fennel reed and took part in other bizarre displays.[27]

[18] 'With the benefit of this training, he sailed to Italy. He was hardly off the boat when he started in on everyone, especially Antoninus Pius, secure in the knowledge that the emperor was mild and indulgent. As expected, Antoninus scarcely took note of this campaign of slander; he expected such abuse from anyone flying the philosopher's colours, especially professional scolds like the Cynics. Our man's reputation, though, only increased. The plebeians, especially, admired his impudence. At last he was banished by the city prefect, a man of sound judgement, who felt that he had overstepped the bounds of free speech, and who declared the city better off without such a philosopher. But what do you know, this only served to enhance the man's reputation. Now he was on everyone's lips as the philosopher who had been expelled for his frank speech and

candour, so that in this respect he deserved to be ranked alongside Musonius, Dio, Epictetus, and anyone else ever subject to
a similar fate.

[19] 'And thus it was he came to Greece and Olympia specifically. At times he directed his attacks against the Eleans.
Sometimes he tried to incite the Greeks to rebel against the
Romans. And sometimes he chose to malign one person in particular,[28] a man of great culture and social standing who had
benefited Greece in many ways, not least by bringing water to
Olympia and preventing visitors to the site from dying of thirst.
"Greece has grown degenerate," he cried. The spectators of the
games should have done without water, even died if necessary,
which many certainly would have done, owing to the virulence
of the diseases formerly caused by the aridity of the place. And
he said this while helping himself to the very same source of
water!

[20] 'When the mob rushed him and threatened to stone him
to death, our hero only survived by taking refuge at the altar of
Zeus. At the next Olympics, he gave the Greeks a speech that
he had spent the four previous years composing. In it he now
praised the man who had brought water to the site and defended
himself for running off on the previous occasion.

'By now, however, people had lost all interest in him and he
no longer enjoyed the same respect. His act was too familiar
and he couldn't come up with any fresh surprises to amaze
people who came in his way, or inspire the kind of awe and
adulation that he showed a profound need for all his life. So he
conceived this last great exploit involving the funeral pyre. He
announced to the Greeks immediately after the last Olympics
that he would stage his own immolation when the games were
next held.[29]

[21] 'And now, they say, he is already putting on quite a
show, digging a pit, collecting logs, and promising a really awe-
some display of endurance. In my opinion, he should have
waited until his time came and not have devised a means to
escape life at all; but if he was determined to do away with
himself, instead of resorting to self-immolation or any such tragic effect, he might have chosen another form of suicide from a

host of options. If however, it had to be fire because that was
how Heracles went, why didn't he quietly choose a densely for-
ested mountain and cremate himself there in solitude, taking
along only one other person to serve as his Philoctetes,[30] such
as Theagenes here? But no, it is in Olympia, at the height of the
festival, when attendance is at its peak, all but in the theatre
itself, that he intends to barbecue himself. At least justice will
be served, by Heracles, if parricides and unbelievers should pay
for their crimes. But he seems very leisurely even in this respect;
long ago he would have had to submit to a protracted death
inside the bull of Phalaris[31] by way of a fitting punishment,
instead of opening his mouth to the flames and dying immediately. For according to everything I've been told, no death is
quicker than fire: you have only to breathe in the fumes and
it's over.

[22] 'Now everything involved in the spectacle is calculated,
I believe, to evoke the greatest awe – a man burning himself on
consecrated ground, where it is sacrilegious even for bodies
already dead to be buried. But I suppose you have heard of the
man who long ago burned the temple of Artemis at Ephesus
just to become famous, being incapable of making a name for
himself by any honourable means. Peregrinus himself has
something similar in mind, so great is his instinctive need for
notoriety.

[23] 'He says, though, that he is doing it for the benefit of all
mankind, to teach them to scorn death and brave the most
daunting of fates. For my part I would like to know – address-
ing you now, not him – what if the criminal caste affected this
courage of his, and learned to despise the prospect of death by
fire or other frightful means? I am sure you would not want
this result. And how is Proteus going to discriminate between
honest and dishonest men, so as to improve the character of the
former without at the same time rendering the latter more dan-
gerous and daring? [24] Let's even suppose that it is possible to
arrange it so that only people likely to profit by his example are
witnesses to the proceeding. Again I ask: would you like it if
your children chose such a man as a model? I doubt it.

'But why bother asking the question, when not even one of

his acknowledged pupils will dare do the same thing? Theagenes, to take the most obvious example, could be taxed for
adopting all his teacher's habits but declining to follow him as
he sets out, as he puts it, "to join Hercules". After all, he has
only to jump head-first into the flames to gain the summit of
happiness.

'Imitation does not consist in having the same kind of staff,
backpack and mantle. Anyone can do that, it is both safe and
easy. Genuine discipleship involves one's end and culmination.
It means constructing a pyre of fig tree logs as green as one can
find, then suffocating in the smoke that it emits. Fire, after all,
is not the exclusive reserve of Hercules or Asclepius; we see
temple robbers and homicides subjected to the same ordeal in
the ordinary process of the law. Smoke is better. It's less common and is the death of only you and your kind.

[25] 'Besides, if Heracles really did venture any such act, he
did it because he was unwell, because the blood of the Centaur,
as the tragedy has it,[32] was eating away his flesh. But what
motivates this man to consign his body to the flames? Of
course – to prove his strength, like the Brahmans![33] For Theagenes saw fit to draw the comparison, as if there could not be
found fools and glory hounds even in India. Well, let him really
imitate them, then. Onesicritus, Alexander's pilot, witnessed at
first hand the fiery death of Calanus, and he says that they do
not leap into the pyre. When they have built it, they position
themselves nearby and stand motionless while they endure the
scorching heat. Then, mounting the pyre, they settle down on
it and are incinerated while maintaining perfect composure,
never shifting an inch from their chosen position.[34]

'As for our protagonist – so what if he jumps in and is overcome by fire? We cannot dismiss the possibility that he will
jump out half baked, unless, as they say, he sees to it that the
pyre is built inside a deep pit. [26] There are reports that he has
actually changed his mind, citing dreams to the effect that Zeus
forbids a holy place to be polluted. But he can rest easy on that
score. I would personally swear to it that none of the gods
would be offended if Peregrinus suffered a gruesome death.
Besides, he cannot easily back down now. His Cynic colleagues

cheer him on, collectively pushing him in the direction of the fire and bringing his resolve to fever pitch. They will not tolerate any backsliding. And if he should drag a couple of them along with him into the fire when he jumps, that would be the only thing about his performance worthy of applause.

[27] 'Word is that he thinks the name "Proteus" no longer appropriate. He has changed it to "Phoenix" because the Indian bird that shares that name is reputed to mount a pyre when it approaches the limit of its drawn-out life. He tells tales too and cites certain oracles of old forecasting his role as a guardian spirit of the night. It is obvious that he wants altars built in his name and expects gold statues of him to be erected.

[28] 'By Zeus, it should surprise no one if, among all the fools out there, some should be found claiming that they were cured of malaria by him, and that in the dark they had encountered this "guardian spirit of the night". Then I suppose these pitiful disciples of his will build an oracular shrine, with an inner sanctuary, on the spot where he went up in smoke. After all, the original Proteus, son of Zeus, had the gift of prophecy. Mark my words, priests of his will also be named, armed with whips, branding irons, or who knows what other strange attribute. Or perhaps a nocturnal mystery rite will be established in his honour, including a torch festival at the site of his cremation.

[29] 'Theagenes, as I have been told by one of my friends, recently said that the Sibyl had made a prediction about all this. He even quoted the verses from memory:

> But when the time shall come that Proteus, noblest of Cynics,
> Ignites a blaze in the precinct of Zeus, Lord of Thunder,
> Leaps into the flame, and reaches lofty Olympus,
> Then I urge all alike who eat of the fruit of the Earth
> To honour the great hero that walks abroad at night,
> Enthroned alongside Hephaestus and lord Heracles.

[30] 'That's the oracle that Theagenes says he heard from the Sibyl. Now I'll give him one of Bacis' own on the same subject. Bacis speaks very much to the point as follows:

When the time comes that a Cynic of many names
Leaps into a roaring fire, his spirit possessed by the
    Fury of ambition
Then it is time that the others too, the fox-dogs who
    follow in his steps,
Mimic the passing of the late-lamented wolf.
But if a coward among them shrinks from the might
    of Hephaestus,
Let him straightaway be pelted with stones by every Achaean,
To teach a timid soul not to use bold words,
He whose satchel is stuffed with gold from indiscriminate loans,
Who owns thrice five talents in the fair city of Patras.

What do you think, gentlemen? Is Bacis in any way inferior to the Sibyl in his powers of prophecy? It is time, then, for these wondrous followers of Proteus to look around for a place to "etherize" – to use their own expression for incineration.

[31] When he had said this, all the bystanders shouted: 'Let them be burned right now; it's all they are good for!' And the man got down again laughing. *But Nestor caught the sound of the uproar.*[35] It is Theagenes to whom I refer. When he heard the shouting he came at once, mounted the stage, and barked out a whole series of slanders against the man who had just stepped down – I'm afraid I don't know the name of the gentleman. For my part, I left Theagenes, just about bursting with anger, behind, and went off to see the athletes, as the Hellanodicae were said to be already in the Plethrium.[36]

[32] Well, there you have what happened at Elis. When we reached Olympia, we found a crowd in the temple's rear chamber split among critics of Proteus and supporters of his plan. Feelings ran so high that many actually came to blows. After the Heralds' contest, in came Proteus himself with a sizeable entourage. He delivered a speech, all about himself – the life he had led, what dangers he had faced, the sort of agonies he had endured for philosophy's sake. He went on for what seemed like days, but I caught only a little owing to the crush. Then, because I saw many in danger of being suffocated, I slipped through the crowd and departed. By then I had had enough of

this suicidal sophist who was delivering his own eulogy before
he was even interred.

[33] This much, however, I overheard: he said that he wanted
to cap a glorious life with a glorious end. One who had lived
like Heracles ought to die like Heracles, and be commingled
with the upper air. 'And I also want to leave mankind a legacy
in the form of a death that will teach men to despise it. To my
Heracles, then, everyone should play my Philoctetes.' The
weaker element in the crowd began to shed tears and cry out:
'Save yourself for Greece!' But the more strong-minded among
them yelled, 'Do what you came to do!' This rattled our hero
not a little because he hoped that his audience would cling to
him and not give him up to the flames. He expected them to
preserve his life – against his will, naturally – and was quite
unprepared for these calls to stick to his resolve. He turned even
paler than usual, although he was already of a sickly cast. By
Zeus, he was even seen to tremble a bit. The upshot was that he
brought his speech to an abrupt conclusion.

[34] You can imagine my amusement; I could feel no pity for
a man beset by vanity, twisted to a degree beyond any other
known victim of that vice. He had a large escort, however, and
gloried in the size of his following. Too bad for him, he did not
know that men led off to crucifixion or in the custody of the
public executioner attract a much larger following.

[35] Now the games were over. I had never seen better performances at Olympia and this was my fourth time attending
the games. But since it was not easy to hire a carriage with so
many people leaving at once, I was regretfully detained. Peregrinus in the meantime had kept pushing back the date of his
show. At last he announced the night on which his self-sacrifice
would take place. Thus it was that I was awakened in the dead
of night and dragged to Harpina by one of my friends to where
the pyre had been built. It is more than two miles from Olympia as one passes the hippodrome heading east. As soon as we
arrived, we found the pyre set in a pit about six feet deep. It
was composed mostly of resinous pine, with dry brushwood
stuck in between as kindling.

[36] When the moon was rising – for it too had to witness

this marvellous event – he came forward, dressed in his usual
fashion and escorted by the most prominent Cynics, especially
the pride of Patras, Theagenes. He carried a torch, this worthy
supporter, as did Proteus himself. Approaching from various
points, they applied their torches to the pyre, which was soon
in full blaze owing to the quantity of torchwood and brush.
Peregrinus – pay attention now – laying aside his satchel, cloak,
and Heracles club, stood there in a shirt that was unspeakably
dirty. Then he called for incense. When someone obliged him,
he tossed the spice onto the fire and, turning to the south – this,
too, was part of his act – said, 'Spirits of my mother and
father, receive me with favour.' With that he leapt into the fire.
He could not be seen, though, as he was engulfed by flames
that had reached a great height.

[37] And again I see you laughing, Cronius, my dear friend,
at the most tragic part of the play. Speaking for myself, I swear
that when he invoked the guardian spirits of his mother I did
not mind much. But when he appealed to the spirit of his father,
I recalled the tales concerning his murder. Then I could not help
but laugh out loud. The Cynics who circled his pyre were not
weeping, it's true, but their grief was evident as they gazed on
the funereal fire in respectful silence. I could take it no more.
'Get out of here, you idiots,' I said. 'There's no pleasure in star-
ing at an old man cooked to a crisp and emitting the vile smell
of burning flesh. Or are you waiting for some painter to come
and sketch you after the fashion of pictures of Socrates in jail
attended by his companions?' Well, this made them pour out
their abuse and anger on me. Several even brandished their
staffs. But I threatened to grab hold of a few of them and toss
them into the fire to join their master and fountain of wisdom.
This checked their aggression and peace was restored.

[38] On my return journey, though, many diverse thoughts
occurred to me, as I reflected on the power that worldly glory
exerts. Even people otherwise deserving admiration are subject
to its allure, let alone a man like Proteus, whose whole life was
disordered, irrational and deserving of the flames.

[39] Then I ran into a crowd of people out to view the spectacle for themselves, since they expected to catch the protagonist

still alive and breathing. You see, on the previous day it had been given out that he would greet the rising sun before mounting the pyre, as the Brahmans, at any rate, are reputed to do. Well, I succeeded in turning most of them back with the word that the performance was already over. But I also ran into people who thought even that was not important. They wanted to see the location for themselves and carry off some souvenir of the event.

That involved me in no end of complication, I can tell you. I related the sequence of events to everyone who asked for precise details and information. When I was questioned by an educated person, I would give a straightforward story, just as I have been reporting the incident to you. But when I was accosted by some idiot, anxious to hear a really interesting account, I added some significant details of my own invention. When the pyre was kindled, for instance (I said) and Proteus spontaneously threw himself in, a great earthquake took place, with a huge rumbling from underground. A vulture then emerged from the blaze and made straight for the skies, but not before saying, in a human voice, 'I abandon Earth to make for Olympus.' These innocent souls blessed the gods, overcome by wonder. They then wanted to know if the vulture was carried east or west; I gave them whichever answer occurred to me first.

[40] I made my way back to the festival, when who should I meet but a man of venerable age and dignified demeanour, with a carefully trimmed beard and a generally imposing presence. Well, Proteus was the only theme of his conversation. The philosopher, it transpired, had appeared to him after the blaze dressed all in white. The old man had just come from seeing him walking in the Portico of Echoes,[37] to all appearances in a state of bliss, crowned with an olive wreath. To cap it all, he added mention of the vulture that he swore he had personally seen emerging from the conflagration, the vulture that I myself had launched into the atmosphere as a joke on fools and naïfs.

[41] Imagine what is now likely to happen to glorify his resting place: bees will be induced to settle there, cicadas will sing on it, crows will flock there as they did to the tomb of

Hesiod – among other marks of veneration. As to statues, I know that many will be set up right away by the Eleans themselves and also by other Greeks to whom, I understand, he supposedly sent letters. These letters, by report, were dispatched to almost every city of significance. They include his will, along with edifying laws and instruction. He appointed a number of ambassadors for this purpose from among his coterie, calling them 'Hades' postmen' and 'couriers among the dead'.

[42] This was the end of that pitiable Proteus, a man, not to waste words, who could not distinguish truth from fantasy, but did and said everything to enhance his name and renown. His self-obsession at last led him to self-destruction, when, alas, he could not enjoy the consequent praise because he was no longer alive.

[43] I shall add one thing more to my narrative before ending, in order to leave you with a good laugh. You have long heard the story I have told about my return journey from Syria and how I was in his company from Troy, in a position to witness at close hand his vice and dissipation. He persuaded a pretty young boy to turn Cynic in order to have his own personal Alcibiades. When we were awakened by a storm that appeared out of nowhere and raised an enormous sea in the middle of the night and in the middle of the Aegean, this model of virtue swelled the chorus of weeping women – he who pretended to be indifferent to death.

[44] Well, shortly before his self-imposed death – perhaps nine days – I suppose that he had a little too much to eat and fell sick during the night with a high fever. I have this from Alexander, his physician, who was called in to examine him. He said that he discovered him rolling on the ground, unable to stand the fever and pleading passionately for cold water. Alexander refused his request and added that if he really wanted to die, here was death, unbidden, at his very door. He had only to attend the summons; there was no need of a pyre. But Proteus said, 'No, that would not be so memorable a death, it is all too common.'

[45] Well, that is Alexander's story. I myself not many days

before saw his eyes smeared with a pungent ointment meant to produce purgative tears. Do you understand? Aeacus[38] does not often welcome people with weak eyes. He is like someone about to be raised on a cross who worries over a cut on his finger. What do you think Democritus' reaction would be if he saw this? He would have laughed at the man to the extent he deserved. But who ever deserved to be laughed at so much? Could even the laughing philosopher have mustered the requisite mirth? Well, dear friend, enjoy your own good laugh, especially when you learn that he commands the admiration of a large crowd of true believers.

EPICTETUS

Unlike most of the selections in this anthology, Epictetus' essay
On Cynicism *is not about any one figure in particular (unless
we count Diogenes, whose example he continually invokes as
the first Cynic not only chronologically but in terms of merit).
In his eyes, his Cynic contemporaries attest to a sad decline in
the moral standards set by the founder of the school and his
successors. So idealized (and sanitized) a picture of Cynicism in
its formative days does Epictetus have, that he doubts anyone
of his own era is worthy to approach it, including the student
who ostensibly motivates the discourse by consulting him as to
the wisdom of adopting the vocation. As there is no ulterior
reason for Epictetus to paint the Cynics of his day in such disparaging terms, it seems reasonable to conclude that many, if
not most of them, did fall short of its founders' standards. But
because Epictetus treats of the subject of Cynicism in the round,
without reference to any one individual, his essay presents us
with one of the fullest contributions to our knowledge of the
subject, even if its viewpoint is mainly nostalgic.*

135 On Cynicism (Discourse 3. 22)

[1] An acquaintance, evidently attracted to Cynicism, wanted
to know who was qualified to be a Cynic and what one could
expect from it.

We will consider the topic at length, Epictetus said. [2] But
this much I can tell you already: whoever undertakes the

project without God's approval is inviting his anger and will only make a public spectacle of himself. [3] I mean, in a well-run household you don't find just anybody presuming to think, 'I should be running the place.' Otherwise the owner, when he turns around and sees someone insolently giving orders, will haul the man outside and have him thrashed. [4] It's no different in the community of God and men: here too there is a master who assigns everything its place. [5] 'You are the sun. You are empowered as you move to make the year and the seasons, cause plants to grow and flourish, rouse the winds or calm them, and keep men's bodies sufficiently warm. Go, revolve, put everything, great and small, into motion. [6] You are a cow. When a lion appears, you know what to do, or you won't even survive to regret it. You are a bull: step out and face the lion, it's your job. It suits you and you have what it takes. [7] You can lead the army to Troy: be Agamemnon. You can take on Hector in single combat: be Achilles.'

[8] If Thersites had presumed to ask for command, either he would have been turned down flat, or he would have made an ass of himself before dozens of witnesses. [9] You need to consider the present business carefully because it isn't what you think. [10] 'Already I wear a tattered coat like the Cynic's, and I already sleep on the ground, just as I will when I turn Cynic. I have but to add a satchel and a staff to become an itinerant beggar who hectors everyone who crosses his path. If I see a man who shaves his body hair, I'll be sure to lay into him, just like someone elaborately coiffed, or strutting around in fancy clothes.' [11] If that's how you picture Cynicism, it's better to keep your distance. In fact, don't go anywhere near it, the position is not for you.

[12] If you picture it realistically, however, and don't think yourself unworthy, consider next the project's scale. [13] To begin with, you have to set a different example with your behaviour. No more blaming God or man. Suspend desire completely, train aversion only on things under your control. Banish anger, rage, jealousy and pity. Be indifferent to women, fame, boys and tempting foods. [14] Other people indulge in these things protected by walls or the gloom of night. They have

many ways of hiding; they can lock the gate and station someone outside their chamber: 'If anyone comes, tell them, "The
master's out" or, "He's occupied." ' [15] The Cynic, in contrast,
only has his honour to protect him.¹ Without it he will be
exposed to shame – naked and out of doors. Honour is his
house, his gate, his guards, his cloak of darkness. [16] He must
not have anything personal he wants to hide; otherwise, farewell – he has killed the Cynic, the free spirit, the man of the
open air. He has begun to fear factors outside his control and
crave concealment, which he cannot have even if he wants to
because he has no place or means to hide. [17] If this teacher
and trainer at large has the bad fortune to fail, what mortifica-
tion must he feel! [18] With all this weighing on his conscience,
how is he going to find the complete confidence he needs to give
other people advice? There's no way, it just is not possible.

[19] To begin with, then, you must purify your intellect by
training your thoughts: [20] 'My mind represents for me my
medium, like wood to a carpenter, or leather to a shoe-maker.
The goal in my case is the correct use of impressions. [21] The
body is irrelevant to me, as are its members. Death, too,
whether of the whole body or a part, can come when it likes.
[22] And exile? Where can they send me? Nowhere outside the
world, since, wherever I end up, the sun will be there, as will
the moon and stars. There will still be dreams, birds of augury,
and other means of staying in touch with the gods.'

[23] Disciplining the mind, though, is just the start of the
true Cynic's duty. He has to realize that he has been sent by
God as a messenger for the benefit of others, by bringing them
to an awareness of how confused they are about what is good
and bad, and how this causes them to look in vain for the good,
having no clue as to its true location. The Cynic should realize
that in addition to being a messenger he is also a spy.² [24] He
needs to be like Diogenes, when he was captured in the battle
of Chaeronea, and dragged before Philip.³ [25] The Cynic is a
bona fide spy; he reports back on who is friend and foe. He
must check and double-check before he returns with the truth,
to guard against fear and false rumours. [26] He should be prepared, if necessary, to mount the podium and, like Socrates,

say, 'Where are you going, poor souls, and what are you doing? You drift about as if you were blind. You forsake the right road for a cul-de-sac. You look for peace and happiness in the wrong places; and are suspicious of anyone who tries to point you in the right direction.'

[27] Don't look for it in externals; it isn't in the body, and, if you doubt me, just look at Myron and Ophellius.⁴ It isn't in wealth, look at Croesus or at the rich of today: you'll see how unhappy they are. It doesn't lie in office, otherwise those who have been consuls multiple times would be happy, which they are not. [28] Whom are we going to trust on this score – you, who see only the surface and are dazzled by wealth and power, or these people personally? What do they tell us? [29] Just hear them groan and complain; they say their lives are worse and less safe for having been consul more than once, thereby attracting fame and notoriety. [30] Being king is not the answer either, otherwise it would have made Nero and Sardanapalus⁵ happy. Even Agamemnon, a better man than either of them, was not happy. When his men were still snoring away, what was he doing? *He pulled many a hair from his head, roots and all.* What did he say? *I pace up and down . . . My spirit is troubled, and my heart is pounding right out of my chest.*⁶ [31] Poor man, what's worrying you? It can't be money, *You are rich in gold and bronze.*⁷ Nor can it be your health, you're fine. Your problem is that you have neglected and ruined the faculty with which we exercise the will to get or to avoid, to act or not to act. How? [32] By not learning the true nature of the good to which it is born and of the nature of evil, or learning where its interest lies. Whenever something that is none of its interest goes awry, it thinks, 'Poor me, the Greeks are under attack.'

[33] Too bad for your mind, though, the one thing you have neglected out of indifference. 'They are going to die at the Trojans' hands.' And if they are not killed by the Trojans, won't they die regardless? 'Yes, but not all at once.' What difference does that make? If death is bad, then it is bad whether they go singly or together. After all, death signifies nothing more than the separation of soul and body. [34] And if the Greeks die, do they thereby close the door to Hades behind them? Can't you

die too? 'Yes.' So why complain, 'Alas, to be king and have to
carry Zeus' sceptre'? A king can no more be unfortunate than
God. So what does that make you? [35] A shepherd – that is
how you react, anyway, like a shepherd complaining when a
wolf makes off with one of his sheep. And your subjects too –
alas, they are sheep in spirit if not in actual fact.

[36] Why did you come? Your desire was not in danger, was
it, or your choice, impulse or aversion? 'No, Paris ran off with
my brother's wife.' [37] Wasn't that a blessing in disguise, to rid
your brother of the tramp he was tied to? 'Well, should we just
let the Trojans insult us?' Are the Trojans wise or foolish? If
they are wise, do not quarrel with them; if they are fools, ignore
them. [38] 'If it's not in any of these things I've been protecting,
then where is the good located? Pray tell us, Great Messenger
and Spy.' It isn't where you imagine, or where you'd think to
look. Otherwise, you would find that it's within you; and you
wouldn't go wandering off among externals, which are none of
yours. [39]

Turn your attention on yourself, examine your belief system.
What is the good as you feature it? 'It means serenity, happiness and independence.' Very good. [40] But doesn't it also
appear naturally great in your imagination, priceless and
impervious to harm? Where are you going to find serenity and
independence – in something free, or something enslaved?
'Free.' And your body, is it free or a slave? 'I don't know.' You
are aware, I presume, that it is subject to fever, gout, rheum and
dysentery, not to mention despots, fires and swords – anything,
in a word, that is physically stronger? 'I agree, it is subject to
these.' [41] So how can the body or any of its parts be considered free – or great, or priceless? In essence it is a corpse, a
thing of mud and dust. Do you have anything that is free? [42]
'Well, now I am inclined to think not.' Look, can you be forced
to assent to what appears to you wrong? 'No.' Or to dissent
from the plain truth? 'No.' Then you see you do have within
you a share of freedom. [43] And can any of you have the will
to desire or avoid, choose or refuse, plan or anticipate, if you
don't first formulate the impression of something advantageous or improper? 'No.' So here, too, you have a measure of

freedom and independence. [44] Poor devil, why not try focusing on that, why not look after that for a change; that's where
you should go in pursuing the good.

[45] Now, how can someone who has nothing – no clothes,
no hearth or home, no luxuries, no slaves, no city he can call
his own – how can a person like that be happy? [46] Well, God
has sent among you a person who will prove by example that
it can be done. [47] 'Look at me, I have no home, no city, no
property, no slave; I sleep on the ground; I haven't a wife or
children, no officer's quarters, only earth, sky – and one tattered cloak. What more do I need? [48] I am cheerful, I am
tranquil, and I am free. You've never seen me fail to get what I
want, or get stuck with what I want to avoid. I have never been
angry with God or a fellow human being; I've never yelled at
anyone. Have you ever seen me with a sad expression? [49]
The people before whom you bow and tremble – when I meet
them, I treat them as if they were slaves. In fact, whenever they
see me, without exception they all think that they are in the
presence of their lord and master.'8

[50] There you have the words of the authentic Cynic, words
that faithfully reflect his purpose and personality. Most of you,
however, identify the Cynic with trivial details like his satchel,
his stick and large jaws – large, I suppose, the better to wolf
down the food he's given (if he doesn't hoard it) – or with his
embarrassing habit of shouting abuse at passers-by, or with the
broad shoulder he leaves bare.9

[51] You see how big the project is you propose to take on.
First, get a mirror; look at your shoulders, check out your loins,
examine your thighs; you are about to sign up for the Olympics, not some half-hearted practice match. [52] If you lose at
the Olympics, you cannot just leave; you have to suffer the
indignity of having the whole world watch, and not just Athenians, Spartans or the citizens of Nicopolis, but people from
everywhere. A casual contestant will be trounced, but not
before he suffers thirst, endures heat exhaustion and swallows
mouthfuls of sand. [53] Plan carefully, know your limits, be
reasonable and don't go forward without god's say-so. If he
picks you, be aware that in addition to greatness, his plans for

you entail a good deal of discomfort. [54] Because this is a particularly charming clause in the Cynic contract: you are going to be beaten like a donkey and have to love your tormentors as if you were their brother or father. [55] Or would you rather invoke the emperor in their presence: 'Caesar, you may have brought peace to the world, but look at the violence I have to put up with! Take me to the proconsul at once.'[10] [56] Caesar and the proconsul mean nothing to the Cynic; he only calls upon Zeus, whom he serves as ambassador. If he suffers some hardship, he is confident that it is only Zeus putting him through his paces. [57] I mean, Heracles did not wallow in self-pity when he performed his labours for Eurystheus; he did what he was told without delay. So the Cynic, who takes his orders from Zeus, and has earned the right to carry the staff of Diogenes – should we expect him to dawdle or complain? [58] Listen to how Diogenes, laid low with fever, still lectured passers-by: 'Idiots, where are you going in such a hurry? You travel a great distance to see those damned athletes compete; why not stop a bit to see a man do combat with illness?' [59] A man of his mettle is not one to accuse God, who chose him, of unfairness in making him ill. He positively prides himself on his hardships and is bold enough to be a roadside attraction. What would he blame God for? That he cuts such an admirable figure? And what would the charge be? That his virtue is too glaringly bright? [60] Here, just remember what he says about poverty, death and pain; how he compares his happiness with that of the Great King.[11] Or rather, he doesn't think there is any comparison. [61] For where you find unrest, grief, fear, frustrated desire, failed aversion, jealousy and envy, happiness has no room for admittance. And where values are false, passions inevitably follow.

[62] The young man asked, if he got sick, whether as a Cynic he should consent to receive a friend to help take care of him. Yes, but where are you going to find a Cynic's friend? [63] He would have to be someone just like him to deserve being called his friend. He would have to share equally in the sceptre[12] and the kingdom. It is a worthy minister indeed who deserves a Cynic's friendship, as Diogenes was worthy of Antisthenes, and

Crates of Diogenes. [64] Don't imagine that it is enough just to go up to a Cynic and introduce yourself to become his friend and be invited into his home. [65] If that's your plan, you'd better start looking for a nice rubbish dump in the event of illness, one protected from the north wind, so you don't catch your death of cold. [66] Friendship, it seems to me, means no more to you than moving in with somebody and sponging off him or her indefinitely.¹³ You have no business contemplating so great a project as Cynicism.

[67] 'Well,' the young man said, 'what about marriage and children: will the Cynic choose to take those duties on?' Give me a state composed of wise men, and you may not be able to find a single person adopting the profession of Cynic. For whose sake, after all, would one adopt so rigorous a way of life? [68] Still, if we suppose that there is a Cynic there, I see no reason why he should not marry and have children. His wife will be wise, like him and like her father; and their children will grow up to be the same. [69] But with things as they are – in a virtual crisis – it's better, perhaps, that the Cynic not be occupied with domestic duties.¹⁴ He needs to focus on his sacred ministry, and be free to move around, not tied down by personal obligations that he cannot well ignore, but which, if he honours, will detract from his role as messenger, scout and herald of the gods. [70] Consider the responsibilities he owes to his father-in-law and his wife's other relations, to his wife as well; in the end, he is reduced to the role of nurse and provider. [71] To give just a few examples: he has to find a pot to heat water for the baby, and a tub to bathe it in; wool for his wife after she's given birth, together with oil, a cot, a drinking cup – already we have a long list of accessories. [72] And he has other duties and distractions. In the end, what's left of that king devoted to the commons – *the king who has the people in his care, and so many concerns?*¹⁵ Where is the king whose duty it is to watch over others who have married and got children, to see which of them is treating his wife well, which badly, who is quarrelling, which households are prospering, which are in decline? In effect, he makes rounds like a doctor, taking his patient's pulse, alternately saying, [73] 'You have a fever, you

have a headache, you have gout; you should fast, you should eat, you should not bathe; you need an operation, you have to be cauterized.' [74] How is someone encumbered by private duties going to find time for this? And he has to put little coats on his children's backs, and send them off to school with little notebooks and little pens, and make up a little bed for them at night; because, after all, his children will not be Cynics from the womb.[16] If he does not do all this for them, he would have done better to expose them at birth rather than kill them by prolonged neglect. [75] Now look at the condition we've reduced our Cynic to – he's more butler than king. [76] 'Yes, but Crates had a wife.'[17] You are talking about a circumstance that arose out of love, and a wife who was Crates' virtual twin. We, on the other hand, are discussing normal marriages, not special circumstances; and our analysis has not discovered, in our present state, that marriage is advisable for the Cynic.

[77] 'Then how will he help the community carry on?' For god's sake, who benefits society more, people who produce two or three brats with runny noses to survive them, or those who supervise in their contemporaries' lives what they care about, or mistakenly neglect? [78] Who benefited the Thebans more, those who gave them children, or Epaminondas, who died childless? Did Priam, with his fifty worthless sons, or Danaus, or Aeolus, contribute more to society than Homer?[18] [79] Their contribution to society as poet, or general, is considered more than a fair return for their failure to marry or have children. Should not the kingdom of the Cynic be reckoned reasonable exchange as well? [80] I fear we don't appreciate its importance, nor do we have a fair idea of Diogenes' character. We are influenced by the sad spectacle of today's Cynics, *these dogs who beg at table and hang about the gate*,[19] who have nothing in common with the Cynics of old except maybe for farting in public and not much more. [81] Because, if we did, we wouldn't be surprised or disappointed if a Cynic does not marry or procreate. My friend, he fathers everyone: every male is his son, every woman his daughter. That is how he regards everyone, and how much he cares for them. [82] Don't think he browbeats strangers because he was born to be surly; he is acting

like a brother or father – like the vicar of God, the father of everyone.

[83] Now go on, ask me whether he will take part in public life. [84] Look, is any form of public life superior to his? Why should he stoop to preparing speeches about income and expenditures for the Athenians, say, when he is called upon to address everyone – Athenians, Corinthians, Romans – and not about debits and credits, or war and peace, but about happiness and unhappiness, success and misfortune, freedom and slavery? [85] You are asking me if someone will take part in politics when they are already engaged in politics on a prominent scale. Ask me further if he will hold office, and again I will ask you. 'Fool, what office is superior to the one he has?' [86] Furthermore, the Cynic's body should be in good shape, since his philosophy will not carry as much conviction coming from someone sickly and pale. [87] He not only needs to show his qualities of soul in order to convince ordinary people that it is possible to be a gentleman without the material goods they usually admire, he also has to prove, with his physique, that his simple, frugal life outdoors is wholesome. [88] 'What I testify to, my body testifies to as well.' Which is what Diogenes did: he went about with a healthy glow on his face, and his body alone was enough to win the common people over. [89] A Cynic who excites pity is taken for a beggar; everyone is disgusted and walks around him. The Cynic shouldn't be so filthy that he drives people away;[20] his very ruggedness should be of a clean and pleasant kind.

[90] The Cynic ought to be naturally sharp and witty, too (otherwise he's just a boring windbag), to be equal to every occasion that calls for a quick reply, [91] the way Diogenes responded to the man who greeted him with, 'So Diogenes, you don't believe the gods exist?' with 'How can you say that, when I know that you are headed for hell?' [92] Or again, when Alexander the Great stood over him while he was resting, and recited: *A man charged with making decisions shouldn't sleep the night away*, Diogenes, still half-asleep, responded: *Who has the people in his care, and so many concerns.*[21] [93] Above all, though, his mind should be purer than the sun, because anyone

guilty of wrongdoing who presumes to lecture others can only be considered slick and unscrupulous. [94] For you see how it is: the kings and tyrants of this world, even if they are corrupt, can reprimand and punish offenders by virtue of their arms and soldiers; instead of weapons and bodyguards, his conscience gives the Cynic the same authority. [95] For he works overtime on his fellow man's behalf. What sleep he gets only leaves him purer than when he first lay down;²² his thoughts are never unworthy of a friend and minister of the gods, and he shares in Zeus' administration. 'Lead me, Zeus, lead me, Destiny' is always on his lips, as well as 'If it pleases the gods, so be it.' [96] Conscious of all this, why shouldn't he venture to speak truth to his own brothers, his own children – his own relations, in a word?

[97] A person of his conscience is neither bossy nor officious; he is not poking into other people's business when he looks after the common welfare, he is tending to his own. If you disagree, then by your lights a general who inspects, drills and oversees his troops, punishing those who get out of line, is officious as well. [98] If, however, you reprimand others with a bit of cake under your arm, I will say, wouldn't you rather go and wolf down in secret what you've stolen there? [99] What are other people's affairs to you? Who are you – the bull, or the queen of the hive? Show me proof of your authority, such as the queen is endowed with by nature. If you are a drone disputing control over the bees, expect your fellow citizens to get rid of you, just as worker bees get rid of the drones.

[100] The Cynic's powers of endurance should be such that he appears to most people insensible, a veritable block of wood. As far as he's concerned, nobody insults or hits or hurts him. He has personally surrendered his body to be used or abused however anyone likes. [101] He knows that whatever is inferior, in that respect in which it is inferior, must yield to what is superior; and that his body is inferior to the crowd – what's physically weaker, in other words, is inferior to what is physically more robust. [102] So he never condescends to compete with them on that level. He has completely renounced things outside himself and makes no claim to things that are by nature

enslaved. [103] But when it comes to matters of the will and the use of impressions, then you'll see how many eyes he has: enough to make Argus²³ seem blind by comparison. [104] With him there is no premature assent, mistaken impulse, frustrated desire, misdirected aversion or unrealized purpose; hence no blame, envy or humiliation. [105] All his effort and energy go into this. As for the rest, he yawns away, in a state of perfect indifference. Of free will there can be neither thief nor tyrant; [106] of the body, however, yes. Of material things? Yes. Of honours and offices – yes. Which is why he is not interested in them. 'When someone tries using these things to affect him, he says, 'Go look for children to intimidate; masks are meant to frighten them; I know that nothing is behind them.'

[107] This, then, is the nature of Cynicism. You consider undertaking it; then please take some time to judge your aptitude. [108] And remember what Hector said to Andromache:²⁴ *No, go inside, and see to your weaving instead. Men will see to war – men, and me in particular.* [109] He sensed both his own endowment, you see, as well as his wife's limitations.

JULIAN

As discussed in the Introduction, the Emperor Julian was not a
Cynic. But he fought a rearguard action in defence of paganism
against the encroachment of Christianity, and he seemed to
have a soft spot for Cynicism as a relic of the classical tradition.
Against the Ignorant Cynics *was provoked by a renegade Cynic
who presumed to criticize Diogenes – the man himself – for
carrying his primitivist programme too far and venturing at the
cost of his life to eat an octopus without first cooking it. The
treatise* To the Cynic Heracleios *is also written in a spirit of
controversy, this time reacting to what Julian takes to be the
illegitimate introduction of myth into philosophical discourse.*

*Like Epictetus, Julian evinces nothing but scorn for the con-
temporary generation of Cynics, and harks back to the ideal
standards of the movement in the late Classical era. In the process he tells us much of what Cynicism had come to stand for
over the course of its 600-plus-year history, and what it continued to mean for him, even though he was not a professed
member of the order.*

136 Against the Ignorant Cynics (Oration 9)

[181] 'The rivers are running backwards,' to quote the famous
line.[1] Here is a professed Cynic saying that Diogenes' ambition
was over-reaching. This man won't bathe in cold water, in case
he might catch something, although he is quite strong, healthy,
and in the prime of life, and the sun god is approaching

summer solstice.² He mocks Diogenes for eating raw octopus and calls his death fit punishment for his stupidity and conceit – the way Socrates was justly punished for drinking hemlock, I suppose. He is so far advanced in philosophy that he knows for certain that death is evil, something the wise men Socrates and Diogenes after him did not pretend to know.

When Antisthenes was suffering from a long and incurable illness, Diogenes gave him a dagger and said, 'In case you could use a friend's assistance.' Evidently he did not look upon death as sad or distressing. But although we have our authority from him, in our greater wisdom we presume to know that death is terrible beyond dispute. Disease, we say, is even worse. But what's even worse is being cold. Patients, after all, are sometimes coddled, and then their illness is immediately transformed into a kind of self-indulgence, especially if they are rich.

To be sure, I have personally witnessed people who indulge themselves more when they are sick than when they are healthy, and they indulge themselves when they are healthy quite a bit. I was moved to remark to friends that such people would be better off being slaves than masters, and luckier if they were as poor and unadorned as a lily of the field than rich as they are now. Poverty, you see, would have brought their life of luxury to an end. The fact is, some people think it's a fine thing to play the pampered invalid. But does that mean that whoever endures the cold and heat is really worse off than convalescents? Well, it's true that the latter have sympathizers at their bedside whereas the poor and homeless enjoy no such moral support.

Let us make public what we learned from our teachers concerning the Cynics, for the benefit of people potentially interested in our way of life. If they are won over, [182] I will know that the next generation of Cynics will be worthy successors of our masters. If they are not won over but commit to some other fair goal, shouting me down, as it were, by their actions, what I say will do nothing, at least, to obstruct them.

But if there are slaves to gluttony, sex, or bodily pleasure in general, people who mock my words and laugh in my face, like dogs that piss in front of schools and law courts – well, 'It's all one to Hippocleides.'³ We are likewise indifferent to the antics of these puppies.

I will organize my speech into chapters, giving each point its due, the better to complete my task, and the easier for the reader to follow. Since Cynicism is a type of philosophy – not the worst or meanest either, but rivalling the best – I will begin by saying something about philosophy.

What the gods gave mankind through Prometheus, with Hermes' help – the gift of glowing light from the sun – in reality stands for the share they gave us in mind and reason. Prometheus, you see, represents providence, which orders human affairs. Fire is the fiery breath that permeates nature as a cause, and gives everything a bit of incorporeal reason.⁴ And things partake of reason to the extent that each is able. For lifeless bodies this amounts to mere existence. Plants have life in addition. Animals have a soul, and mankind has a rational soul.

Now, some people believe that there is a single nature suffusing all these types of being, while others think that each type is essentially different. That does not concern us yet – in fact, not in the least at the present moment. [183] And the different ways philosophy is defined – as the art of arts and science of sciences, or becoming as much like god as possible, or, to quote Apollo, 'Know yourself' – that does not matter to us either. Ultimately, all these definitions seem to agree and correspond.

However, let us make a start with 'Know yourself', since this commandment has a divine origin. Whoever comes to know himself must know about the soul, and must know about the body. And it is not enough to know that man is a soul using a body. We must grapple with the nature of soul itself, and trace its faculties. Even this is not enough: there is the question of whether something superior even to the soul exists in us, which without being told we believe to be of divine origin and all alike imagine is fixed in heaven.

Then there is the nature of body to consider, whether for example it is simple or complex. And in due course one must explore its coherence, its powers and affects, all the qualities, in short, that guarantee its survival. The nature of the arts that assist in the body's survival should be explored, such as medicine, agriculture and the like.

Whoever undertakes to research the question properly will not completely ignore certain meaner and less important arts that have been devised to cater to the emotional side of our souls. He will not dwell on these subjects, since he thinks it is beneath him to do so and does not want to seem in any way devoted to them. But he will acquire some knowledge of what these arts are, and what parts of the soul they serve.

Reflect, therefore, whether 'Know yourself' does not involve every art and every science, and whether it does not also entail knowledge of universals, [184] since divine things are known through the divine part of us, mortal things through the mortal part. Moreover, according to the oracle, man is an animal that straddles these two categories, being individually mortal, but immortal as a race. And individuals and the human race as a whole are both composed of mortal and immortal elements.

That becoming as much like God as possible means acquiring as much knowledge as possible is clear from the following. We do not account the gods happy on the basis of wealth or any of the other so-called goods, but because, as Homer says, *The gods know all things.*[5] Of Zeus in particular he writes, *Zeus was older and wiser.*[6] It is in respect of knowledge that the gods surpass us.

And if, as seems likely, self-knowledge holds a special place among the gods as well, their self-knowledge would be better than ours to the degree that they themselves are better. So please, let no one divide philosophy into many parts or carve it into many pieces or, rather, make it many when it is one. For, as truth is one, so philosophy is one.

It is hardly surprising, though, if we come at it in different ways. A stranger, or, for that matter, a long-time resident wishing to travel to Athens can choose to either walk or sail. On land he has a choice between the main roads and short cuts with more rugged terrain. Sailing, he can either hug the shore or, like the old man of Pylos, *cleave the open sea.*[7] And let no one bring it as an objection against us that a few men on these roads have lost their way and wound up somewhere else, lured by pleasure, praise, or some other temptation, [185] as if by Circe or the Lotus-eaters, with the result that they stopped making progress and stopped short of their goal. Look at the leaders in each of the philosophical schools, and their principles will be found to agree.

Therefore, Apollo at Delphi commands us to 'Know yourself' and Heraclitus says, 'I searched myself'. Pythagoras and his successors, including Theophrastus and Aristotle, bid us become as much like god as possible. Because what we sometimes are, this god always is. It would be absurd if he did not know himself. In that case he would not know anything, since he himself is everything, having in and near himself the causes of every sort of being, immortal causes of immortal things, and causes of mortal things which are not themselves mortal, being the eternal cause of perishable things' constant regeneration. But this is thought too lofty for the moment.

Now, truth is one and philosophy is one, and the men I just mentioned are its lovers, one and all. By rights I should add another school, namely the Stoics, followers of Zeno of Citium. They saw that the cities of Greece recoiled from the uncompromising purity of the Cynic's freedom. For this reason they drew curtains, so to speak, around the Cynic philosopher, with duties like management of a household, gainful employment, marriage, children – in order, I suppose, to position him better as a bulwark of society.

You can satisfy yourself that the Stoics put 'Know yourself' at the head of their philosophy from books they wrote on this very topic. [186] But how they defined the goal of philosophy – life in agreement with nature – furnishes even more compelling proof, because this goal cannot be attained by anyone who does not know who he is or what his nature is like.

Such a person will not know the right way to act, any more than he would know whether iron was good for cutting, or what he would need to make iron meet his requirements if he knew nothing about iron at all. This is enough, however, to show that philosophy is one and that practically all philosophers have a single aim, although they take different routes to reach it. It is time, now, to look into Cynicism.

If the Cynics had written books with a serious rather than a playful purpose, my thoughts on the subject should be compared with theirs and if they agreed, I should not be accused of false witness. If they disagreed, they ought to be barred from a hearing, the way Athenians exclude forged documents from their Metröon.

But no such document exists. The much-discussed tragedies of Diogenes reportedly are the work of one Philiscus of Aegina. And even if they were by Diogenes, there is nothing out of the ordinary in a philosopher being facetious. Many have been known to act that way. Even Democritus, they say, would laugh at people he found in a serious mood.

But let's not give our attention to these squibs. In that case we are no better than people who have no desire to learn anything important. Here they are, such men, come to a shining city on a hill, full of holy men and holy mysteries, with countless priests inside tending countless sacred precincts. Everything that is common, low and superfluous has been pushed to the outskirts to keep the city pure – things like markets, baths and brothels. These men, however, get only as far as this and do not enter the city proper.

Surely we should pity anyone who, arriving in this quarter, [187] mistakes it for the whole city and at once turns on his heel. Even more to be pitied, though, is someone who settles there when he might, by taking just a step across the threshold, come face to face with Socrates himself. I will borrow those same words Alcibiades used in his praise of Socrates, and say that Cynic philosophy is 'just like the Silenus figurines seen in statuary shops, which are made with pan-pipes or flutes in their hands. Open them up, though, and they are found to contain images of the gods.'[8]

To avoid the same fate by supposing that what he wrote in jest was intended in earnest – not that there isn't much truth spoken in jest, but Cynicism is different, as I presently hope to show – let us explore it from the practical viewpoint, like dogs on the hunt for game.

It is not easy to discover who the founder of Cynicism was. Some people say Antisthenes, others think Diogenes deserves the credit. At any rate, Oenomaeus with good reason asserts that 'Cynicism is neither Antisthenism nor Diogenism.' The better class of Cynics says that the great Heracles, mankind's chief benefactor in this as in other respects, gave us the best example of the Cynic life.

But while I certainly wish to speak well of the gods, and of men who attain to the status of gods, I am convinced that Cynicism was practised even before Heracles, and not just in Greece. It seems to be a kind of universal philosophy and the most natural, requiring no special study at all.

The choice of an ethical life is all that is needed – a desire for virtue and aversion to evil. It is not necessary to con a lot of books. 'Great learning,' as they say, 'does not teach understanding.'⁹ Nor do we have to go through what the adherents of other schools do. [188] We need only commit two commandments of Apollo to heart: 'Know yourself' and 'Deface the currency'. So the founder of our philosophy is none other than the source of all the Greeks' blessings, Greece's universal leader, law-maker and king, the god of Delphi. And because it was hardly right that anything escape him, Diogenes' talent came to Apollo's attention.

The advice he gave him differed from his usual mode of expressing himself. He did not cast his advice in verse, but made known what he wanted through metaphor in telling him to 'Deface the currency'. 'Know yourself' was not meant for Diogenes alone, he directed these words of wisdom towards others, and still does; the phrase, after all, is inscribed above the god's own temple.

We have discovered, then, the founder of our philosophy, as Iamblichus also says, along with the principals of the school, Antisthenes, Diogenes and Crates. The goal and aim of their life was to know themselves, to despise empty opinion, and to grasp the truth with their whole mind, since truth 'is responsible for all good things among gods and men equally'.¹⁰ All the labour of Plato, Pythagoras, Socrates, Aristotle and his school, and Zeno as well, was devoted to truth. They wanted to know themselves and not be misled by vain opinion, but to track truth among things of real substance.

So it is clear that Plato and Diogenes cherished aims that were not different but identical. If you were to ask Plato what store he set by the commandment 'Know yourself', I am certain he, too, would say, 'Everything'. In fact, he says precisely that in the *Alcibiades*. 'Tell us next, divine Plato, son of the gods, what view should we take of popular opinion?' He will start by giving the same answer. Then he will recommend that we read in full a particular dialogue of his, the *Crito*, where Socrates is shown encouraging us to take no notice of conventional ideas. At any rate, he is quoted there as saying, [189] 'But why, dear Crito, are we so concerned about what the mass of men believe?'

Now, are we to ignore all this evidence, and arbitrarily choose to divide and segregate men whom the love of truth, indifference to opinion and a shared passion for virtue have united? And if Plato used words to realize his aims, whereas for Diogenes actions alone sufficed, does he therefore deserve your contempt?

Stop to consider whether his way is not, in fact, altogether best. Plato himself seems to renounce writing when he says, 'There is no composition by Plato, nor will there ever be, and what circulates under his name by rights belongs to Socrates.'[11] Then why not study Cynicism on the basis of Diogenes' actions?

Now a body consists of parts such as eyes, hands and feet; but there is in addition a class of secondary things like hair, nails and other forms of excrescence. Although a human body cannot exist without them, it would be absurd for someone to take note of these parts instead of what's really valuable and important, I mean the organs of sense and eyes and ears especially, since these faculties contribute most to our understanding.

They assist the soul in the process of thinking, whether we are to imagine the soul buried deep inside, the better to remain pure by virtue of the unmoved and unalloyed power of thought; or, as others believe, it uses these senses to communicate with the outside world. For the soul, they say, collects individual sense perceptions and stores them in memory, and from that the different branches of knowledge gradually develop.

My own view is that if there were no such capacity enabling us to apprehend the outside world, whether it be imperfect, or perfect but hindered by a host of different factors, such apprehension would not be possible. But this line of reasoning little pertains to our present theme; [190] so let us return to the question of Cynic philosophy and its divisions.

Evidently the Cynics agreed with Plato and Aristotle in dividing philosophy in two, its practical and theoretical sides. The explanation, no doubt, is that they realized that man is made both for action and the exercise of reason. Although Cynics refrained from studying natural philosophy, this does not detract from my argument. Socrates, it is true, and many others are often shown engaged in abstract argument, but always with a view to how best to behave. For them 'Know yourself' means learning what responsibilities to assign to the mind and body respectively. They rightly put mind in command, relegating the body to a subordinate role.

Therefore our sources represent the Cynics as pledged to self-control, modesty and freedom, and opposed to malice, cowardice and superstition. But this is not how we have come to think of them ourselves. In the popular imagination they make light of the most serious things and casually expose them to undue risk. The body, for instance, they completely neglect, in line with Socrates' definition of philosophy as 'a rehearsal for death'.

If this were their usual study, then I would be the first to warn against following them and to acknowledge that they were cranks. But if they had a sound reason for facing such ordeals, what was it? To gain renown, you say? And how is eating raw meat designed to win the public's approval? Certainly you don't advocate the practice. And supposing you imitate a Cynic by affecting a folded mantle and matted hair, the way the Cynics are shown in pictures; do you thereby hope to gain a reputation with the crowd – you, who can't hide your antipathy towards their way of life?

There may have been one or two who applauded Diogenes at the time, but countless more were overcome with nausea and disgust and turned away, having lost all taste for food. Only

when they were plied with sweets, scents and spirits did they
manage to collect themselves, [191] so great was the shock the
great man caused with that foolish act,[12] *foolish to men such as
they are today.* Explained in light of Diogenes' purpose, however, it does not seem so daft.

Socrates claimed that he took up the life of examining his
fellow citizens in deference to Apollo, since he felt he had to get
to the bottom of the oracle the god had proclaimed involving
him.[13] Diogenes, too, knew that he came to philosophy by way
of the Pythian oracle, and so thought it was his duty to put
everything to practical test and not rest content with received
opinion, which could easily be right or wrong.

Not even if 'Pythagoras (or someone of like stature) said
so'[14] was this enough to persuade Diogenes. He reckoned that
god, not man, brought philosophy into being.

And what, you may ask, has this to do with eating an octopus? I'll explain. Some people regard the eating of meat as
natural. Others think that no practice is less suited to human
beings. The question has been much debated, and has even produced a small library of books[15] that you can scrutinize at your
leisure. Diogenes saw fit to correct them by writing something
of his own about it. His view was that eating meat, if done with
no more fuss or preparation than is done by animals that are
naturally carnivorous, and if it does not lead to discomfort or
lasting harm but works to the body's benefit, then the custom
was without question in accordance with nature. But if anyone
were harmed as a result, then Diogenes allowed that it was
probably wrong for him and that such a person should avoid
meat as far as was practical.

Here, then, is one rather perfunctory view of the matter.
Diogenes also gave it a more personal and original treatment.
But appreciating it requires that I go into the principles of Cynicism in more detail. [192] Cynics aimed to be indifferent to
pleasure and pain, like the gods. Now Diogenes found that he
could tolerate food of almost any kind; only raw meat made
him queasy and nauseous, still governed, as he himself supposed, by received ideas instead of reason. Meat, after all, was
still meat no matter how often it was cooked or how many

sauces were poured over it. And he thought it was his duty to defeat this fear by confronting it squarely, exactly the way other kinds of cowardice (for that is what his squeamishness was, a kind of cowardice) are defeated.

By Demeter, if we eat cooked flesh, then explain why don't we partake of any flesh, be it cooked or raw? Because that is the custom and we have always done it that way – that is all anyone can offer by way of explanation. I can hardly suppose that what exists in its pure state, as nature made it, is made purer by the act of burning it to cinders. Then what was the right thing for Diogenes to do? Remember, he had been appointed God's agent on earth to revise the common currency and decide questions solely by the standards of truth and reason.

So should he have conformed to convention and announced that it was all right to eat cooked flesh because it was clean and fit for use; whereas meat that had not been exposed to fire was somehow vile and repulsive? Can anyone be so stupid and thoughtless? What you call Diogenes' ostentation, I call his seriousness of purpose and his commitment to serving Apollo with all his heart. And may I remind you that for the one raw octopus he ate you have put away any number of pickled sea urchins, *along with fish and birds and whatever else is at hand*.[16] You, after all, are an Egyptian, and not an Egyptian priest either. You therefore have licence to feed on anything, *like the grass in the field*. [193] (I presume you recognize the words of the Galilaeans.[17]) I almost forgot to add that many people who live by the ocean, and even some distance inland, regularly gulp sea urchins, oysters, clams and shellfish of all kinds without so much as warming them up. You envy them their raw delicacies, while Diogenes you regard with disgust and disrespect. Look, octopus is animal flesh the same as shellfish, only without the hard outer covering. It is bloodless, like hard-shelled fish, and the latter are also animate things like the octopus. It can sense pain and pleasure, which is the distinctive mark of animals. (For present purposes we can ignore the passage where Plato attributes soul to plants as well.[18])

But now, I think, it is evident to those who are in any way

able to follow an argument that what the excellent Diogenes did was not out of the way, irregular or at odds with your own habits, when judged, not on the basis of hardness and softness, but on the basis of taste. And so it is not after all the eating of raw food that disgusts you, since you do the same thing not only with bloodless animals but also with those that have blood. There is also this difference between you, perhaps, that he thought he ought to eat such food just as it was and in the natural state, whereas you think you must first prepare it with salt and many other things to make it pleasant, thereby doing violence to nature.

So much on that subject. Now the end and aim of the Cynic philosophy, as indeed of every philosophy, is well-being, but well-being that consists in living according to nature and not in accordance with vulgar opinion. Plants and animals of every kind experience well-being when they are allowed to attain the end designed for them by nature. Even among the gods this is the definition of well-being, or happiness, that they should be left to themselves, in their natural state.

[194] So it stands to reason that humans need not look outside themselves for some secret source of happiness. Neither the eagle nor the plane tree – no plant or animal, in fact – worries about leaves or wings of gold, silver branches or iron (much less steel) barbs or spines. If the equipment they inherit at birth is strong and adequate for speed or defence, then they consider that they themselves are well off and well provided for. Then how is it rational for human beings to waste time running after happiness outside themselves, making much of money, birth, the influence of friends and all that sort of thing? If nature had only given us a body and a soul like that of other animals, then we could be content with physical advantages and look for our happiness there, troubling ourselves with nothing further.

But the soul that has been implanted in us is quite different. Maybe it is essentially different, maybe it is just functionally superior, the way pure gold outshines gold that is mixed with sand. Both views are held. What we know for certain is that we are smarter than other animals. Like the myth in the *Protagoras* says,[19] nature lavished physical advantages on the beasts,

like a true mother. As compensation, however, Zeus gave us the
gift of reason. In reason, then, the best and most important
part of us, our happiness must be found.

Wasn't Diogenes a man of this conviction? He was unspar-
ing in subjecting his body to hardship to make it stronger than
it was by nature. He only thought [195] to do what reason
judged best. And he ignored the feelings that this covering, the
body, often excites to try and force us to give it our attention.
By means of such self-discipline he acquired a body stronger, I
dare say, than any Olympic athlete's. His soul was so disposed
that he was at least as happy, and as much of a king, as the
Great King himself (to use the same title used by the Greeks of
his day to refer to the king of Persia).

Does it seem to you trivial to be able to say that of a man
who was

> *without a home, without a country,*
> *having neither a penny, a dollar, nor a single slave of his own?*[20]

He didn't even have a loaf of bread – and Epicurus said that
with a loaf of bread he was hardly less happy than the gods.
But Diogenes was not vying with the gods but with the man
generally considered happiest, and claiming that his own life
was more sublime. And if you don't believe him, experience it
in person and you will see. But let us examine it with arguments first.

Presumably you believe that freedom is the foundation of all
the most celebrated goods. Who can doubt it? After all, without freedom such things as money, property, birth, health and
beauty belong, not to their apparent owner, but to whoever
owns him. Then who is a slave? You will say, of course, the
person we buy for a certain amount of silver or gold. Why?
Because we have paid money for him to the seller. [196] But in
that case hostages of war whom we ransom should count as
slaves as well.

Furthermore, these men by law are free once they come
home safely. And the whole purpose of our ransoming them is
that they won't have to be slaves but may be free again. So you

see that paying down money for someone is not enough to establish that he is a slave. The real slave is anyone whom another is in a position to command and compel to do whatever he wants, and if he refuses, to punish, and in Homer's words, to *visit great pains upon*.[21]

Consider next whether we don't have as many masters as there are people whom it is necessary for us to play up to, to avoid suffering the consequences of their displeasure. Or do you think that the only form of punishment is when a man brings his staff down on a menial's head? And not even the harshest masters go so far with all their slaves, often a word or threat is sufficient. So never think that you are free, my friend, as long as you are ruled by the belly and nether regions. They are masters who can either furnish you the means of pleasure or take them away. And even if you prove stronger than them but remain enslaved to the opinions of the crowd, you have not yet reached freedom or tasted of its nectar, 'I swear by him who entrusted me with the secret of the tetrad.'[22]

By that I do not mean to imply that we should act shamelessly in front of everyone and do what's indecent. I only mean that what we do, or refrain from doing, should be done (or not done) because reason and the god within us, the mind, commands it, not because the mob judges such actions moral or immoral. For the majority of people, following common opinion is fine. It is certainly better than acting shamelessly, [197] and mankind is naturally inclined to the truth. But anyone who has attained to a life of reason, who can make sound decisions, should not be governed by conventional ideas about good and bad behaviour.

Now, one part of our souls is more divine, which we call mind and intelligence and silent reason. Its herald is expressive reason – speech – which uses words and phrases and proceeds by way of the voice. Teamed with it is the other half of the soul, a many-headed monster of protean appearance, a mix of appetite and emotion. Until we have tamed this beast and taught it to obey the god within us – the divine part – it's best not to give the opinions of the masses any regular attention. But this is what many of Diogenes' followers have overlooked. The result is that they turned out disgusting, no better than one of the beasts. And to prove that this is not my own theory, first I will relate to you something Diogenes did. Most will laugh at it, but to me it seems quite admirable.

Once a young man farted in a crowd that happened to include Diogenes. Diogenes hit him with his stick and said, 'So, swine, you've done nothing to deserve taking such liberties in public, and still you choose this large crowd to demonstrate your new-found contempt for what other people think?' So convinced was he that we should subdue pleasure and passion before our third and final encounter – with common opinion, the scourge of the multitude.

You know how people deter young men from the study of philosophy by repeating some rumour about it. Pythagoras' legitimate students, along with those of Plato and Aristotle, are called quacks, sophists, charlatans and frauds. [198] If there is some honest Cynic among the bunch, he is regarded with pity. I remember my tutor once saying to me when he saw my friend Iphicles with his hair matted, his chest sunken in, wearing next to nothing in bad weather, 'What evil spirit can have brought him to this sorry state, while giving his parents, who raised him with great care and gave him the best education possible, even more cause to grieve? Now he goes about like this, completely destitute, no better than a tramp.' At the time I put him off with some sarcastic remark. But I assure you that most people hold such views about real Cynics.

That is not so bad. But you see that they also teach them to love wealth, hate poverty, and tend to the belly's needs. They teach them to endure anything for the body's sake, to fatten up that jailer of the soul. They teach them to keep a lavish table and never sleep alone at night, and to do all this in secret so no one will see them. Is not this worse than Tartarus? Wouldn't it be better to sink beneath Charybdis or Cocytus, or ten thousand fathoms underground, than fall into a life of enslavement to the belly and the groin? And not the simple enslavement of the beasts, either; these men must do their deeds in the dark, to escape notice. Surely it would be best to refrain from such conduct altogether.

If you cannot manage that, however, the advice of Diogenes and Crates on these matters is not the worst: 'Lust is conquered by fasting, and if you cannot starve yourself, then hang yourself.'[23] Those men, you must know, behave as they did to give us a model of the frugal life. [199] To quote Diogenes, 'You don't find tyrants eating bread, only costly dinners.' Crates composed a hymn to frugality:

> Hail, goddess and queen, Frugality,
> beloved of wise men, child of honoured Abstinence.

The Cynic, then, should not be like Oenomaus – shameless, shocking, scornful of every convention human and divine. Let him be like Diogenes and honour religion. After all, Diogenes obeyed the Pythian oracle and never regretted it. If he did not visit temples or worship statues or at altars, this is not proof of atheism, as some might argue. He simply did not have incense, or offerings, or money to buy them with. He held right opinions about the gods and that alone is sufficient. He worshipped them with his whole soul, thereby giving them the most valuable gift he had, the dedication of his soul through his thoughts.[24] Rather than act scandalously, the Cynic should follow reason and first subordinate the passionate side of his soul. Let him destroy it so completely that he is not even conscious of being indifferent to pleasure. For it is best to get to the point where we don't even know that we experience it. And we can only get there through training. Let me quote you a few lines from Crates' lighter verse, lest anyone think I say this unsupported:[25]

> Glorious children of Memory and Olympian Zeus,
>> Muses of Pieria, listen to my prayer.
> Always give me food for my belly, which has made
>> My life simple and free from slavery... [One or more
> lines have dropped out.]
>> To my friends make me useful rather than pleasant.
> I do not wish to accumulate conspicuous wealth by seeking
>> the beetle's portion

[200] *Nor do I hanker after the substance of the ant.*
I want a share of justice, and to make only as much money as is
    Easily carried, easily gained, and well-suited to virtue.
Give me these, and I will gratify Hermes and the holy Muses,
    Not with expensive gifts but pious virtues.

If you find this apt, I could quote more from the man. But since Plutarch of Chaeronea has written a life of Crates[26] you won't have to be satisfied with cursory knowledge about him from me.

But let us go back to what we were saying earlier. The Cynic apprentice should start with ruthless self-scrutiny and self-examination. He must ask himself honestly if he enjoys expensive meals, if he cannot do without a soft bed, if has a weakness for praise or applause, if he craves public notice and thinks it important, however vain the honour.

He must avoid yielding to the influence of the mob. He should not touch vulgar pleasure even with the fingertip, as the saying goes, before he succeeds in trampling it underfoot. Then he may sample it if it happens to come his way. By way of analogy, less powerful bulls, I hear, will leave the herd for a time and pasture alone to gradually recruit their strength. Only later do they return to challenge the head of the herd, more assured of their own fitness to lead.

The prospective Cynic, then, should not just affect [201] the school's doubled cloak, knapsack, staff and matted hair, like a man walking around unshaved and illiterate in a village with neither a barbershop nor school. He must realize that reason rather than a staff, a definite way of life and not the Cynic rucksack, are the trademarks of our philosophy. Frank speech should be avoided until he has proven his worth, as Crates and Diogenes, in my opinion, did.

These men bore the threats of fortune, whether we are to regard such threats as wanton insults or mere teasing, with such good grace that Diogenes joked with the pirates who captured him. Crates the cripple gave away his money to his native city[27] and made fun of his own lame leg and protruding shoulders. When his friends hosted a dinner, he used to go, invited or not, and would reconcile relatives he saw estranged. If he had

to criticize, he did it lightly and gently so that he seemed eager
to help, not harass, the objects of his criticism, along with any
chance bystanders.

Yet this was not their principal aim. As I said, mainly they
searched for personal happiness. They concerned themselves
with others, I believe, only insofar as they recognized that man is
by nature a social and gregarious animal. And they helped their
friends not just by setting them an example but also by giving
them advice. So whoever wants to be an honest Cynic should
start by taking himself in hand and, like Diogenes and Crates,
expelling every passion from every part of the soul. Then he
should commit his life to the control of mind and right reason.
Because this, I think, is Diogenes' thought in a nutshell.

If he visited a prostitute, it was a few times at most. [202]
Anyone who chooses to do the like openly and in plain sight
must prove himself like Diogenes in seriousness of purpose.
Then we will not blame him for it or take him to task.

But first let us see him match Diogenes for intelligence, wit,
freedom in other respects, independence, fairness, sobriety, piety,
charm and concern to do nothing thoughtlessly or irrationally.
These traits are also integral parts of the man's philosophy.

Then he may trample on pretence,[28] and make fun of people
who tend to nature's needs, like the excretion of waste, in hiding, but perpetrate the crudest and most unnatural crimes in
the very heart of our cities. I refer to things like theft, false witness, unjust prosecution and similarly deplorable acts.

On the other hand, when Diogenes farted or relieved himself
or did anything else of that kind in public, as is commonly
reported of him, he was trying to trample on pretence and
teach such people that their practices were much worse and
more savage than his own. What he did, after all, accorded
with our common humanity. Their acts, by contrast, are merely
perverse and agree with no one's nature.

Today, however, they only seize on what is easiest to imitate in
Diogenes and fail to see his better side. As for you, in your desire
to be more dignified than Diogenes and his followers, you are so
at odds with his outlook that you regard him with contempt.

If you do not believe all I have to say about the man, a man

the Greeks of Plato and Aristotle's day rated alongside Socrates
and Pythagoras, whose pupil taught the wise and noble Zeno –
and it is not likely that they all were wrong about a person as
low as you make him out to be in your travesty – well, dear sir,
[203] you might have done a better job of researching him for
yourself. Was there a single Greek who did not stand in awe of
Diogenes' resilience – a resilience that had in it the nobility of a
prince – and of his capacity for hardship?

The man used to sleep better in his barrel or on a bed of
straw than the Great King did on his soft couch under his
gilded roof. He ate his bread with more relish than you now eat
your Sicilian dishes. He bathed in cold water and let the air dry
him instead of using the linen towels with which you rub yourself down, O celebrated philosopher.

And well you might mock him because, I suppose, like
Themistocles you defeated Xerxes, or overcame Darius like Alexander of Macedon. If you were at all in the habit of reading, as I
am, despite being a statesman and greatly occupied, you would
know how much Alexander is said to have respected Diogenes'
high-mindedness.[29] But it doesn't seem to me that any of this matters to you. And why, after all, should it matter in the least? It's a
woman's sorry life you admire and want . . .[30] If my work has
been at all successful, you will have gained by it more than I. But
if we accomplish nothing with this breathless composition – the
labour of barely two days, as the Muses, or rather you personally
can attest – then by all means stand by your former views. For my
part, I will never regret having spoken on that great man's behalf.

137 To the Cynic Heracleios (Oration 7)

How a Cynic should behave and whether he should
compose myths (excerpts)

[204] *How much takes place over an extended period of time!*[31]
While recently attending a comedy, I heard that line and was
tempted to shout it aloud. We had been invited to hear a Cynic

lecture, a Cynic, we soon discovered, whose barking lacked all force and significance. He resorted to fables like nursemaids with their charges; and even those tales were not very edifying. Suddenly I was seized by the urge to stand up and cut the proceeding short. But when Dionysus or Heracles is lampooned on the comic stage we endure it. So I sat through the man's speech, not, to be sure, to spare his feelings but those of the crowd. Actually, to be quite honest, I stayed out of consideration for myself. I was determined not to seem unnerved or subject to irrational fear of the gods by taking flight like a timid bird on being exposed to this fellow's trite ideas. And I wanted to show that only pious and rational thoughts can affect me. So I stayed, repeating to myself Odysseus' words of self-encouragement: *Be strong, my heart, you've endured trials worse than this.*[32] For a mere fraction of the day (I told myself) indulge the ravings of a dog; it is not, after all, the first time you've heard the gods maligned. Our state is not so well governed, nor our private lives so well ordered – [205] in fact, we are not so blessed by fortune – that we can insulate ourselves from the expression of such coarse sentiments any more than we can blind ourselves to the spectacle of the crimes against the gods committed by this race of iron men. And as though we needed more such rubbish, the Cynic filled our ears with vile phrases explicitly relating to the supreme god, Zeus, phrases such as we should no more have to listen to than he should be allowed to say.

I propose to teach him, while you look on, first of all that it is the part of a Cynic to write essays, not to fabricate myths; then, if philosophy could really use the addition of myths, I will determine which myths are appropriate and how best to adapt them. Finally, I shall have a few words to say about respect for the gods. That is why I am here before you, despite the fact that I am no writer myself and by preference have always excused myself from public speaking, just as I have always avoided playing the uncongenial role of a sophist. But perhaps it will not be amiss for me to say, and for you to hear, a few remarks about myth as a phase in the annals of education.

[206] In all probability myth was invented by pastoralists, and the habit continues as an essential part of their existence today. We may compare the role that music, particularly the

use of the lyre and flute, plays in their everyday lives. Birds are made to fly, fish to swim, deer to run, and they don't need instructors to show them how. If they are restrained or caged, they will still try to use those parts of the body that they instinctively know they are born to exercise. In the case of man, whose body contains a soul remarkable for knowledge and understanding – faculties that amount to the body's 'potentiality',[33] to use the language of philosophy – learning, study and research are his native drives and pursuits. As soon as a friendly god releases him from the body's confines and potentiality becomes actuality, a person is at once endowed with understanding. Those still tied to the body are subject to false opinion instead of truth; they are like Ixion who embraced an insubstantial cloud in the shape of Hera under the delusion that the goddess herself was in his arms. The fruit of such union takes the form of wind-eggs and those malformed approximations to real knowledge that are no more than shadows and ghostly imitations. Their behaviour counterfeits acts based on true science. They propagate their false values with great conviction, in possession, as they imagine, of some rare and wonderful truth.

But if I must say something in defence of the original creators of myth, they are like nannies who hang leather dolls above the cribs of teething infants, to distract them and alleviate their pain. So those first mythologists supplied a steady stream of stories and legends to the fledgling souls of young men learning to fly and eager to be taught but not yet ready to absorb the undiluted truth. As if they were watering a thirsty field, they were trying to mitigate their pain and irritation [. . .]

[208] Reason, perhaps, bars the Cynic from concocting myths and imaginative tales meant for public performance. He only cares for freedom, so it stands to reason that he will speak nothing but the unembellished truth. But is there not a tradition of rhetorical display beginning with Diogenes and current among Cynics even now? On the contrary, you will nowhere find evidence of any such custom. I pass over for now how the Cynic, in vowing to 'deface the currency', should scorn conventional usage and rely on reason to decide for himself the proper thing to do [209], instead of learning it from others. If

Antisthenes the Socratic, like Xenophon, at times resorted to myth, don't let it misguide you.³⁴ In time I will explain that to you as well. But, by all the Muses, declare yourself at once: is Cynicism a form of madness, is it an inhuman way of life, does it represent a savage attitude of mind that knows nothing of what is good, fair and decent? For Oenomaus would influence many people to hold this view of it. If you had taken the trouble to investigate, you would have undoubtedly concluded this from a reading of that particular Cynic's works *Oracles in their Own Words* and *Against the Oracles* – from becoming familiar with any of his books, in short. This is his mission,³⁵ to do away with reverence for the gods and discredit human piety. He aims to trample on all the laws defending right and justice, as well as the unwritten laws the gods have planted in our souls which, without need of formal proof, persuade us that the gods exist, and compel us to attend to this divine element in a spirit of emulation. For our souls naturally stand in the same relation to this divine element as our eyes do to the sun.

Now, suppose that the second-most sacred law, as judged by the standards of nature and gods, were abolished. I refer to the law that commands us without qualification to keep our hands off other people's property, the law that puts an end to any confusion on this point in words, deeds, even in our private imaginations. And since this law is our principal guarantor of justice, wouldn't its abolition earn whoever is to blame a period of confinement in the pit?³⁶ Advocates for such a measure deserve worse than scapegoats who are driven from the city by physical force: that is too mild a fate for such offenders. Death by stoning would be more appropriate. [210] Tell me, after all, how are such wretches any better than pirates lurking in remote locations, or positioned on shore to attack and plunder vessels passing by? Well, some would say, their attitude shows that they despise death. As though this same manic courage were not characteristic of pirates!

So, at least, says the man who among you is accounted a poet and mythologist, but who is esteemed no less than a hero or god by certain bandits who consulted the oracle of Apollo – I mean Homer, and I am thinking specifically of the line where he refers to *pirates who roam the deep, risking their very lives.*[37] What more authoritative witness can there be to the desperate courage of the criminal caste? Only, one might say that the criminals are more courageous than such Cynics, and say that the Cynics are more audacious. Pirates, you see, favour lonely spots as much from consciousness of their outlaw status as from fear of death. Cynics, on the other hand, go about in the open, boldly challenging convention, and not by promoting a cleaner or more sophisticated life but actually a cruder and more squalid one.

As to the tragedies assigned to Diogenes, it is true that they are acknowledged to be the work of a Cynic. Disagreement, however, exists as to whether they are by Diogenes, the master, or by his pupil Philiscus. One has only to read them, however, to reject them. Their depravity is such as to make a prostitute blush. But then let him turn to the productions of Oenomaus, for he wrote tragedies to match his disquisitions. He will find that they are beyond deplorable and set new standards for filth. I am at a loss to describe them. It would be vain to invoke the horrors of Magnesia,[38] the wickedness of Termerus,[39] or the [211] whole of tragedy, with every satyr play,[40] mime and comedy thrown in for good measure. That is how much care the man has taken to reproduce every form of scandalous and outrageous behaviour, and in their most dramatic form.

Now, if someone wished to show us the nature of Cynicism using these works as testimony – dramas in which the gods are maligned and no one is spared the Cynic's malicious bark – then away with him, let him go wherever he wants and equally as far away. But if he does as Apollo told Diogenes to do and 'alters the currency', then takes as his own guiding principle the order Apollo first laid on Diogenes, I mean the command to 'Know yourself' – advice which Crates as well as Diogenes plainly tried to live by – then I am already prepared to say that this identifies someone with aspirations to rule as well as philosophize. For what was the god trying to say, do we even know? He urged Diogenes to ignore common opinion and alter – not the truth – but custom and received ideas. Now which description fits the motto 'Know yourself'? Can we call it conventional?

Is it not rather the truth in a nutshell? The proverb indicates a new way to 'alter the currency'. After all, a person who has challenged social rules out of respect for the truth does not expect to find the truth about himself discoverable in common opinion, but in established fact. So whoever can truly be said to know himself will derive this knowledge not from vulgar views, but from conviction grounded in reality. Whatever is popularly said about him, of this he will know nothing and care even less. So can we not conclude that Apollo speaks the truth and that Diogenes knew it? Because he put his faith in him, he advanced from the status of a mere exile to become – I don't say Alexander's equal, but someone Alexander could admire. And this is the Alexander who had smashed the Persian empire,[41] challenged comparison with Heracles for outstanding deeds, and modelled his life on Achilles. So let us get to know Diogenes and learn the truth about his attitude [212] towards gods and men, not from the writings of Oenomaus or the tragedies of Philiscus – who did a signal disservice to the great man by signing his name to those scurrilous works – but from the established facts of his biography.

Why in heaven's name did he go to Olympia? To see the athletes compete? Couldn't he have seen the same athletes perform at the Isthmian games or the Panathenaic festival, and with far less trouble to himself? Or was he moved by the wish to see men of renown in the flesh? But could he not meet such luminaries closer to home in Isthmia? No, you cannot discover any motive besides his wish to honour the god.[42] Unless, that is, a thunderstorm put such fear of God into him that he went in a spirit of superstition. Really, I personally have been witness to many such signs from Zeus without being overcome by awe. But I am in awe of the gods all the same. I love them, adore and venerate them. In short, they affect me as benign masters, teachers, parents, guardians and other such caring and commanding presences. So the other day it was all I could do to keep from getting up and walking out when I heard you lecture. But these reflections came upon me I don't know how and I was moved to share them, even though I might have done better to keep them to myself.

Though poor and short on resources, Diogenes nevertheless went to Olympia on foot. He insisted that Alexander visit him there, if we can credit Dio.[43] This shows that he felt personally obliged to make a pilgrimage to the gods' shrines, but that it was incumbent upon the most politically powerful man of his day to come to him if he sought an interview. And the advice he addressed to Archidamus, isn't it as regal and commanding as any decree of Alexander's? His actions, too, prove his devotion to the gods. He preferred to live in Athens. But when a divine voice sent him to Corinth he felt duty-bound to remain there, [213] even after his Corinthian master had set him free. He was convinced that the gods took an interest in his affairs, and that he had been sent to Corinth not by accident or without good reason. The gods, he believed, had a part in summoning him there. He could see that the city was morally more corrupt than Athens, and could benefit from the presence of a better reformer than any Athens would be left with in his absence [. . .]

[222] To return to [the subject of myth and its place in philosophy]. Whenever myths on sacred topics are not well adapted to the message that they aim to convey, they practically scream at us not to take them at face value but to probe a bit to discover their hidden meaning. In the case of such myths, the jarring element counts for more than the superficial narrative. In the latter, to be sure, the gods are depicted as moral, powerful and attractive; but this has the unfortunate consequence of virtually turning them into people. Whereas, when the meaning is somewhat at odds with the narrative, there is the chance that readers will look beyond the words' obvious sense. Then our more refined intelligence may be moved to a better understanding of the gods' distinctive nature, which transcends all earthly realities.

[223] This explains the use of language that is exceptionally earnest and devout in that branch of philosophy dealing with rites and mysteries. With respect to the message, however, the exposition may assume a more exotic character. But whoever invents moral fables intended to improve the character of the reader, and incorporates myths to that end, must see that their proper audience is not grown men but children, whether we are

to judge children by age or by intelligence. Either way, children benefit most from myth. But if you mistake us for children – and here I include not just me but Memmorius and Sallust and everyone else in due order – then you need a trip to Anticyra.[44]

Why not speak to you frankly? By the gods, by the power of myth itself, and most especially by the sun who rules over everything everywhere, please tell us, what accomplishment, great or small, can you point to with pride? When did you ever assist a person unfairly in trouble with the law? Name one grieving person whom you comforted by telling them that death is not an evil, either for the deceased or for their family? What dissolute young man will thank you for taking him in hand, introducing him to a life of regular habits, and making him beautiful inside and out? What practical discipline do you adhere to? What have you done to earn the staff of Diogenes, to say nothing of his freedom of speech? Do you honestly think that carrying a staff, letting your hair grow out, moving from city to city or camp to camp and insulting the rich and prominent in all such places while associating with society's dregs – do you honestly think, I say, that this amounts to anything great or glorious? Before Zeus and the audience here, who have been alienated from philosophy because of you and your kind, please explain: why did you visit the late lamented Emperor Constantius[45] in Italy but did not get as far as Gaul? If you had come to me, at least you would have had the company of someone better able to understand your language. What's with this incessant moving about, pushing pack mules to the limits of their endurance? From what I hear, you also drive the mule drivers to exhaustion, so that even more than soldiers they dread the patronage of Cynics. By report, you make more brutal use of your staff in urging them on than soldiers do with their swords. No wonder they dread you more.

Long ago I thought up a name for you; now I am of a mind to commit it to writing. The name is 'monk'. It is applied to certain members of the god-forsaken Christian sect. Most of these characters sacrifice little to gain much – everything really, and from every quarter. They are blessed in addition with honours, a corps of bodyguards, and scores of admirers. Something

like this describes your condition, except, perhaps, for the
money-making. But this is not your custom, it is ours. For we
are shrewder than those dimwits. Perhaps there is this difference too, that you have no pretext for collecting tribute on
specious grounds, the way they do – tribute they refer to as
'charity' or 'alms', I don't profess to understand why. But in all
other respects you are much alike. Like them, you left your city
to go wandering off in all directions. In my camp you made a
bigger nuisance of yourselves than they did, and were more
impertinent. At least they had been invited, whereas we were
compelled to ask you to leave. And what benefit have you
derived from this? What advantage, in fact, have any of us
gained thereby? . . .

[225] You are no better off for wearing your hair long and
carrying a staff. You have even managed to diminish the prestige of philosophy in general. The least accomplished orators,
ones whose powers of expression King Hermes himself could
not excel, and whose intelligence Athena herself could not
improve upon, even with Hermes there to help, acquired the
little they know from chance encounters in public places. They
do not appreciate the truth of the proverb, 'Grape ripens near
grape'.[46] Then they rush into Cynicism, which they equate
merely with a staff, mantle, matted hair, contempt for learning
and good manners, insolence, et cetera. They say that they are
taking the short, intensive course in virtue. I wish you were taking the long one! That way you would reach your goal more
easily. Don't you realize that short cuts involve great hardship?
On the public roads a traveller who can manage a shorter, more
direct route will handle the longer, circuitous route with relative ease; but, conversely, conquering the circular route is no
assurance that someone can successfully negotiate the short
one. Likewise in philosophy, approaches may differ, but there
is only one goal and one starting point for all: self-knowledge
and imitation of the gods. The beginning is self-knowledge, the
end is assimilation to the heavenly powers.

The prospective Cynic turns his back on the familiar usages
and prejudices of mankind, to focus primarily on himself and
god. To him gold is not gold or sand sand if they are judged by

their exchange value, and it is left to God to decide their inherent worth.[47] [226] For he knows that both are merely earth.
That one is rare while the other is plentiful – both discoveries,
he thinks, we owe to man's vanity and simple-mindedness.
Actions should not be categorized as good or bad by the degree
of praise (or blame) they arouse; their value lies in their nature.
The Cynic practises moderation in his diet, and refrains from
sex. When the needs of the body call, he is not the slave of
opinion, nor does he need to be served by a cook, require fancy
sauces, or expect his food to send forth a sweet aroma. He is
not on the lookout for Phryne, Lais,[48] another man's wife or
daughter, or a household slave, to satisfy his lust. As far as possible he answers the body's demands with whatever is nearest
to hand. He resists its insistent demands and from the heights
of Olympus, as it were, looks down upon the mass of men
Wandering blind in the valley of confusion.[49] For the sake of a
few pleasures they suffer agonies worse than those that the
cleverest poets describe the souls undergoing in the rivers Cocytus and Acheron. The true short cut to philosophy is this: a
man must step outside himself and know that the soul within
him is divine. He must ever and always train his mind on clean,
pure and holy thoughts. His body he must despise; he should
think of it, to quote Heraclitus, as 'more disposable than dirt'.[50]
Its needs should be met by the simplest means so long as God
wants it to survive and function as a tool.[51]

Glossary

Academy. Originally a sanctuary of Athena (goddess of wisdom), located in northern Athens, it gained prominence in the fourth century BC as the site of Plato's school, and the name became synonymous with the school itself, which survived until the sixth century AD.

Acheron. In Greek myth, one of the three rivers, along with Styx and Cocytus, running through the underworld.

Achilles. The pre-eminent Greek warrior in Homer's *Iliad*.

Acrocorinth. The acropolis (citadel) of Corinth, situated to the southwest of the ancient city and rising to an elevation of 1883 ft (574 m).

Aeacus. Along with Minos and Rhadamanthys, one of the judges of the dead in Hades.

Aegina. A small island in the Saronic Gulf, seventeen miles off the coast of Athens.

Aeolus. Mythical ruler over Thessaly, father of a large family, although their exact number varies in different versions of the myth.

Aeschylus. Fifth-century BC Athenian tragedian, author *inter alia* of the *Oresteia*.

Agathoboulos. Cynic philosopher (*fl.* AD 125), teacher of Demonax and Peregrinus Proteus.

Agathocles. Peripatetic philosopher of the second century AD.

Ajax. One of the foremost soldiers on the Greek side in Homer's *Iliad*, second only to Achilles in terms of brute strength.

Alcibiades. Brilliant but erratic and unprincipled Athenian aristocrat and general, who played a vital role in the Peloponnesian War, on both the Athenian and Spartan sides at different times; originally a member of Socrates' inner circle.

Alexander the Great. Fourth-century BC Macedonian king and general, successor to Philip II of Macedon. Conqueror of the Persian empire and commander of a realm extending from Greece to present-day Pakistan.

Amazons. A race of female warriors in Greek mythology.

Amphiaraus. Greek mythical hero prominently featured in the Theban cycle; saved (in a sense) by being swallowed by the Earth while in flight from his arch-enemy Periclymenus.

Andromache. In Homer's *Iliad*, wife of the Trojan warrior Hector.

Anticyra. A Greek town in the district of Phocis, known for the hellebore that grew in profusion. The plant's reputation as a cure for madness gave rise to the saying 'You should visit Anticyra' – prompted when a person spoke or acted foolishly.

Antigonus. References in the text to Antigonus are to Antigonus II Gonatas, member of the Antigonid dynasty that succeeded to control of Greece after Alexander's death.

Anytus. Along with Meletus, Athenian citizen who charged Socrates with impiety and corruption of the city's youth, resulting in the philosopher's execution.

Aphrodite. Greek Olympian goddess whose province was erotic and romantic love.

Apollonius. A common Greek name, in Cynic sources invariably a reference to the Stoic philosopher of the second century AD.

Argus. Mythical creature endowed with a hundred eyes.

Aristides, aka Aristides the Just. Athenian politician and general (lived 530–468 BC), who as a military commander made a signal contribution to Greece's victory in the Persian Wars.

Aristippus. Founder of the Cyrenaic school of philosophy, *fl.* fourth century BC. Originally from Cyrene, he was induced by Socrates' reputation to relocate to Athens to benefit from first-hand association with the man. In the event, the Cyrenaic school he founded came to be identified with a kind of lenient ethics that indulged and even encouraged the cultivation of pleasure – a moral position Socrates would most likely have disowned.

Aristogeiton. See under **Harmodius**.

Ariston of Chios. Unorthodox third-century BC Stoic, whose uncompromising distinction between things good and bad seems to reflect the influence of the stark value system of the Cynics.

Aristophanes. Athenian comic playwright of the fifth century BC.

Asclepius. Ancient Greek god of healing.

askêsis. Greek word denominating the varieties of physical self-discipline submitted to in the course of preparing for the rigours of Cynic life.

Astypalaea. Greek island in the Dodecanese chain.

Atalanta. A figure from Greek myth: raised in the wild, she was celebrated for her speed and proficiency in the hunt.

Athenaeus. Greek composer of epigrams, cited by Diogenes Laertius at 6.14 and 7.30.

Atreus. A scion of the Pelopidae, who in Greek mythology reigned over the important Bronze Age city of Thebes. Atreus became embroiled in a fraternal feud with Thyestes. Atreus went so far as to serve Thyestes' murdered sons in a stew at a feast arranged by Atreus with the ostensible purpose of making peace with his brother.

Attica. Region of Greece dominated by the capital, Athens; bordered by Boeotia on the north, the Saronic Gulf on the west, and the Aegean Sea to the east.

autarkeia. Self-sufficiency or independence, a condition the Cynics gained chiefly by reducing their material needs to a minimum.

Bactra. Ancient Middle Eastern city now named Balkh and located in northern Afghanistan; part of the Persian empire in the age of Cyrus the Great and his Achaemenid successors.

Battle of Chaeronea. Fought in 338 BC, near the city of Chaeronea in Boeotia, between Philip II of Macedon and an alliance of Greek city-states, ending in a decisive Macedonian victory.

Belbina or Belbinites. Small Greek island, very lofty and difficult of access, situated at the entrance of the Saronic Gulf.

Boeotia. Region of central Greece bordering Attica on the south; home of the city of Thebes.

Busiris. Mythical king of Egypt who routinely sacrificed intruders into his realm and whose slaying by Heracles counted among the latter's twelve labours.

Calanus. One of the gymnosophists whom Onesicritus encounters on the embassy arranged by Alexander to meet with representatives of their order and learn their philosophy.

Calchas. Mythical Greek seer, a character in Homer's *Iliad*.

Caligula. Roman emperor of the Julio-Claudian dynasty, reigned from AD 37 to 41.

Callias. Fifth-century BC head of a wealthy Athenian family.

Callisthenes. Fourth-century BC philosopher, a relative of Aristotle. This connection secured him a place in Alexander's military campaigns. He criticized Alexander, however, for encouraging Oriental habits of sycophancy among his subordinates, including his fellow Greeks. The personal tension led to his execution around 328 BC.

Chalcis. Largest city on the Greek island of Euboea.

Charon. In Greek mythology, the ferryman who transported souls of the dead across the river Styx to Hades.

Charybdis. A sea monster, later rationalized as a whirlpool and a natural hazard to ships negotiating the Strait of Messina between Italy and Sicily.

Chiron or Cheiron. Name of one of the best-known Centaurs, hybrid creatures, half-man, half-horse. According to legend, Achilles' tutor.

chreia. A particularly popular Cynic trope, usually an anecdote capped by a Cynic's pithy and sardonic remark.

Chremonides. Athenian third-century BC statesman and general. He issued the Decree of Chremonides in 268 BC, creating an alliance between Sparta, Athens and Ptolemy II.

Chrysippus. The leading theorist of Stoicism, *fl.* third century BC, honoured as the Stoics' 'second founder' (after Zeno of Citium). Some of his writings, lost but paraphrased in other sources, betray the influence of the early Cynics.

Cinyras. A famous Cyprian hero. According to tradition, he was a son of Apollo and priest of the Paphian Aphrodite. He was married to Metharne, the daughter of the Cyprian king Pygmalion, by whom he had several children, Adonis among them.

Circe. A mythical sorceress, featured in a central episode in Homer's *Odyssey* in which, by a touch of her magic wand, several of Odysseus' companions are transformed into pigs.

Cleomenes. A Cynic philosopher who wrote a work on education, quoted by Diogenes Laertius (at 6.75 and 95).

Cocytus. A river in the underworld in Greek mythology.

Constantius II. Roman emperor from AD 337 to 361, second son and successor of Constantine the Great. Promoted his cousin Julian to the rank of Caesar, but when Julian claimed the rank of Augustus in 360, Constantius moved against him but took ill and died (361) before battle was joined – not, however, before naming his opponent as his successor.

Craneum. A district outside the Greek city of Corinth, location of a gymnasium by tradition frequented by Diogenes the Cynic.

Critobulus. An obscure member of Socrates' circle.

Cynosarges. A gymnasium located outside Athens, a favourite haunt of Diogenes the Cynic and proposed by some as the source of his epithet, since it translates something like 'white dog'.

Cyrus. Sixth-century BC founder of the Persian empire.

Danaids. Literally 'daughters of Danaus', fifty in number, who by an enforced arrangement married their father's nephews. All but one killed their husbands on their wedding night, and, by way of punishment, eventually came to spend eternity in Hades vainly trying to transport water in leaky urns.

Danaus. Mythical king of Argos who fathered fifty daughters, the so-called Danaids.

Darius. Name of three kings of the Achaemenid dynasty that ruled over the Persian Empire until Alexander the Great defeated the last of the line, Darius III, in 331 BC.

Delian oracle. Originally applied to the prophetic site devoted to Apollo and located on the Greek island of Delos; later applied to any oracular site in Greece where Apollo was supposed to exercise his powers of prognostication.

Delphi. Site of the Delphic oracle, dedicated to the god Apollo, located in the central Greek region of Phocis.

Demeter. Greek Olympian goddess, associated with agriculture and food generally.

Demetrius of Magnesia. First-century BC Greek biographer.

Demetrius of Phalerum. Fourth/third-century BC Athenian orator and statesman, appointed ruler of Athens by Cassander, a member of the Argead dynasty to which Alexander the Great belonged. He was deposed by Demetrius Poliorcetes, an enemy of Cassander, in 307 BC, and relocated to Thebes.

Demosthenes. Famous Athenian orator of the fourth century BC, whose best-known speeches are probably those urging his fellow citizens to prepare for attack from the north by Philip II and his son Alexander the Great.

Diocles of Magnesia. Greek doxographer who composed digests of the lives and opinions of eminent Greek philosophers before his day; his own works are lost but Diogenes Laertius' *Lives of the Ancient Philosophers*, which does survive, borrows from him extensively.

Diomedes of Thrace. Keeper of man-eating horses, which Heracles tamed and brought back to Eurystheus – traditionally the eighth of the twelve labours he accomplished at the latter's behest.

Dionysius I. Fifth/fourth-century BC tyrant of the Greek city of Syracuse in Sicily.

Dionysius II. Fourth-century BC successor of Dionysius I to rulership of Sicily; like his father, he was cultivated by Plato in an (abortive) effort by the philosopher to induce the tyrant to convert to his own moral and political ideals.

Dionysus. One of the twelve Olympian gods, associated with wine, women and song; according to Greek myth he also ventured into Egypt and Asia as far as India, subduing the native populations but also introducing them to viticulture.

Ecbatana. Ancient city now called Hamadan and located in north-western Iran; under the Persian kings of the Achaemenid dynasty it served as their favoured summer residence.

Echo. Name of a nymph in Greek mythology.

Eleusis. Town in west Attica, about 18 km northwest of Athens, best known for having been the home of the Eleusinian Mysteries, which were devoted to the goddess Demeter and her daughter, Persephone.

Elis or Eleia. District on the Peloponnesian peninsula in Greece, site of Olympia and the Olympic games.

Empedocles. Fifth-century BC Greek philosopher, a native of Acragas (Agrigentum) in Sicily. Legend has it that he committed suicide by leaping into an active volcano (Mt. Aetna in Sicily).

Epaminondas. Fourth-century BC Theban general who defeated Sparta in a series of important battles.

Epicurus (341–270 BC). Greek philosopher who founded one of the most important schools of the Hellenistic age. In physics he revived the atomism of the fifth-century BC philosopher Democritus, while he may be described as a principled hedonist so far as his ethics are concerned.

Eratosthenes. Third-century BC polymath at the court of the Ptolemies. He was put in charge of the famous library at Alexandria, but is perhaps best known for devising a means to estimate the circumference of the Earth, arriving at a figure accurate to within 1 per cent of modern science's calculations.

Eubulides. Fourth-century BC Greek philosopher of the Megarian school.

Euclides. Fourth-century BC Greek philosopher. Originally a student of Socrates, after the master's death he moved to Megara and founded the Dialectic school.

Eumolpus. Mythological figure of Thracian origin, founder by tradition of the Eleusinian Mysteries.

Eurystheus. Figure of Greek myth, variously reported as king of either Tiryns or Argos; famous chiefly as author of the twelve labours he imposed on Heracles.

Favorinus. Roman sophist and philosopher who flourished in the mid-second century AD and wrote on a great number of subjects, although little of his output survives. He is described as a hermaphrodite by birth.

Geryones or Geryon. A monster with three bodies, ruler over a kingdom in the far west ('Hesperia'), who kept a herd of oxen that Heracles was instructed to capture and bring to Eurystheus as one of his twelve labours.

Glaucon. An Athenian who seems to have distinguished himself in the Chremonidean War, 263 BC. After Athens' defeat he, along with Chremonides, was received at the court of Ptolemy Philadelphus where he ascended to a position of power and prestige.

Gorgias. Greek philosopher and instructor in rhetoric, active in the fifth century BC.

gymnosophists. Greek name (meaning 'naked sages') for the Indian rishis or holy men.

Harmodius. With Aristogeiton, by tradition one of the young men native to Athens who contrived the assassination of Hippias, last of the Peisistratid dynasty, leading to the liberation of Athens and the establishment of democracy.

Hecato. Stoic philosopher who flourished in the second/first century BC, of whose writings only fragments remain from citations in other surviving sources.

Hector. In Homer's *Iliad*, leader of the Trojan forces against the Greeks.

Helen. Mythical wife of the Spartan king Menelaus; the Trojan prince Paris ran off with her to Troy, precipitating the war with Greece.

Hellanodicae. The judges in the Olympic and Nemean games.

Heracles. Legendary Greek demigod, whose twelve labours helped rid the world of malefactors; his endurance and self-control in the cause of *philanthropia* made him a virtual 'Cynic saint'.

Heraclitus. Greek philosopher from Ephesus in Ionia, on the coast of Asia Minor; lived *c.*535–*c.*475 BC.

Hermes. One of the twelve Olympian gods in Greek religion, father of Pan.

Herminus. Peripatetic philosopher, a contemporary of Demonax.

Hermippus. Fifth-century BC Athenian author of Old Comedy.

Herodes Atticus. Famous Athenian aristocrat who lived from AD 101 to 177. He served as a Roman senator and also composed speeches (now lost) that qualified him as a representative of the Second Sophistic. From a wealthy background, he personally underwrote public works such as the Odeon in Athens, a stadium in Athens, and an aqueduct in Italy. He had a close, some say romantic, relationship with Polydeuces, whose untimely passing is said to have affected him deeply and hastened his own death.

Hesperides. In Greek mythology, nymphs in the far western corner of the world who tended a grove of trees bearing golden apples. Heracles traversed Europe and retrieved the apples in fulfilment of his eleventh labour.

Hicesias. Father of Diogenes, the founder of Cynicism. Official moneyer of Sinope on the Black Sea until he was implicated in a scheme to debase the currency.

Hippocleides. An Athenian, one of the suitors for the hand of Agarista, daughter of Cleisthenes of Sicyon. He proved himself a man of good parts and earned Cleisthenes' favour, until the day of decision came when he gave himself up to indecent dancing and acrobatic tricks. To his host's remark, 'You have danced away your marriage,' he said simply, 'It's all one to Hippocleides' and carried on with his dancing and tumbling routines – a remark that came to symbolize a capricious or happy-go-lucky attitude. (Herodotus 6. 127–9)

Hippolyte. Legendary queen of the Amazons, who tried to seduce Heracles but whose advances Heracles successfully resisted, capturing and returning her girdle to Eurystheus to complete his ninth labour.

Hippomedon. Son of Agesilaus, a leading politician in Sparta in the middle of the third century BC who fell out of favour leading to his – and his son's – exile. Hippomedon must have redeemed his reputation, however, because by report he later served Ptolemy, king of Egypt, as governor of the cities subject to that prince within the confines of Thrace.

Hyperides. Celebrated Attic orator of the fourth century BC.

Isocrates. Fifth/fourth-century BC Athenian orator, philosopher and rhetorician.

Isthmian games. One of the Panhellenic athletic festivals of ancient Greece, named after the Isthmus of Corinth where they were held every other year.

Jason. Greek mythical hero, leader of an expedition to fetch the Golden Fleece; becomes involved *en route* with the sorceress Medea.

karteria. Greek word usually translated 'patience' or 'endurance', one of the characteristic Cynic virtues.

Kythera. Greek island off the southern coast of the Peloponnese.

Laertes. Father of Odysseus, the Greek hero of epic.

Lais. Name of two famous Greek courtesans (fifth to fourth centuries BC), whom surviving sources seem frequently to confuse.

Lechaeum. Village about 5 km west of Corinth.

Lycinus. A native of one of the Greek colonies in Italy, he was exiled from his native city, but entered the service of Antigonus Gonatus and was entrusted with command of the Macedonian garrison at Megara *c.* 270 BC.

Lysander. Spartan general who defeated the Athenians at Aegospotami in 405 BC and, the following year, forced the Athenians to capitulate, bringing the Peloponnesian War to an end.

Lysias. Athenian orator of the fifth century BC.

Maeander. River in southwest Asia Minor, present-day Turkey.

Marathon. Village in Attica, site of the first battle of the Persian Wars (490 BC), in which the Athenian army defeated a much larger Persian force.

Megara. Ancient city in the district of Attica, 42 km west of Athens.

Meletus. See under **Anytus**.

Menedemus. Greek Cynic philosopher of the third century BC.

Menelaus. King of Sparta; the loss of his wife to Paris led to the ten-year Trojan War.

Menippus. Third-century BC Cynic philosopher and originator of a literary genre alternating passages of prose with poetry. His own efforts in this hybrid genre are lost, but many well-known examples by imitators survive. They include Petronius' *Satyricon*, Boethius' *Consolation of Philosophy*, and Martianus Capella's *Marriage of Philology and Mercury*.

Metrocles. Cynic philosopher (*fl. c.* 325 BC), converted by Crates to his school.

Minos. See under **Aeacus**.

Musonius. Stoic philosopher of the first century AD, teacher of Epictetus among others.

Mykonos. Greek island, part of the Cyclades.

Neanthes. Third-century BC polymath and prolific writer, author *inter alia* of a work entitled *Lives of Famous Men*.

Nestor. In the *Iliad*, leader of the Greek contingent from Pylos in the Trojan War, depicted as advanced in age and valued most for his wisdom and advice. With Zeus' help he sailed home safely after the war and lived out the balance of his life in peace, surrounded by many worthy sons and grandchildren.

Oenomaeus. Cynic philosopher of the second century BC, a native of Gadara in northern Palestine; author of a work attacking the reliability of oracles, long extracts of which are preserved in the writings of the Christian polemicist Eusebius of Caesarea.

Olympia. A sanctuary of Zeus in the Greek region of Elis; best known for hosting the quadrennial Olympic games.

Pan. The god of flocks and shepherds among the ancient Greeks; he is depicted with goat features from the waist down, of human aspect above except for horns and a billy-goat beard.

Pandora. The first woman according to Greek myth. She was in possession of a box which she opened out of curiosity, releasing all the evils afflicting mankind, leaving only the palliative power of hope behind.

Paris. Trojan prince who brought about the Trojan War by running off with Helen, wife of Menelaus, king of Sparta.

Parium. A coastal town on the Hellespont in northwest Anatolia, present-day Turkey.

Parnassus. Mountain in central Greece that towers above Delphi, north of the Gulf of Corinth.

parrhêsia. Candour or freedom of speech, a character trait for which the Cynics were notorious.

Patras. Peloponnesian city on the coast of the Corinthian Gulf.

Peiraeus. The port of Athens, situated on the east coast of the Saronic Gulf.

Pelopidae. Literally 'the ancestors of Pelops'. In Greek mythology, the extended family that ruled in Bronze Age Thebes, including Oedipus and his sons Eteocles and Polyneices, who were cursed by Oedipus, leading to a civil war over control of the city-state.

Peloponnese or **Peloponnesus.** Name of the large Greek peninsula west of the isthmus of Corinth.

Pelops. Legendary king of Pisa in Elis, after whom the Peloponnese supposedly derived its name. His father Tantalus butchered him and served him in a stew to the Olympian gods, in a test of the gods' omniscience. All passed the test and refrained from partaking of the dish except Demeter, who consumed Pelops' shoulder. Hermes gathered the remains and put them in a cauldron, restoring him to life and his former appearance. Demeter made amends by replacing the missing shoulder with one of ivory.

Penelope. Odysseus' wife, who remained faithful to him during his long absence first while fighting in the Trojan War, then while he wandered for ten years in his effort to reach his home in Ithaca.

Perdiccas III. Ruled Macedon from 368 to 359 BC; his successor was Philip II, father to Alexander the Great.

Peripatos or Peripatetic School. School of philosophy founded by Aristotle in Athens *c.* 335 BC.

Persaeus. Stoic philosopher of the third century BC, who secured a position of influence at the Macedonian court of Antigonus II Gonatas. He sought to undermine Bion of Borysthenes' philosophical career by waging an (unsuccessful) smear campaign against him, focusing especially on his humble origins (see section **99** §§46–7).

Perseus. Mythical founder of Mycenae and traditional ruler over most of Bronze Age Greece. He got the better of the Gorgons, daughters of Phorcys, including Medusa.

Phalaris. Sixth-century BC tyrant of Acragas (Agrigentum) in Sicily, described by Cicero as the 'cruellest of all the tyrants.' No circumstance connected with him is more notorious than the brazen bull in which he is said to have burnt alive his enemies.

Pheidias. Renowned fifth-century BC Greek sculptor.

Philemon. Fourth/third-century BC Athenian playwright of the New Comedy.

Philip II. King of Macedon from 359 BC until his assassination in 336 BC. It was he who launched the Macedonian strategy of expansion into northern and central Greece in campaigns in which his son Alexander took an active part and who, in turn, extended his father's imperial policies well beyond Greece.

Philiscus. Cynic philosopher from Aegina of the third century BC. Some ancient sources assign to Philiscus some, if not all, of the tragedies of Diogenes of Sinope, but this probably reflects confusion with Philiscus the tragic poet active in the fourth to third centuries BC.

Philoctetes. Soldier on the Greek side in the Trojan War. As a close companion to Heracles, he assisted in his suicide by erecting and igniting a pile on which Heracles immolated himself.

Philonides. Third-century BC Stoic philosopher, a student of Zeno of Citium, the founder of Stoicism.

Phoenix. A minor figure in Homer's *Iliad*, mentor to Achilles.

Phrygia. In antiquity, a kingdom in the west central part of Anatolia, in what is now modern-day Turkey.

Phryne. Famous Athenian courtesan of the fourth century BC.

Plethrium. The wrestling ground at Olympia.

Polycleitus. Eminent Greek sculptor in bronze of the fifth and early fourth century BC.

Polydeuces. Student of Herodes Atticus in the art of rhetoric (second century AD); Atticus was especially (perhaps romantically) attached to him, and after the youth's early death honoured him with lavish games, inscriptions and public monuments, besides continuing to reserve a place for him at table when he hosted dinner parties.

Polyxena. In Greek mythology, the youngest daughter of King Priam of Troy. After the Greek victory in the Trojan War, she was sacrificed at the behest of Achilles' ghost, who claimed that the winds demanded her death if the Greeks were ever to arrive home.

Poseidon. One of the twelve Olympian gods, associated especially with horses, earthquakes and the sea.

Priam. Mythical king of Troy in Homer's *Iliad*.

Prometheus. In Greek mythology, a demigod, son of the Titan Iapetus. A 'culture hero', he is credited with introducing man to the use of fire, writing, the domestication of animals, metallurgy and other civilized arts.

Propylaea. Monumental marble gateway, built in the fifth century BC, at the entrance to the Athenian acropolis.

Proteus. Figure in Greek mythology, distinguished by his power of assuming any shape at will.

Pythagoras. Greek philosopher of the fifth century BC.

Pythian. The Pythia was originally the female mouthpiece for Apollo's oracles at Delphi; 'Pythian' later came to connote Apollo generally in his sage and clairvoyant capacity.

Rhadamanthys. See under **Aeacus**.

Salamis. Island in the Saronic Gulf about 1 nautical mile (2 km) off the west coast of Peiraeus.

Sallustius. Praetorian prefect under the Emperor Julian, like him a pagan to whom Julian dedicated his fourth oration. Author of a Neoplatonic treatise, *On the Gods and the Cosmos*.

Sardanapalus. Seventh-century BC king of Assyria, by tradition the last of his dynasty. Notorious for a life of self-indulgence that contributed to his death and his empire's dissolution.

Socrates. Athenian philosopher (469–399 BC), who wrote nothing but whose confidence in man's innate powers of reason, as dramatized in the dialogues of Plato and other near contemporaries, had a profound effect on Greek philosophy for centuries after his death.

Solon. Athenian statesman and elegiac poet of the seventh to sixth centuries BC.

Sophocles. Fifth-century BC Athenian tragedian, author *inter alia* of *Antigone* and *Oedipus Rex*.

Sosicrates. Second-century BC Greek historical writer, who contributed to the tradition of *Diadochai*, that is, books chronicling the succession and pedigree of philosophers, their teachers and their own students in turn. His work in this genre is lost but is drawn on and expressly credited in Diogenes Laertius' *Lives of the Ancient Philosophers*.

spoudaiogeloion. Greek word literally meaning 'serious-funny', applied to the Cynic style of teaching, which frequently employed humour in the treatment of weighty topics.

Sunium or **Sounion**. A promontory located 69 km (43 miles) south of Athens, at the southernmost tip of the Attica peninsula.

Susa. One of the four capital cities of the Achaemenid Persian Empire founded by Cyrus the Great, located in the lower Zagros Mountains about 250 km (150 miles) east of the Tigris River.

Tantalus. A figure of Greek myth, punished, for reasons variously reported, in Hades by being placed in a lake whose waters receded whenever he tried to drink from it, with fruit trees overhead whose branches were always blown out of reach when he tried to pick from them, and threatened by a huge rock poised directly above him.

Taxiles. Hellenized version of the name of the ruler over the Punjab region at the time Alexander invaded India in 326 BC.

Telemachus. Only son of the legendary Greek hero Odysseus.

Telephus. A son of Heracles.

Termerus. A highwayman whose slaying is ascribed to either Heracles or Theseus depending on the source.

Theagenes. Minor Cynic philosopher, described by Lucian as Peregrinus Proteus' attendant and chief disciple.

Themistocles. Athenian politician and general (lived *c.* 524–459 BC), whose planning and strategy in his military capacity contributed most to victory in the Persian Wars.

Theodorus. Fourth/third-century BC philosopher of the Cyrenaic school (founded by Aristippus). He was known as Theodorus the Atheist, but the epithet may only mean that his writings challenged traditional Greek religion on certain points.

Theognis. Sixth-century BC Greek gnomic and elegiac poet.

Theophrastus. Lived *c.* 371–*c.* 287 BC; Aristotle's successor as head of the school he founded in Athens, the Peripatos.

Theopompus. Fourth-century BC Greek historical writer.

Thersites. Greek foot soldier in Homer's *Iliad*, represented as ugly, weak and insolent towards his superiors.

Theseus. Legendary Athenian hero, whose philanthropic exploits are modelled in large part on those of the Doric Heracles.

Thesmophorion. Temple in Athens dedicated to Demeter, accessible to women only.

Thessaly. Region of central Greece, bordering Macedonia on the north, Epirus on the west, and the Aegean Sea on the east.

Timocrates of Heraclea. Member of the Second Sophistic (*fl.* first century AD), similar to Dio Chrysostom and other representatives of the movement in wedding philosophy to rhetoric.

tribôn. Greek name for the rough mantle that was a traditional part of the Cynic attire.

tuphos. Literally 'smoke' or 'vapour', the typical Cynic term for vanity or self-indulgence.

Xanthippe. Wife of Socrates, a proverbial nag.

Xeniades. Master of Diogenes the Cynic in Corinth after Diogenes' ship was reportedly captured by pirates – probably fictional like the story of Diogenes' enslavement as a whole.

Xenocrates. Greek philosopher, scholar of the Platonic Academy from 339 to 314 BC.

Xenophon. Athenian polymath and prolific author of the fourth century BC, an associate of Socrates who commemorated his master's life in his *Memorabilia*.

Xerxes I. Persian king in the Achaemenid line, reigned 485–465 BC. He led an invasion of Greece in 480–479, the failure of which effectively put an end to Persian designs on Europe.

Notes

[Lucian], the Cynic

1. *It follows that the gods ... hardly anything at* all: Cf. 2 §104 for a close parallel.

Antisthenes

1. *The very mother of the Gods is Phrygian*: Cybele, otherwise known as Rhea.
2. *we don't bar bad men from participation*: The criticism applies particularly to Athenian democracy, where political office was assigned by lot.
3. *Cynosarges*: In Greek *Cynosarges* means 'white dog'.
4. *the city they afterwards built*: For a symbolic description of this 'city', compare section 84.
5. *But it's nearly always the same thing*: This line makes little sense in context, but no convincing suggestion for emending the text has been suggested.
6. *to Troy against his will*: When Helen was abducted, Menelaus called upon her other suitors to honour an oath to retrieve her, leading to the Trojan War. Odysseus tried to get out of the shared commitment by feigning insanity.
7. *more cowardly than one*: The 'one' in question is Odysseus himself.
8. *if ever there arises a poet*: The reference, of course, is to Homer and the *Iliad*.

Diogenes

1. *Argead*: The so-called Argead dynasty ruled Macedon from around 700 to 310 BC.

2. *gymnosophists*: The gymnosophists – literally, 'naked wise men' – are the Hindu rishis whom Onesicritus meets and describes in section 113.

3. *Isthmus*: the Corinthian district.

4. *Sicily*: Sicily was famous for its cuisine, but Diogenes is merely teasing Plato in suggesting that this was behind his several trips there; in reality he tried unsuccessfully to interest Dionysius I and Dionysius II (his son) – the tyrants of Syracuse – in the study of philosophy.

5. *ordered to remain standing*: The easier, presumably, for buyers to assess his physical condition.

6. *trained them to hunt*: Other favourable references to hunting are at sections 124 § 11, and 136 § 187.

7. *Even fair-haired Niobe . . . in the flower of youth*: Homer, *Il.* 24. 602–4.

8. *the 113ᵗʰ Olympiad*: 324–321 BC. That Diogenes and Alexander died on the same day, as little as they ostensibly had in common during their lives, hints at some deeper, spiritual brotherhood, no doubt related to the several accounts of their meeting in Corinth that usually end with Alexander expressing the wish that if he were not Alexander, he would like to be Diogenes. The coincidence of dates is a transparent invention to lend colour to this (itself rather doubtful) moral bond.

9. *Not to have to cook meat*: The tradition that Diogenes brought about his own death by eating a raw octopus – which even some later Cynics condemned as unnatural (it did, after all, kill him) – is discussed (and defended) at length by Julian in section 136 below.

10. *Ichthyas*: A proper name.

11. *The only genuine country . . .*: Similar cosmopolitan sentiments can be found in sections 1 §15, 55 and 56.

12. *no use for military arms in his republic*: When men's needs were reduced to essentials, and property (and family) were shared among the citizen body, the usual motives to war were eliminated, so naturally the instruments of war could serve no useful purpose. Compare section 84.

13. *Atreus, Oedipus and Philiscus*: Judging from their titles, we infer that in these plays cannibalism and incest featured as prominent themes.

14. *Athens' civic centre*: The civic centre is the *agora*, a sacred space on account of the many shrines situated there.

15. *the functions of Demeter and Aphrodite alike*: I.e., eating and engaging in sexual behaviour.

16. *Plato in the* Republic: The specific reference is *Rep.* 375e.

17. *Metroön*: hall of public records.

18. *A man without a home or country . . . living hand to mouth*: Evidently a quote from an unknown tragedy; compare sections 135 §45 and 146 §195.

19. *Harmodius and Aristogeiton*: Youths who assassinated the Athenian tyrant Hipparchus. Bronze statues of the pair were on display in Athens' pottery quarter.

20. *alleviate hunger pains so easily*: For this most shocking aspect of Diogenes' public behaviour, compare sections 34, 37, 64, 123 §17 and 134; but contrast section 71 below (sceptical).

21. *Euclides' school*: Euclid (or Eucleides) of Megara, a Greek Socratic philosopher who lived around 400 BC and founded the Megarian school of philosophy, best known for its progress in logic.

22. *Perdiccas*: Perdiccas III, king of Macedonia from 368 to 359 BC.

23. *Callisthenes*: Callisthenes of Olynthus, *c.* 360–328 BC: a Greek historian. He was the great-nephew of Aristotle by his sister Arimneste. They first met when Aristotle tutored Alexander the Great. Through his great-uncle's influence, he was later appointed a professional historian to attend Alexander on his Asiatic expedition and memorialize his achievements.

24. *Against the poets*: Perhaps 'poets' (*poiêtas*) should be emended to 'ruffians' (*ponêrous*).

25. *no place where one could spit*: Virtually the same anecdote recurs in section 60.

Crates and Hipparchia

1. *113ᵗʰ Olympiad*: 328–324 BC.

2. *Antisthenes*: Not Antisthenes the nominal founder of Cynicism but an historian from Rhodes who lived *c.* 200 BC.

3. *Telephus*: Telephus was the son of Heracles, like his father of noble birth and character. In Euripides' name play he disguises himself as a vagrant and visits Clytemnestra, hoping to excite her

sympathy and elicit her help. The motif recalls the story that Odysseus pretended to be a homeless beggar when he returned to Ithaca. Why his character impressed Crates to the extent of taking up the Cynic satchel and mantle we can only guess. Perhaps it was the nobility of his character and background that survived the (provisional) loss of his name, wealth and social standing, suggestive of a kind of moral aristocracy that not only survived such misfortune but tested and enhanced it insofar as Telephus bore his circumstances bravely. Crates found a reflex in the Cynic movement of his own day and enlisted.

4. *I know a fair city, Pera by name*: The lines are modelled on a passage in Homer's *Odyssey* describing the island of Crete. They are a good example of seriocomic literary style favoured by Cynics. *Pera* in Greek is the name for the Cynic satchel. So Crates is not describing a place, but, under the pretence of such a description, in reality is giving an account of the Cynic life; cf. section 136 §§ 186–187. Life on Pera is austere. But the needs of its inhabitants (i.e., the Cynics), are few because they have learned to make do with the bare essentials; and a great advantage to this self-discipline is that the usual motives to war with one's neighbours are eliminated. In his *Republic* Diogenes also claimed that there was no place for the instruments of war in a state organized on Cynic principles; compare section 33.

5. '*Pay the cook a hundred pounds . . .*' A satire, of course, on conventional society's inverted values.

6. *Zeno*: The founder of Stoicism.

7. *Hipparchia*: Crates' wife. Most Cynics abstained from marriage, as they did from bourgeois life in general; for the reason see section 135 §76 *infra*, where Cebes' special case is also cited and rationalized. Hipparchia, for her part, was admitted into the Cynic fold on equal terms with men, a privilege rarely extended to women by other ancient schools of philosophy – one more proof of Cynic disdain for empty convention.

Bion

1. *Who among men are you . . . your parents?*: Homer, *Odyssey* 19. 325.

2. *Persaeus and Philonides*: Persaeus was a Stoic philosopher; Philonides is otherwise unknown.

3. *If your wife is ugly . . . sharing*: The jest is also credited to Antisthenes at section 3 §4.

4. *Danaids*: In Greek mythology, the Danaids, in punishment for having killed their husbands, were condemned to the never-ending task of trying to carry water in leaky jars.

5. *Misers of this sort ... good it does them*: Compare section 128 §§33 seq.

6. *Because it humbles a man ...*: Euripides, *Hippolytus* 424.

7. *O gentle Archytas ...*: A parody of Homer, *Il.* 3. 182–3.

8. *three classes of student ... silver and bronze*: Bion draws on the myth of the three races of man outlined in Hesiod, *Works and Days*, 109–201.

9. *a bad or foolish fellow*: Homer, *Od.* 6. 187.

10. *gods grant you happiness*: Homer, *Od.* 24. 402.

Onesicritus

1. *Alexander was well advised to concentrate his forces in the center of his empire*: A clear warning against carrying the campaign into India on the pretext that Alexander would stretch his forces too thin and incur the risk of losing control of the lands he had conquered in his progress east.

2. *Once fountains yielded an abundance of water, milk – even honey, wine and olive oil*: In assigning to the gymnosophists belief in a distant golden age, very much like the Cynics' own belief in such a blessed age, Onesicritus is probably exercising his wonted liberties as an historian, here in repeating and thereby lending support to the analogous Cynic myth.

3. *Taxiles*: Taxiles (fourth century BC) was the Greek chronicler's name for the prince who ruled over the Punjab region of India at the time of Alexander's expedition.

4. *abstention from meat*: At the time of Alexander's expedition most of India nominally adhered to Buddhist principles, which forbade the killing and eating of animals.

5. *remains perfectly still until he dies*: Compare section 65.

Demetrius

1. *every seventh year marks a new stage in a human life*: The periodization of human life into seven-year intervals, each with its own distinctive strengths and weaknesses, was given definitive expression in Solon's elegiac poem tracing the progress of a

person who proceeds through ten stages to attain the age of seventy.

2. *their different destinies*: The putative mystery stems from belief in the tenets of astrology.

3. *corrected*: Reading *corrigi* for *corripi*.

4. *agents of such slaughter*: That the very inaccessibility of precious ores is proof that nature did not intend us to mine them is also argued at section 1 §§8, 15; and again at section 123 §60.

5. *like me he does not profess to know virtue but is conscious of lacking it*: Likening himself to Demetrius may be intended to defend Seneca himself against the charge he reports in connection with Demetrius, since Seneca professed to be a follower of Stoicism, with its low estimate of material goods, while personally possessed of fabulous wealth.

Dio Chrysostom

1. *which accounts for its name:* The point depends on the verbal similarity between Attike, the peninsula where Athens is located, and *aktê*, the Greek word for beach.

2. *Craneum*: A cypress grove outside Corinth where a gymnasium was located.

3. *the latter city's proportions*: According to Herodotus, the walls of Babylon were some forty miles in diameter.

4. *half in jest*: An illustration of characteristic Cynic *spoudaiogeloion*: humour in the service of a serious point.

5. *Diogenes was not neglectful of his body*: Compare section 135 §86.

6. *most piquant and satisfying sauce*: Compare section 126 §7.

7. *the sons of Asclepius*: I.e., professional doctors.

8. *Prometheus*: Prometheus was a mythical 'culture hero' credited with the discovery of fire and other innovations associated with the advance of civilization. In Cynic sources he often comes across less like a hero and more like a male Pandora, responsible for alienating man from nature and for many of his subsequent ills; compare §30 below.

9. *their devotion to self-interest brought them to dreadful ends*: Consistent with his 'softer' Cynicism, Julian credits Diogenes with a more tolerant and nuanced attitude towards technological progress and cultural gains at section 136 §183.

10. *they regularly show up in autumn*: In Greece, as in other places

with a Mediterranean climate, planting is done in the autumn, when the rains resume. Aristotle describes the migration of cranes in *The History of Animals*, adding an account of their fights with Pygmies as they wintered near the source of the Nile.

11. *the golden plane tree*: Xerxes found near the Maeander river a plane tree so splendid that he decorated it with golden ornaments and placed it under the care of one of his Immortals (a corps of elite warriors).

12. *armed men*: Reading ἐνόπλους for ἀνόπλους.

13. *the horse in the fable*: Zenobius gives the proverb in full: 'To the ageing horse assign the easier courses.'

14. *Spartan hounds*: Fast and aggressive hunting dogs, Diogenes refines on the standard comparison of a Cynic to a dog.

15. *purify the community*: A reference to the ritual of purification performed at Athens and other Greek cities, involving a 'scape-goat' (Greek *pharmakon*: either human or animal), charged with the collective sins of the community and ceremonially cast out of the city.

16. *and not for the benefit of a sprig of parsley . . . or pine*: Victors at the Isthmian and Nemean games were crowned with parsley, Olympic victors were honoured with sprigs of wild olive, while at the Isthmus winners were crowned with pine.

17. *Battle was now joined fiercely . . . broadswords double-edged*: Homer, *Iliad* 15. 696, 711–12.

18. *Heracles' labours either*: Heracles is featured at length here as a (proto-)Cynic hero, but allusions to his iconic status among historical Cynics can also be found at sections 1 §13, 3 §§2, 16–17, 10, 31, 124 §27 and 136 §187.

19. *meting out justice to good and bad alike*: Heracles' labours are featured allegorically, along Cynic lines, to elaborate on the moral dimension of his heroism.

20. *his liver would swell*: Here, liver is the seat of emotion; we would say 'heart' or '(swollen) head'.

Teles

1. *just as the Greeks did with Ajax*: Compare sections 5 and 6 for a rhetorical setting of the personal calamity that beset Ajax and set the Greeks to gloating. Teles, however, probably has in mind the treatment of the myth in Sophocles' *Ajax*, especially at ll. 955

seq., where the *Schadenfreude* of certain Greek chieftains – Odysseus of course prominent among them – is described.

2. *No one else brought this upon me ... responsible*: Source unknown.

3. *Look at sailors*: The same analogy is developed at section 131 §53.

4. *if one of us succumbed to sleep ...*: There appears to be a gap here following the text.

5. *On Exile*: Many philosophical treatments of exile survive from antiquity, arguing in the main that it is not the misfortune it is popularly supposed to be. Brief allusions to the same view are found at sections 7 §21, 86, 133 §8 and 135 §22, where Cynic cosmopolitanism is adduced in support of this reassuring position.

6. *Stilpo*: A member of the Megarian school of philosophy, originally a pupil of Socrates, later the teacher of Zeno the Stoic for a time.

7. *Phoenix*: A minor figure in Homeric epic: he was cursed and banished by his father Amyntor, settled in Thessaly, where he became tutor to Achilles (Peleus' son) and accompanied Achilles to Troy.

8. *To Peleus I came ... large retinue*: Homer, *Iliad* 9. 479 seq.

9. *Themistocles*: An Athenian general prominent in the Persian Wars. He was exiled from Athens in 472 BC, and eventually settled at the Persian court.

10. *Lycinus*: An Italian Greek who was exiled from his native city and entered the service of Antigonus Gonatas, who appointed him to command the garrison at Megara sometime around 270 BC.

11. *Hippomedon*: Hippomedon was forced to leave Sparta along with his father, the Spartan king Agesilaus, in 241 BC.

12. *Chremonides*: Chremonides and his brother Glaucus played leading roles in the Greek revolt against Antigonus and then must have sought the protection of Ptolemy II (308–246 BC), who gave them positions of honour in his regime. The so-called Chremonidean War, named after him, in which Ptolemy allied himself with Athens and Sparta against Antigonus, began in 267 and ended in 261 with Antigonus' defeat of Athens.

13. *Thesmophorion*: The Thesmophorion was a temple of Demeter that only women were permitted to enter; the temple of Ares was only accessible to men.

14. *Kythera, Mykonos or Belbina*: Small islands of little importance politically or culturally.

15. *metic*: A metic was a resident alien in Athens with limited civic rights.

16. *You, metic . . . enslaved*: From a lost tragedy, possibly Euripides' *Cadmus*.

17. *Bury me, mother . . . ruling house to ruin*: Euripides, *Phoenissae* 1447 seq.

18. *But to lie beneath a mound . . . thing*: A verse from an unknown tragedy.

19. *Close my eyes . . . mother*: Euripides, *Phoenissae* 1451.

20. *other races*: The reference is clearly to the Egyptians: cf. Herodotus 2. 136. 2.

21. *IVA – A Comparison of Poverty and Wealth*: This and the following discourse may originally have been one but by chance have been transmitted separately.

22. *Wallowing in filth*: Homer, *Odyssey* 4. 716 seq.

23. *dark clouds and out of reach*: Homer, *Odyssey* 11. 591 seq.

24. *superstitious as well*: Superstitious because he fears arbitrary loss of his wealth; see below, §42.

25. *Corrupt men are never content*: Theognis 109.

26. *Youth is always dear to me . . . Mount Aetna*: Euripides, *Heracles Furens* 637 seq.

27. *Indeed, it is no small thing . . . subservience*: Text and translation of the last sentence are uncertain.

28. *IVB – A Comparison of Poverty and Wealth*: For the title and numeration of this discourse, see note at the beginning of the section on Teles.

29. *Many more people . . . having too little*: Theognis 605.

30. *his reputation would not suffer for associating with philosophers*: Popular prejudice against philosophers is vividly documented in Aristophanes' *Clouds*. Despite the efforts of Plato and Aristotle to reform its reputation, well-born Greeks and Romans were suspicious of philosophy as foreign, subversive and declassé; Cynicism, because of its nonconformism, met with the greatest resistance in certain quarters.

31. *the present war*: Presumably the Chremonidean War, 265–261 BC.

32. *Your anguish is for yourselves alone . . . entire city*: Apparently quoting from memory, Teles condenses lines 62–64 of the *Oedipus Rex* into two.

33. *Aristides*: Aristides 'the Just' commanded the Athenians at Marathon, then served Athens as a public official.

34. *But in the city of Argos . . . honour*: Euripides, *Suppliants* 873, slightly altered.

35. *My youth was dear to me . . . Mt. Aetna*: Euripides, *Hercules Furens*, 637–8; also cited at section 128 §§153–4.

36. *resilient in circumstances good or bad*: An hexameter verse of unknown provenance.
37. *With an old slave woman . . . food and drink*: Homer, *Odyssey* 1. 191–2.
38. *His humble bed strewn with fallen leaves*: Homer, *Odyssey* 1. 194.
39. *The good does not lie . . . repletion*: Euripides, *Suppliants* 865–6.
40. *Self-indulgence . . . food*: From an unknown play.
41. *But you . . . stain your cheek*: From a lost tragedy.
42. *our own women*: Presumably Teles means the women of his home town, Megara.
43. *But in the face of such misfortune*: Text uncertain.
44. *To quote Socrates . . . the same uncertainty*: The text is uncertain, the translation partly conjectural.

Lucian

1. *He slept under the stars . . . places previously inaccessible*: All Cynic traits, of course, the connection confirmed by comparison with Heracles, the legendary Cynic paradigm.
2. *He cared enough to reconcile feuding relatives . . . wives*: Compare section 83 §22.
3. *Persuasion seemed to live upon his lips*: Eupolis, fr. 94. 5 Kock.
4. *the Eleusinian Mysteries*: A secret cult centred on Demeter. Eleusis was a town located just outside Athens. Diogenes similarly exempted himself from participation in their rites (DL 6. 39).
5. *I did not imagine she needed anything from me*: Compare sections 1 §12 and 2 §104.
6. *the following dilemma*: I.e., either way he would make known their content, which was reason enough for him to exempt himself, since the Mysteries were supposed to be secret (the word *mystery* comes from the Greek word meaning 'to keep silent'.) That the Mysteries contained obscene elements, after the manner of a fertility cult, is alleged by early Christian critics.
7. *a sampling of his witty and well-timed remarks*: Anecdotes – *chreiai* – follow, through §62.
8. *judged philosophers by their beard*: To 'judge a philosopher by his beard' means to recognize them by superficial attributes, like the characteristic beard or, in this case, their ostensive membership in an established school, which Demonax ironically disclaims. Favorinus was a eunuch and therefore beardless.
9. *ring*: 'Ring' in the second instance is a euphemism for 'anus'.

10. *Arcesilaus*: The name evokes *arktos*, the Greek word for 'bear'.

11. *the upside-downers*: The Antipodeans.

12. *Herodes Atticus*: Herodes Atticus of Athens (*c.* 101–177 BC) was the most celebrated sophist of his age.

13. *Apollonius*: A Stoic philosopher who tutored Marcus Aurelius. Demonax makes a double joke, on the coincidence of his name with that of Apollonius Rhodius, author of the *Argonautica* that describes Jason's quest for the Golden Fleece; and Apollonius the philosopher's analogous pursuit of wealth.

14. *the immortality of the soul*: Demonax presumably refers to the ultimate indestructibility of matter; most ancients believed that the soul was composed of matter, air (or breath: Greek *pneuma*).

15. *we don't have a single soul*: Demonax must refer to Plato's belief in a tripartite soul, only one part of which was intelligent.

16. *Regilla and Polydeuces*: Regilla was Herodes' wife; Polydeuces was his favourite. In honour of their memory, after their deaths Herodes continued to reserve places for them at dinners that he put on.

17. *the Spartan he saw beating his slave*: Spartan youths had to endure initiation rites such as whipping en route to full citizenship.

18. *Danaë . . . Acrisius' daughter*: The Danaë of myth was daughter to Acrisius, whose name in Greek means 'lawless'.

19. *Kynegeiros*: An Athenian who lost an arm at the Battle of Marathon.

20. *one of your own daughters*: The point of the rejoinder is that Epictetus was unmarried and childless.

21. *the Altar of Pity*: A monument located in the Athenian agora.

22. *Hero and coward both meet the same end*: Homer, *Iliad* 9. 320.

23. *two noblest masterpieces that the world has seen*: The reference is to the giant chryselephantine cult statue of Zeus created by Pheidias and installed inside Zeus' temple at Olympia.

24. *another man*: All indications are that this unnamed man who rebuts Theagenes' extravagant defence of Peregrinus is to be identified with Lucian himself.

25. *radish had been thrust up his anus*: A standard penalty for adulterers.

26. *eating food . . . forbidden to them*: Probably meat sacrificed to 'idols', that is, to pagan gods. Considering how opportunistic and superficial his allegiance was to different religions and philosophies of his day (did his nickname 'Proteus' reflect this doctrinal flexibility?), it is not surprising that he would be caught on at least one occasion violating this taboo.

27. *took part in other bizarre displays*: Compare sections 3§37, 64, 123 §§16–20 and 126 §§10–11).

28. *one person in particular*: The object of Peregrinus' ill-judged attack was the millionaire benefactor and philhellene Herodes Atticus.

29. *when the games were next held*: AD 165.

30. *Philoctetes*: Philoctetes assisted Heracles in his suicide by igniting the pyre.

31. *Phalaris*: Phalaris, tyrant of Acragas in Sicily, roasted his enemies inside a bronze bull placed over a flame.

32. *the tragedy has it*: The reference is presumably to Sophocles' *Trachiniae*.

33. *like the Brahmans*: Or gymnosophists, as they are referred to in Onesicritus; compare section 114 §65.

34. *from their chosen position*: Compare section 114 §65.

35. *But Nestor caught the sound of the uproar*: Homer, *Iliad* 14. 1.

36. *Plethrium*: The wrestling ground at Olympia; the Hellanodicae were the games' chief judges.

37. *Portico of Echoes*: A stoa in the Olympian complex.

38. *Aeacus*: Aeacus, along with Minos and Rhadamanthys, was one of the three judges in Hades.

Epictetus

1. *his honour to protect him*: Epictetus bowdlerizes traditional Cynicism by replacing *anaideia* (shamelessness), a characteristic Cynic feature, with its antithesis *aidôs*, 'dignity', or – as it's translated here – 'honour'.

2. *he is also a spy*: For the comparison of the Cynic to a spy, compare sections 6 §8, 65 and §38 below.

3. *dragged before Philip*: Philip II of Macedon established Macedonian control over half of Greece as a result of his victory in the battle of Chaeronea in 338 BC; for Diogenes' defiant attitude towards the new ruler, see section 65.

4. *Myron and Ophellius*: Myron and Ophellius were athletes or gladiators who were contemporary with Epictetus and, like Croesus, presumably came to a bad end. Reference to the plight of 'the rich of today' may allude to the practice of the first emperors of charging prominent citizens with treason (*maiestas*), with the covert goal of appropriating their assets for the imperial coffers. These paradoxical unfortunates may overlap with the

statesmen who drew unwelcome attention to themselves by holding more than a single consulship.

5. *Sardanapalus*: Sardanapalus was the last king of Assyria, and proverbial for luxury.

6. *He pulled many a hair ... my chest*: The quotes relating to Agamemnon are from the *Iliad* 10. 15, 91, and 94–5.

7. *You are rich in gold and bronze*: Homer, *Iliad* 18. 289.

8. *in the presence of their lord and master*: Compare sections 24 to 26.

9. *the broad shoulder ... bare*: A Cynic characteristically wore his signature rough mantle (the *tribôn*) with one shoulder exposed; this helps, for instance, to identify Diogenes in Raphael's painting, *The School of Athens*. Sarcastic reference to 'large jaws' evokes the popular reputation of the Cynic as a parasitic glutton, a malicious parody of his true nature for which the writers of comedy were no doubt responsible.

10. *proconsul at once*: The proconsul functioned as a judge in the provinces of the Roman Empire.

11. *the Great King*: The common designation for the king of the Persian empire, proverbially the most fortunate person on earth; but compare section 123 §35 for Diogenes' self-comparison with the Great King to the latter's detriment.

12. *sceptre*: The Cynic's signature staff is here featured as a royal sceptre, in line with the paradoxical presentation of the Cynic as the true king; compare §34 above. At the same time he is 'minister' to Zeus, who sent him to rule among men; compare §69 below.

13. *sponging*: As the Cynic was lampooned in ancient comedy as a parasite, so Epictetus represents parasitism as antithetical to the Cynic ideal of independence.

14. *Cynic not be occupied with domestic duties*: Epictetus' equivocation concerning the compatibility of Cynicism with marriage is refracted through conflicting sources; compare section 3 §11 with 78.

15. *the king who has the people ... many concerns*: Homer, *Iliad* 2. 25.

16. *Cynics from the womb*: That is, they are not yet ready to survive on the Cynic's limited regimen; they still have many material needs.

17. *Crates had a wife*: On the singular *kynogamia* (Cynic marriage) that Crates contracted with Hipparchia, compare section 89.

18. *Epaminondas ... Homer*: Epaminondas was a fourth-century

BC Theban general who scored several notable victories over Sparta. Priam, Danaus and Aeolus are figures from the Greek epic cycle, which is why they are here contrasted with Homer, their chronicler. Like Priam, Danaus and Aeolus were mythical kings credited with epic-sized families; Homer, according to tradition, lacked both home and family.

19. *these dogs who beg at table and hang about the gate*: Homer, *Iliad* 22. 69; the word 'Cynic', of course, comes from the Greek word for dog.

20. *The Cynic shouldn't be so filthy that he drives people away*: Another revisionist aspect of Epictetus' presentation of the Cynic, this time presenting squalor as alien to his persona.

21. *Diogenes, still half-asleep, responded . . . many concerns*: Homer, *Iliad* 2. 24–5; cf. §72 above. Diogenes' ability to give the next line of Homer's text and promptly complete Alexander's thought demonstrates that he was not 'sleeping the night away', in fact, but even when ostensibly sleeping was in reality half-awake – as Homer said a leader of men ought to be.

22. *What sleep he gets only leaves him purer than when he first lay down*: That is, his reason does not desert him even when asleep, so that, unlike the regular run of people, he is not prey to indecent dreams.

23. *Argus*: Argus was a mythical creature endowed with a hundred eyes.

24. *what Hector said to Andromache*: Homer, *Iliad* 6. 490 seq., partly paraphrased. The number of Homeric citations in this discourse is remarkable and indirectly reflects the Cynics' facility in quoting Homer promptly and to the point.

Julian

1. *the rivers are running backwards*: Euripides, *Medea* 410.

2. *the sun god*: As part of his programme of religious reformation, Julian promoted worship of the sun. At the beginning of his *Oration to the Lord Sun* he declares himself a votary of the solar cult (*To the Sun*, §219).

3. *Hippocleides*: From a story in Herodotus (6. 129), in which Hippocleides loses his chance at a highly advantageous marriage after getting drunk and making a public spectacle of himself.

4. *Fire is the fiery breath . . . incorporeal reason*: Principles of Stoic physics.

5. *The gods know all things*: Homer, *Odyssey* 4. 379.

6. *Zeus was older and wiser*: Homer, *Iliad* 13. 355.

7. *cleave the open sea*: Of Nestor, Homer, *Odyssey* 3.174.

8. *images of the gods*: Plato, *Symposium* 215.

9. *Great learning . . . does not teach understanding*: Julian quotes Heraclitus, fr. 40 DK.

10. *among gods and men equally*: Plato, *Laws* 730b.

11. *There is no composition by Plato . . . to Socrates*: Plato, Second Letter 314c (slightly misquoted).

12. *that foolish act*: That is, eating raw octopus. See Homer, *Iliad* 5. 304.

13. *the oracle*: I.e., that he was the wisest man. Socrates expected to prove the oracle wrong by interviewing every class of contemporary, but discovered that they did not know as much as they thought they did, whereas he, at least, was aware of his ignorance – and wiser, at least, on that account.

14. *Pythagoras . . . said so*: 'Pythagoras said so' or 'He himself (i.e., Pythagoras) said so' was a formula in Pythagorean circles meant to settle questions out of hand.

15. *a small library of books*: The best-known books that survive from Julian's age advocating vegetarianism are both by the Neoplatonic philosopher Porphyry (AD 234–c. 305): *On Abstinence* and *On the Impropriety of Killing Living Beings for Food*.

16. *along with fish and birds and whatever else is at hand*: Homer, *Odyssey* 12. 331.

17. *the words of the Galilaeans*: Genesis 9:3. Note that by the time of Julian the Tanakh was considered part of Christian scripture.

18. *Plato attributes souls to plants as well*: *Timaeus* 77b.

19. *the myth in* Protagoras *says*: Plato, *Protagoras* 321a–b.

20. *without a home . . . single slave of his own*: Compare section 44.

21. *visit great pains upon*: Homer, *Iliad* 5. 766.

22. *I swear by . . . the secret of the tetrad*: A Pythagorean oath. The tetrad is the first four numerals or, more precisely, their sum (i.e., 10).

23. *if you cannot starve yourself, then hang yourself*: Compare section 51.

24. *worshipped them with his whole soul . . . through his thoughts*: Generally speaking, the Cynics seemed to have worshipped the gods in their own way, which did not involve much participation in popular ritual: compare sections 1 §12, 2 §104 and 133 §1.

25. *Let me quote you a few lines . . . unsupported*: What follows is a parody of Solon, fr. 13 West.

26. *Plutarch . . . has written a life of Crates*: The work is lost.
27. *Crates . . . gave away his money to his native city*: Compare sections 81–83.
28. *pretence*: Greek *tuphos*.
29. *Diogenes' high-mindedness*: Compare sections 11–13.
30. *It's a woman's sorry life you admire and want . . .*: A small section of the text following these lines is corrupt and has been omitted from the translation.
31. *How much takes place . . . period of time*: From the comic poet Eupolis, Kock 356.
32. *Be strong, my heart . . . worse than this*: Homer, *Od.* 20. 18.
33. *potentiality*: The term derives from Aristotle's *Metaphysics*; cf. 1045 b19, etc.
34. *If Antisthenes the Socratic . . . misguide you*: Julian may include the speeches he composed for Ajax and Odysseus among the myths Antisthenes composed.
35. *This is [Oenomaus'] mission*: Long extracts from Oenomaus' attack on oracles are quoted by Eusebius; his criticisms, coming from a pagan, provided potent ammunition for early Christian polemicists.
36. *the pit*: The pit in Athens served as a jail and form of punishment.
37. *pirates who roam the deep . . .lives*: Homer, *Odyssey* 3. 73.
38. *the horrors of Magnesia*: A proverbial phrase for something disgusting or horrific.
39. *Termerus*: A savage robber whom Theseus killed.
40. *satyr play*: Satyr plays are cited for their bawdy element. By 'comedy' Julian must mean the Old Comedy of Aristophanes with its sexual themes and frequent profanity; few examples of ancient mime survive but the mimes of Herondas are notable for their indecent subject matter and salty humour.
41. *Alexander who had smashed the Persian empire*: As discussed in the Introduction, if, according to tradition, Alexander and Diogenes met in Corinth, the meeting would have predated Alexander's conquest of Persia, and this anachronism throws doubt on the whole tradition of their meeting.
42. *the god*: Zeus, patron god of the Olympic games.
43. *if we can credit Dio*: Dio Chrysostom, *Or.* 4. 12.
44. *you need a trip to Anticyra*: A city in Phocis. Hellebore, supposed to be a cure for madness, grew there in profusion – hence the proverb.
45. *Emperor Constantius*: Third son of Constantine the Great,

Constantius became emperor of the East in 337. In 355, he promoted Julian to the rank of Caesar of the Gauls. But Julian rose up against him in Paris in 361 and Constantius met his death in the expedition that he led to put the rebel down.

46. *the proverb 'Grape ripens near grape'*: Referring to the habit of mindlessly accepting whatever views one happens to overhear.

47. *left to God to decide their inherent worth*: God here is equated with nature.

48. *Phryne, Lais*: The names of prostitutes.

49. *Wandering blind in the valley of confusion*: Empedocles fr. 388 DK.

50. *to quote Heraclitus, as 'more disposable than dirt'*: DK 96.

51. *function as a tool*: A tool, that is, of the soul. Although the whole passage demonstrates a Platonic contempt for the body, it also forbids suicide insofar as the soul needs the body to put its designs into effect. So the body has real, if subordinate value and should not be wholly despised (or destroyed).

Penguin Classics

ELECTRA AND OTHER PLAYS
SOPHOCLES

Ajax/Electra/Women of Trachis/Philoctetes

> 'Now that he is dead,
> I turn to you; will you be brave enough
> To help me kill the man who killed our father?'

Sophocles' innovative plays transformed Greek myths into dramas featuring complex human characters, through which he explored profound moral issues. *Electra* portrays the grief of a young woman for her father Agamemnon, who has been killed by her mother's lover. Aeschylus and Euripides also dramatized this story, but the objectivity and humanity of Sophocles' version provided a new perspective. Depicting the fall of a great hero, *Ajax* examines the enigma of power and weakness combined in one being, while the *Women of Trachis* portrays the tragic love and error of Heracles' deserted wife Deianeira, and *Philoctetes* deals with the conflict between physical force and moral strength.

E. F. Watling's vivid translation is accompanied by an introduction in which he discusses Sophocles' use of a third actor to create new dramatic situations and compares the different treatments of the Electra myth by the three great tragic poets of classical Athens.

Translated with an introduction by E. F. Watling

PENGUIN CLASSICS

THE GREEK SOPHISTS

'In the case of wisdom, those who sell it to anyone who wants it are called sophists'

By mid-fifth century BC, Athens was governed by democratic rule and power turned upon the ability of the individual to command the attention of the other citizens, and to sway the crowds of the assembly. It was the Sophists who understood the art of rhetoric and the importance of being able to transform effective reasoning into persuasive public speaking. Their inquiries – into the gods, the origins of religion and whether virtue can be taught – laid the groundwork for the next generation of thinkers such as Plato and Aristotle.

Each chapter of *The Greek Sophists* is based around the work of one character: Gorgias, Prodicus, Protagoras and Antiphon among others, and a linking commentary, chronological table and bibliography are provided for each one. In his introduction, John Dillon discusses the historical background and the sources of the text.

Translated by John Dillon and Tania Gergel with an introduction by John Dillon

PENGUIN CLASSICS

THE ODYSSEY
HOMER

'I long to reach my home and see the day of my return. It is my never-failing wish'

The epic tale of Odysseus and his ten-year journey home after the Trojan War forms one of the earliest and greatest works of Western literature. Confronted by natural and supernatural threats – shipwrecks, battles, monsters and the implacable enmity of the sea-god Poseidon – Odysseus must test his bravery and native cunning to the full if he is to reach his homeland safely and overcome the obstacles that, even there, await him.

E. V. Rieu's translation of *The Odyssey* was the very first Penguin Classic to be published, and has itself achieved classic status. For this edition, his text has been sensitively revised and a new introduction added to complement E. V. Rieu's original introduction.

'One of the world's most vital tales. *The Odyssey* remains central to literature' Malcolm Bradbury.

Translated by E. V. Rieu

Revised translation by D. C. H. Rieu, with an introduction by Peter Jones

---

PENGUIN CLASSICS

THE ILIAD
HOMER

> 'Look at me. I am the son of a great man. A goddess was my mother.
> Yet death and inexorable destiny are waiting for me'

One of the foremost achievements in Western literature, Homer's *Iliad* tells the story of the darkest episode in the Trojan War. At its centre is Achilles, the greatest warrior-champion of the Greeks, and his refusal to fight after being humiliated by his leader Agamemnon. But when the Trojan Hector kills Achilles' close friend Patroclus, he storms back into battle to take revenge – although knowing this will ensure his own early death. Interwoven with this tragic sequence of events are powerfully moving descriptions of the ebb and flow of battle, of the domestic world inside Troy's besieged city of Ilium, and of the conflicts between the gods on Olympus as they argue over the fate of mortals.

E. V. Rieu's acclaimed translation of Homer's *Iliad* was one of the first titles published in Penguin Classics, and now has classic status itself. For this edition, Rieu's text has been revised, and a new introduction and notes by Peter Jones complement the original introduction.

Translated by E. V. Rieu

Revised and updated by Peter Jones with D. C. H. Rieu

Edited with an introduction and notes by Peter Jones

PENGUIN CLASSICS

THE RISE OF THE ROMAN EMPIRE
POLYBIUS

> 'If history is deprived of the truth,
> we are left with nothing but an idle, unprofitable tale'

In writing his account of the relentless growth of the Roman Empire, the Greek statesman Polybius (*c*. 200–118 BC) set out to help his fellow-countrymen understand how their world came to be dominated by Rome. Opening with the Punic War in 264 BC, he vividly records the critical stages of Roman expansion: its campaigns throughout the Mediterranean, the temporary setbacks inflicted by Hannibal and the final destruction of Carthage in 146 BC. An active participant in contemporary politics, as well as a friend of many prominent Roman citizens, Polybius was able to draw on a range of eyewitness accounts and on his own experiences of many of the central events, giving his work immediacy and authority.

Ian Scott-Kilvert's translation fully preserves the clarity of Polybius' narrative. This substantial selection of the surviving volumes is accompanied by an introduction by F. W. Walbank, which examines Polybius' life and times, and the sources and technique he employed in writing his history.

Translated by Ian Scott-Kilvert

Selected with an introduction by F. W. Walbank

PENGUIN CLASSICS

THE POLITICS
ARISTOTLE

'Man is by nature a political animal'

In *The Politics* Aristotle addresses the questions that lie at the heart of political science. How should society be ordered to ensure the happiness of the individual? Which forms of government are best and how should they be maintained? By analysing a range of city constitutions – oligarchies, democracies and tyrannies – he seeks to establish the strengths and weaknesses of each system to decide which are the most effective, in theory and in practice. A hugely significant work, which has influenced thinkers as diverse as Aquinas and Machiavelli, *The Politics* remains an outstanding commentary on fundamental political issues and concerns, and provides fascinating insights into the workings and attitudes of the Greek city-state.

The introductions by T. A. Sinclair and Trevor J. Saunders discuss the influence of *The Politics* on philosophers, its modern relevance and Aristotle's political beliefs. This edition contains Greek and English glossaries, and a bibliography for further reading.

Translated by T. A. Sinclair
Revised and re-presented by Trevor J. Saunders

PENGUIN CLASSICS

THE BIRDS AND OTHER PLAYS
ARISTOPHANES

The Knights/Peace/The Birds/The Assemblywomen/Wealth

> 'Oh wings are splendid things, make no mistake:
> they really help you rise in the world'

The plays collected in this volume, written at different times in Aristophanes' forty-year career as a dramatist, all contain his trademark bawdy comedy and dazzling verbal agility. In *The Birds*, two frustrated Athenians join with the birds to build the utopian city of 'Much Cuckoo in the Clouds'. *The Knights* is a venomous satire on Cleon, the prominent Athenian demagogue, while *The Assemblywomen* considers the war of the sexes, as the women of Athens infiltrate the all-male Assembly in disguise. The lengthy conflict with Sparta is the subject of *Peace*, inspired by the hope of a settlement in 421 BC, and *Wealth* reflects the economic catastrophe that hit Athens after the war, as the god of riches is depicted as a ragged, blind old man.

The lively translations by David Barrett and Alan H. Sommerstein capture the full humour of the plays. The introduction examines Aristophanes' life and times, and the comedy and poetry of his works. This volume also includes an introductory note for each play.

Translated with an introduction by David Barrett and Alan H. Sommerstein

PENGUIN CLASSICS

CONVERSATIONS OF SOCRATES
XENOPHON

Socrates' Defence/Memoirs of Socrates/The Estate-Manager/The Dinner-Party

'He seemed to me to be the perfect example of goodness and happiness'

After the execution of Socrates in 399 BC, a number of his followers wrote dialogues featuring him as the protagonist and, in so doing, transformed the great philosopher into a legendary figure. Xenophon's portrait is the only one other than Plato's to survive, and while it offers a very personal interpretation of Socratic thought, it also reveals much about the man and his philosophical views. In 'Socrates' Defence' Xenophon defends his mentor against charges of arrogance made at his trial, while the 'Memoirs of Socrates' also starts with an impassioned plea for the rehabilitation of a wronged reputation. Along with 'The Estate-Manager', a practical economic treatise, and 'The Dinner-Party', a sparkling exploration of love, Xenophon's dialogues offer fascinating insights into the Socratic world and into the intellectual atmosphere and daily life of ancient Greece.

Xenophon's complete Socratic works are translated in this volume. In his introduction, Robin Waterfield illuminates the significance of these four books, showing how perfectly they embody the founding principles of Socratic thought.

Translated by Hugh Tredennick and Robin Waterfield and edited with new material by Robin Waterfield

---

PENGUIN CLASSICS

PROMETHEUS BOUND AND OTHER PLAYS
AESCHYLUS

Prometheus Bound/The Suppliants/Seven Against Thebes/The Persians

> 'Your kindness to the human race has earned you this.
> A god who would not bow to the gods' anger – you
> Transgressing right, gave privileges to mortal men'

Aeschylus (525–456 BC) brought a new grandeur and epic sweep to the drama of classical Athens, raising it to the status of high art. In *Prometheus Bound* the defiant Titan Prometheus is brutally punished by Zeus for daring to improve the state of wretchedness and servitude in which mankind is kept. *The Suppliants* tells the story of the fifty daughters of Danaus who must flee to escape enforced marriages, while *Seven Against Thebes* shows the inexorable downfall of the last members of the cursed family of Oedipus. And *The Persians*, the only Greek tragedy to deal with events from recent Athenian history, depicts the aftermath of the defeat of Persia in the battle of Salamis, with a sympathetic portrayal of its disgraced King Xerxes.

Philip Vellacott's evocative translation is accompanied by an introduction, with individual discussions of the plays, and their sources in history and mythology.

Translated with an introduction by Philip Vellacott

Penguin Classics

THE FROGS AND OTHER PLAYS
ARISTOPHANES

The Wasps/The Poet and the Women/The Frogs

> 'This is just a little fable, with a moral: not too highbrow for you, we hope,
> but a bit more intelligent than the usual knockabout stuff'

The master of ancient Greek comic drama, Aristophanes combined slapstick,
humour and cheerful vulgarity with acute political observations. In *The Frogs*,
written during the Peloponnesian War, Dionysus descends to the Underworld to
bring back a poet who can help Athens in its darkest hour, and stages a great debate
to help him decide between the traditional wisdom of Aeschylus and the brilliant
modernity of Euripides. The clash of generations and values is also the object of
Aristophanes' satire in *The Wasps*, in which an old-fashioned father and his loose-
living son come to blows and end up in court. And in *The Poet and the Women*,
Euripides, accused of misogyny, persuades a relative to infiltrate an all-women
festival to find out whether revenge is being plotted against him.

David Barrett's introduction discusses the Athenian dramatic contests in which
these plays first appeared, and conventions of Greek comedy – from its poetic
language and the role of the Chorus to casting and costumes.

Translated with an introduction by David Barrett

THE STORY OF PENGUIN CLASSICS

Before 1946 ... 'Classics' are mainly the domain of academics and students; readable editions for everyone else are almost unheard of. This all changes when a little-known classicist, E. V. Rieu, presents Penguin founder Allen Lane with the translation of Homer's *Odyssey* that he has been working on in his spare time.

1946 Penguin Classics debuts with *The Odyssey*, which promptly sells three million copies. Suddenly, classics are no longer for the privileged few.

1950s Rieu, now series editor, turns to professional writers for the best modern, readable translations, including Dorothy L. Sayers's *Inferno* and Robert Graves's unexpurgated *Twelve Caesars*.

1960s The Classics are given the distinctive black covers that have remained a constant throughout the life of the series. Rieu retires in 1964, hailing the Penguin Classics list as 'the greatest educative force of the twentieth century.'

1970s A new generation of translators swells the Penguin Classics ranks, introducing readers of English to classics of world literature from more than twenty languages. The list grows to encompass more history, philosophy, science, religion and politics.

1980s The Penguin American Library launches with titles such as *Uncle Tom's Cabin*, and joins forces with Penguin Classics to provide the most comprehensive library of world literature available from any paperback publisher.

1990s The launch of Penguin Audiobooks brings the classics to a listening audience for the first time, and in 1999 the worldwide launch of the Penguin Classics website extends their reach to the global online community.

The 21st Century Penguin Classics are completely redesigned for the first time in nearly twenty years. This world-famous series now consists of more than 1300 titles, making the widest range of the best books ever written available to millions – and constantly redefining what makes a 'classic'.

The Odyssey continues ...

The best books ever written

PENGUIN 🐧 CLASSICS

SINCE 1946

Find out more at www.penguinclassics.com